AN INTRODUCTION TO
THE
TECHNIQUE OF PALESTRINA

Eus tu conuersus viuifi-

ca-   bis

nos   viuifi-   ca-   bis nos viuifi-

ca-   bis nos   & plebs tua lætabi-

tur in te   & plebs tua   lætabitur in te   ostende nobis

Domine   misericordiam tuam & salutare tuum   da no- bis   & salu-

tare tuum da no-   bis ostende nobis Domine   misericordiam tu-

am & salutare tuum   da no- bis   & salutare tuum da no- bis.

AN INTRODUCTION TO

THE

TECHNIQUE OF PALESTRINA

BY

H. K. ANDREWS
(*Lecturer in Music, Oxford University*)

LONDON
NOVELLO AND COMPANY LTD
160 WARDOUR STREET W.1

The frontispiece is taken from the
Cantiones Sacræ Quinque vocum (Offertories)
in the Peter Phalèse (Antwerp) Edition of 1603
(Bodleian Library)

SET IN 12 POINT BEMBO
PRINTED AND BOUND IN GREAT BRITAIN
BY NOVELLO AND COMPANY LIMITED
LONDON W.1

CONTENTS

To Herbert Howells

Ars polyphonica quae olim apud Praenestinos floruit, in ripa Sabrinensi nuper renata est.

PREFACE

FEW will challenge the statement that the Sacred music of Palestrina displays the most highly organized technique of the age of pure vocal polyphony. Apart from its perfection, this technique is of the greatest interest and importance in that it illustrates a definite stage in the transition between the essentially linear counterpoint of an earlier age and the harmonic counterpoint of a later.

Out of the linear counterpoint of his predecessors, which often took little heed of the vertical aspect of music, Palestrina forged for himself a style euphonious in the vertical synthesis and at the same time allowing the horizontal or linear side full scope, which may be regarded as one of the most successful fusions of these two elements of music ever attained. Within the self-imposed limitations of pure vocal ecclesiastical polyphony he covered the whole range of emotional expression from intense jubilation to penitential sorrow with complete technical mastery of his medium and consummate restraint.

There are some who level the charge of over-sophistication and excess of euphony at Palestrina's musical style. The technique is criticized as being too 'smooth' to be capable of real expression. This is mistaking the means for the end. It cannot be denied by anyone with a wide experience of the music that Palestrina's expressive powers are of the highest order, and that his technique is perfectly apt for their expression. If his art is that of pure line drawing rather than of the brilliant colours and sharp contrasts of the dramatic painter, his technique must fit his chosen medium and purpose.

The intention of this book is to make a study of Palestrina's technique in his church music in all its more important aspects. Any book dealing with this subject must owe much to Professor Knud Jeppesen's fine study of Palestrina's treatment of the dissonance (The Style of Palestrina and the Dissonance). His scholarly and painstaking research, and the historical perspective in which he places many of the technical factors of the style are of the greatest value alike to the musical theorist and historian.

R. O. Morris's 'Contrapuntal Technique in the Sixteenth Century' is another pioneer work to which grateful acknowledgment must be made. Morris had an uncanny insight into the sixteenth-century style, and his book is full of illuminating comments which often get right to the root of the most difficult and obscure problems.

Mediaeval and Renaissance theorists have been studied and quoted on some matters, such as Modes and Proportions, where their propositions throw light on obscure places, but the main purpose of the book is to present the particular technical usages of Palestrina *as they appear in his music* to the present-day student of the style, rather than as contemporary theorists might have seen them. For this reason the rulings of contemporary theorists on general technical problems have been little used, since the often contradictory and over-elaborate explanations in which they abound would require so much comment and correlation as to make the book unnecessarily clumsy and unpractical. Furthermore, in the sixteenth-century writers (and, to a lesser extent, in the means of writing adopted by the composers) there is an element of obfuscation—a tendency to make the simplest matter complex and difficult, to surround the art of music with a deliberate cloak of mystery —which is altogether out of place in the present age.

The main proposition on which this examination of Palestrina's technique is based is that linear counterpoint, that is, the interweaving of separate melodic strands conceived mainly in the horizontal plane with other similar strands, is the foundation of the process which produces the musical texture, the vertical aspect being the outcome, though by no means the fortuitous result of this weaving. The refining of the interval technique which controls the progress of the pairs of strands in mutual relationship effects a satisfactory vertical or *harmonic* basis for the sum of the strands and shows clearly a general tendency which was eventually to lead to harmonic thinking in Diatonic tonality.

Part of the great interest of Palestrina's style for the theorist and musical historian lies in the fact that his music stands in the middle of a period of transition; the Modes of Polyphony were a halfway house between the Plainsong Ecclesiastical Modes and the Diatonic scale system; the Proportional time system of earlier Polyphony was giving way to the modern system of note values whose individual speed might be varied, not by mathematical diminutions and augmentations, but by speed indications of a more indefinite kind; the mainly non-harmonic linear counterpoint of the past was taking on vertical responsibilities. In fact, the main facets of musical technique were in a state of flux. Palestrina's achievement in making an almost perfect language in a time of such apparent chaos is a marvel which has scarcely had the recognition it deserves.

Tracing the various technical factors of Palestrina's art back through the earlier stages of Polyphony has had to be abandoned, for the most part, as such a procedure would make the book unpractical or overlong. Fortunately Jeppesen has done a considerable amount of this in ' The Style of Palestrina '.

*   *   *

Unreduced note values have been used in the examples throughout the book because this method coincides with the usage of the ' Haberl ' complete edition as well as with the proportional system. The Haberl edition has been used as the main source of music examples (references are given to the volume and page: P. XX., p. xx) despite its many shortcomings, since the ' Roma ' edition is still incomplete. Cross-references to the ' Roma ' edition are given where possible (ref.: R. X., p. x).

It has been found necessary for the sake of clarity and brevity to use some technical terms belonging to a later period. It is stressed throughout the text that such terms are only used for convenience, and that their implications in the harmonic age must be discounted. Figuring, for example, must be understood to refer to interval combinations measured from the lowest voice (e.g. $\frac{6}{3}$) or below or above a stationary part (e.g. $\overline{2\ 3}$), and not to imply a first inversion of a diatonic triad or other harmonic entity.

Many of the conclusions in the book are the writer's personal opinions. They are offered not as statements of fact, but as hypotheses which the material has suggested. When they differ from the views of other writers, they are put forward with due reservation and humility.

The aesthetic side of this great corpus of music has had to be left virtually untouched, save for a few remarks in the chapter on word setting. It must not, however, be thought that the writer is interested only in the technical and theoretical side of Palestrina's work; he is very much aware of the sheer beauty and expressive power of the music, which can only be fully realized when it is well and intelligently sung.

H. K. A.

Oxford
September 1955

CHAPTER I

THE ECCLESIASTICAL MODES IN POLYPHONY

General Definition of the Style

PALESTRINA'S medium is *linear counterpoint*, based on a modified version of the Ecclesiastical Modal System; the music is composed of rhythmic-melodic strands woven together in accordance with an interval technique which is refined to a point where the synthesis of the strands makes a logical, disciplined, and euphonious texture in its vertical as well as its horizontal aspect. By this process an organized and clearly defined harmonic basis is produced, although harmonic progression in the sense of the diatonic age is as yet a secondary consideration, and the feeling of tonality founded upon harmonic relationships is scarcely more than a shadow.

The chief concern of the technique is the behaviour, rhythmic and according to interval progression, of each separate strand with every other strand, and in particular of the lowest strand (the Bass) with those which lie above it in pitch.

The Modes

It is generally taken for granted that the music of Palestrina is written ' in the Ecclesiastical Modes '. This conception requires considerable modification; Jeppesen* remarks that ' The Ecclesiastical Modes of Polyphony are a transition between the Gregorian (sic) modes and the Major-Minor system ' and suggests the title ' Polyphonic Modes ' for them.

The origin and history of the Mediaeval Modal System,† and the differentiation between Mode and Scale should be studied in books such as ' Music in the Middle Ages ' (Reese), where a detailed and carefully argued account of the theories of modal origins is given. For the present purpose a straightforward table of the modes may prove of use for reference.

Ex.1 AUTHENTIC PLAGAL

DORIAN (Mode i)   Hypo-dorian (Mode ii)
DIAPENTE I   DIATESSARON I   DIAPENTE I   DIATESSARON I
F   M   T   F   M   T

PHRYGIAN (Mode iii)   Hypo-phrygian (Mode iv)
DIAPENTE II   DIATESSARON II   DIAPENTE II   DIATESSARON II
F   M   T   F   M   T

* Jeppesen: ' Counterpoint ', Williams & Norgate, p. 71.

† Jeppesen in the book cited above devotes considerable space to the Ecclesiastical Modes. His views do not always agree with those of other authorities, but are, nevertheless, of great interest.

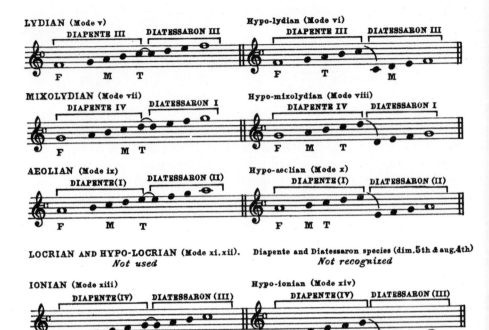

Notes on the above table

1. F, Final of the mode. T, Tenor, reciting note ('Dominant'), also 'confinalis' or 'socialis', a possible note of ending. M, Mediant (secondary reciting note).

2. The modes are grouped in pairs, Authentic and Plagal. Each consists of a characteristic diapente and diatessaron, as shown. The diapente species consist of I, (modes i and ii), Tone, Semitone, Tone, Tone. II, (modes iii and iv), S. T. T. T. III, (modes v and vi), T. T. T. S. IV, (modes vii and viii), T. T. S. T. Modes ix and x have a diapente repeating the interval series of I; modes xiii and xiv that of IV. The diatessaron species are I, (modes i and ii), T. S. T. II, (modes iii and iv), S. T. T. III, (modes v and vi), T. T. S. Modes vii and viii, T. S. T. (as I). Modes ix and x have the interval series of II; modes xiii and xiv of III.

3. Early mediaeval theory recognized four authentic and three plagal modes (i-vii). Hermannus Contractus (A.D. 1013-1054) added mode viii. The final codification was achieved by Glarean (Dodecachordon: 1547), though the additional modes had been in practical use for a considerable time before that date (Modes ix, x, xiii, xiv).

4. Defining characteristics: (i) interval series and melodic outline of diapente and diatessaron-species; (ii) prominence of Final and Tenor (reciting note); (iii) characteristic melodic formulae; (iv) range; (v) the tendency to form cadences on certain notes as melodic points of repose in the line.

Mediaeval and Polyphonic Modes

It is clear that Mediaeval and Renaissance writers were concerned with the application of their modal theories to the single strand of melody even when dealing with polyphonic music; this is wholly true in the case of the former, and for the most part of the latter also, though some attempts to apply modal theory in an over-all form to polyphony will be considered in a long note at the end of this chapter. The modern theoretical idea of 'Polyphonic Modes', in attempting to assess the modality of a polyphonic work as a whole, creates a difficult and, to some extent, anachronistic problem, made inevitable by the way of thinking engendered by years of experience of music dominated by diatonic tonality.

The real crux of the matter lies in the fact that the old modal theories, essentially 'monophonic' in outlook, could not be applied without radical alteration to polyphony of the late fifteenth and sixteenth centuries, and, since tonality in the diatonic system was as yet only in an embryonic stage, theory based upon it was not available. Fortunately composers come first and theorists after them, and the great men of the period knew well how to use the *materia musica* which they had inherited to serve their unerring musical instincts.

Modifications of the Old Modal System

In polyphonic music many characteristics of the 'monophonic' modes were of necessity lost to a considerable extent. Such important factors as range and compass, and the Authentic-Plagal divisions, which were responsible for the definitions 'Tonus Perfectus, Tonus Imperfectus, Tonus Plusquamperfectus' of Tinctoris and other theorists, the strict application of individual diapente and diatessaron species,* the melodic importance of certain degrees of the mode (such as the Tenor and Final), and the concluding notes could no longer play such a decisive part in modal definition, since their strict usage in each individual strand would have made a satisfactory synthesis of all the strands together impracticable. In the case of range and compass, it is obvious that, if unequal voices are used in polyphony, both Authentic and Plagal ranges of the mode are required to secure not only the most effective and natural tessitura of the different voices, but also the best opportunities for sonority and vocal 'lay-out' in the vertical aspect. The strict application of the diapente and diatessaron species to every strand would make freedom of movement of the strands in combination almost unattainable. With the growing awareness of the vertical aspect of polyphony, the melodic importance of certain degrees of the mode in the individual line had to give way to 'harmonic' considerations of sonority and vertical spacing, though this particular characteristic of modal definition was to some extent retained in altered form in the shape of cadence formations on certain degrees (see below).

The vertical aspect of polyphony was responsible for further modification of modal practice. Some of the Modes which were perfectly satisfactory

---

* The use of diapente and diatessaron species foreign to the basic mode in the composition as a whole is discussed at some length in the note at the end of this chapter.

in music consisting of a single melodic line, became intractable in polyphony unless modified. The Lydian B♮, and to a lesser extent, the Dorian B♮ are the most obvious instances. The tendency to flatten the Lydian fourth degree to obtain a perfect fifth below the Final, in addition to the normal melodic reasons for flattening the note, made the B♭ almost an essential part of the mode. Morris states that the flat actually appeared sometimes as a key-signature.* This process equated the interval series of the Lydian octave scale and its diapente and diatessaron species with those of the Ionian in transposed form. †

In the case of the Dorian mode, the flattening of the B, though freely used for both harmonic and melodic reasons, never became such a generally accepted procedure as in the case of the Lydian. The characteristic Dorian melodic formulae, and cadences on particular degrees survived with considerable forcefulness, and many works of undoubted Dorian modality may be found throughout the century. Yet the tendency to equate the Dorian mode with the flattened sixth to the Aeolian (transposed) was there, and may well be regarded as a further step in the emergence of the two-mode major-minor system. Furthermore, the frequent cadential sharpening of the F in the Mixolydian robbed that mode of a good deal of its individuality, and tended to make it merge into the Ionian.

Defining the ' mode ' of a work

Despite the actual fusion of authentic and plagal forms in the over-all aspect of polyphonic music, it is common practice to regard Palestrina's works as being in some definite authentic or plagal mode. The formula generally supplied for finding the mode is perfectly simple, however unsatisfactory and incomplete it may be from the theorist's point of view. The last note of the lowest voice at the end of a work or complete movement is regarded as the Final of the mode; the range of the Tenor part decides whether it is authentic or plagal. This rule, like all over-simplifications, raises all kinds of difficulties and exceptions, but, on the whole it is a workable compromise. It must, however, be noted that when an actual plainsong Cantus Firmus is present in a part other than the tenor, it supersedes the tenor as the indicator of whether the mode is in plagal or authentic form.‡

Transposition of the Modes

The transposition of any of the modes a fourth up or a fifth down is a common practice in Polyphony, and is very often found in Palestrina's works. This transposition is indicated by a B flat in the key signature. Such transposition does not alter the characteristics of the mode or affect its

---

* R. O. Morris: ' Contrapuntal Technique ', page 13.   A good example is to be found in Palestrina's Missa Quinti Toni where the B♭ signature appears.

† Some modern theorists go so far as to dismiss the Lydian mode as an individual mode in polyphony, regarding it as a transposition of the Ionian.   In some cases, however, it does seem to retain at least part of its individuality in the degrees favoured for intermediate cadences, and in characteristic melodic outlines. Jeppesen's arguments for its rejection which follow his statement ' The Lydian mode really exists only in the monophonic ecclesiastical modes ' (' Counterpoint ': page 74) are worth careful consideration.

‡ It must also be realized that the Tenor, except when it is a definite plainsong melody (as a Cantus Firmus), rarely exhibits strict authentic or plagal characteristics even in range.

cadences on specific degrees; it is merely a matter of convenience of vocal range.*

Musica Ficta

The use of chromatically altered notes, written, or implied by the practice generally known as *musica ficta*, plays a restrained but important part in Palestrina's music. The difficult matter of *musica ficta* in its historical minutiae must be the joy and at the same time the nightmare of the honest musicologist, so complex are its ramifications at different periods, so uncertain its exact application. It may be enough for present purposes to attempt to give a set of working rules applicable to the style of Palestrina.

Chromatic alterations, written or unwritten, seem to have been used by Palestrina for two main reasons: (1) melodic; (2) 'harmonic.'

(1) Of the melodic uses the chief are: (*a*) the raising or lowering of a note in order to avoid the tritone or its inversion the diminished fifth either as a direct leap or as the outline of a melodic figure; (*b*) the 'shortening' of whole tone returning steps (A-B-A becoming A-Bb-A, G-F-G becoming G-F♯-G, etc.); (*c*) the growing tendency to use the upward semitone step to the Final in cadences (the modern leading-note cadence) except in the Phrygian mode.

(2) The 'harmonic' considerations influencing chromatic (*musica ficta*) alterations are: (*a*) the perfecting of the diminished fifth between the notes B♮ and F either by lowering the B♮ to Bb or by raising the F to F♯; (*b*) the desire to have a major rather than a minor third in the final chord of every work or important section, which implies the raising of the third degree of the Dorian, Phrygian, and Aeolian modes, and became the normal practice in polyphony throughout most of its history; (*c*) the use of the major 'chord' in intermediate cadences (see below); (*d*) the purely 'harmonic' and expressive effect of a chromatically altered 'chord' (for example, in the opening of the eight-voice 'Stabat Mater'); (*e*) possibly the growing awareness and standardization of the leading-note cadence, demanding a major third for the 'dominant' chord.†

Chromatic notes

The chromatic notes used by Palestrina (sometimes written, sometimes left as *musica ficta* alterations to be supplied by performer [or editor]) were: B flat, E flat, F sharp, C sharp, and G sharp. In very exceptional circumstances he wrote a D sharp (as, for example, in the motet 'Peccantem me quotidie' where the note occurs on the word 'conturbat' in the phrase 'timor mortis conturbat me'), and a G sharp = D sharp in a G-Dorian

---

* See, however, Reese: 'Music in the Middle ages', page 158. The whole matter of key-signatures and transposition is an important and difficult problem, outside the scope of this book.

† Jeppesen lays considerable emphasis on the 'harmonic' aspect of chromatic alteration. Though it is obvious that harmonic perception was advancing in Palestrina's time, there is a danger in reading into the sixteenth century conceptions of a later age. See, however, Jeppesen: 'The Style of Palestrina', p. 32. 'All the accidentals mentioned are employed out of consideration for harmony' (he is referring to the three sharps F♯, C♯, G♯). Reese: 'Music in the Middle Ages', p. 381, quotes the theorist Ugolino d'Orvieto (c. 1400) as giving the following 'harmonic' reasons (among others) for chromatic alteration . . . 'a third expanding stepwise to a fifth, or a sixth to an octave, should be major; a third contracting stepwise to a unison should be minor. If not naturally so, they should be rendered so by alteration.'

madrigal.   A flat does not occur except as = E flat in a transposed mode.*
It must be realized that this limitation of chromatic alteration in Palestrina's
music is a self-imposed restriction.   His predecessors had been much
more lavish in their use of chromatic notes.† A very illuminating remark is
made by Jeppesen‡ in this context: '. . . it does not seem improbable that
Palestrina's art may one day, when all the facts have been finally investigated
and collated, be recognized as the keystone of a great process of diatonic
development'.

Cadences

One of the characteristic features of the Ecclesiastical Modes was the
tendency to form cadences on specific degrees of the particular mode in use.
In fact, this tendency of stressing certain degrees as ' points of repose ' had
much to do with the definition of the mode itself.   This characteristic was
equally important in the Polyphonic Modes (in modified form), replacing
to some extent the defining qualities of prominent single notes such as the
tenor and mediant. Jeppesen goes so far as to say** '. . . the individual character
of each particular mode depends largely upon what cadences it favors (sic)
or avoids.'   These cadences (occurring on degrees other than the Final)
must not be regarded as ' modulations ' in the diatonic tonal sense, though
it may be argued that in them the origin of ' modulations ' and ' transitions '
of a later age may be found.   They should be thought of as emphasizing
certain degrees of the mode, just as ' applied dominants ' are used to emphasize important chords in later harmonic practice of the diatonic age.

' Final ' cadences

The cadences most frequently found at the end of a work or section in
the sixteenth century are, what were later called, the Perfect (dominant-
tonic in modern parlance) and the Plagal (subdominant-tonic).   These
could be formed on the Final of any of the modes in practical use, with the
exception of the Phrygian, where the lack of a D sharp made the Perfect
cadence impossible.   In this case a special cadential form was used in its
place which became known as the ' Phrygian cadence '.   It consisted of
F falling to E in the lowest part, D rising to E (generally in the top part),
and A falling to G sharp completing the formula in three parts.   This
cadence was generally followed by a Plagal close: sometimes the Plagal
close alone was used in the Phrygian mode.

Intermediate Cadences

Intermediate cadences on degrees other than the Final of the mode are
most frequently of the Perfect variety, though the ' Interrupted ' and

---

* Morris: ' Contrapuntal Technique in the Sixteenth Century ', p. 9 (footnote) states, '. . . the
accidental A flat must not be employed in a transposed form of a mode although E flat can be used
freely in the untransposed form '.   Jeppesen quotes one example of A♭ = E♭ in a transposed mode from
a madrigal.   He also says that E flat is generally only found in transposed modes.

† Jeppesen (op. cit.) quotes examples of A♭ and D♭ from Obrecht and Cesaris. Reese (op. cit) states
that ' By the time of Prosdocimus, a complete chromatic scale is arrived at; but D♯ and A♯ are rare '
(early fifteenth century).

‡ Jeppesen (op. cit.), p. 30.

** Jeppesen: ' Counterpoint ', p. 81.

'Phrygian' kinds are also commonly found. In Palestrina's work the Interrupted cadence consists more often of 'Dominant to Subdominant' than of 'Dominant to Submediant' progressions. The Plagal form is hardly strong enough to stand in its own right as an intermediate cadence except on the Final.

These cadence forms have been described here in harmonic terms. This is purely for the sake of brevity. It must be understood that their origin is linear and melodic.

List of Intermediate Cadences

Any list of intermediate cadences must be arrived at by empirical methods, so far as sixteenth-century polyphony is concerned, since the lists of 'regular and conceded modulations' of Mediaeval and Renaissance theorists apply essentially to single-strand plainsong. Authorities differ in detail, but the following table may be regarded as a workable compromise.

Mode	Cadences common	Less common	Rare
DORIAN	D. (Final) A. (Tenor)	G. C. F.	E.
PHRYGIAN	A. E. (Final)	D. C. (Tenor) G.	F.
[LYDIAN	F. (Final) C. (Tenor)	A. D.	]
MIXOLYDIAN	G. (Final) D. (Tenor)	C. A.	F. E.
AEOLIAN	A. (Final) D.	C. G. F.	E (Tenor)
IONIAN	C. (Final) G. (Tenor)	A. D.	F. E.

Characteristics defining the Polyphonic Modes

The chief factors in modal definition in polyphony may be summarized as follows:

1. The interval series of the octave scale of the particular mode which forms the basis of the work.
2. The importance of the Final of the mode as the 'real' bass note at the end of a work or section, and of certain other degrees in the course of the melodic line.
3. The formation of intermediate cadences on the Final and other favoured degrees in a particular mode.
4. The occurence of characteristic melodic outlines and formulae peculiar to each individual mode.
5. The modified use of the diapente and diatessaron species of the particular mode in use. The mixing of these species, which forms a necessary part of polyphonic lines, is given more detailed consideration in the note at the end of this chapter.

B

Palestrina's treatment of the modes

Palestrina's treatment of the modes in polyphony is remarkably conservative when compared with the methods used by many of his contemporaries, especially in England.* A short examination of a typical motet in the Dorian mode and one in the Phrygian may suffice to demonstrate this fact, and also to illustrate the points summarized concerning modal definition in polyphony. It is worth pointing out that the two motets selected for this purpose were the first that came to hand, and were not specially chosen for their conformity to recognized modal usage.

I. ' *Orietur Stella ex Jacob* ' (R. XII, p. 40, et seq.) (P. IV, p. 118 et seq.) is a straightforward example of a (Hypo-)Dorian work for five voices. Taking the points mentioned in the summary given above:

1. The octave species (scale) is Dorian; despite the liberal sprinkling of flattened sixth degrees (B flats) there are enough B naturals to leave no doubt in the hearer's mind that the basis of the work is the true octave species of Mode I. The Tenor voice, though it has a range of only a ninth (G-a) must be classified as ' Tonus plusquamperfectus plagalis ' in the definition of contemporary theorists, since it descends one note below its plagal range. Certain ' Commixtus ' tendencies are also noticeable in the melodic outlines.

2. The Bassus voice ends on the Final (D) and the Final and Tenor (A) are much stressed in the melodic line, especially in the Cantus voice.

3. The chief and most clearly defined intermediate ' Perfect ' cadences occur as follows: 10 on D (the Final), 2 on A (the Tenor), 1 each on G and C, and a less definite instance (in the middle of a phrase) on F. This may be regarded as a normal distribution.

4. Two of the most important characteristic melodic outlines associated with the Dorian mode (Ex. 2) appear in the thematic material of the motet (Ex. 3). One is treated fugally.

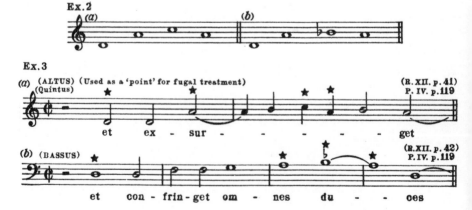

* R. O. Morris: ' Contrapuntal Technique ', p. 65, suggests that English composers at quite an early date in the sixteenth century had practically abandoned the modal system for a two-scale one. He remarks, ' Even the Phrygian mode, which retained a good deal of its individuality (elsewhere) was roughly handled. . . . In Tallis's Lamentations the prevailing mode is Phrygian, but in the middle, at the words " plorans ploravit ", comes a section whose tonality can only be described as the diatonic key of B flat major.'

5. The Dorian diapente and diatessaron species are well represented in the melodic lines of all voices, used as direct leaps, scale passages, and melodic figures. As is inevitable in polyphony, other diapente and diatessaron species appear from time to time, but the true Dorian types are predominant.

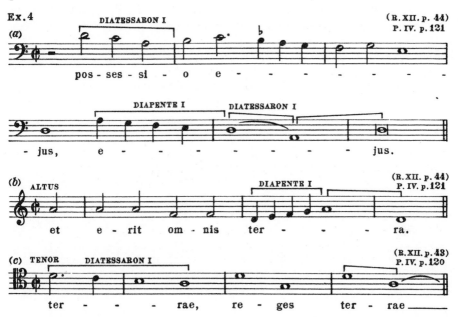

II. ' *Domine quando veneris* ' (R. XI, p. 3, et seq.) (P. V, p. 117, et seq.) is a fairly typical Phrygian motet with a Prima Pars and a Secunda Pars. Examining it as in the case above, the following points appear.

1. Considering the two ' parts ' of the work as a single entity, the octave species is Phrygian; the only chromatic notes are the three customary sharps (mostly in cadence formations) and B flat, either written, or implied as *musica ficta* notes. The range of the tenor is D-f (tenth), so the theorist's classification must be Tonus plusquamperfectus authenticus (' ille qui ultra diapason a suo fine ascendit scilicet ad nonam vel decimam,' as Marchettus of Padua describes it).* It contains ' Commixtus ' elements which will be discussed later.

2. The Bassus voice ends on the Final in both sections of motet, and the Final and Tenor (C) of the mode are prominent in the line in all voices.

3. The intermediate cadences are of special interest. The Final, on which a normal ' Perfect ' cadence cannot be formed through lack of a D sharp, has far less importance as an intermediate cadence point than in the case of the other modes. There are only some five or six important cadences (' Phrygian ' or ' Plagal ') on the Final in the two ' parts '. A, on the other hand is the most favoured degree, and receives at least ten clear-cut ' Perfect '

* M. Gerbert: ' Scriptores, III ', p. 101 (it may be translated: ' that which ascends from its final above the octave as far as a ninth or tenth '.)

cadences and many more where one or other of the cadential ' chords ' is
' inverted ' (to use language of the harmonic age for the sake of brevity).
D seems to be the next favoured degree, with some six ' Perfect ' cadences;
G and C have two each, and some less well defined cadences, interrupted
or in inversion.

4. One of the characteristic melodic outlines of the Phrygian mode can
be found in the melodic material of the motet.*

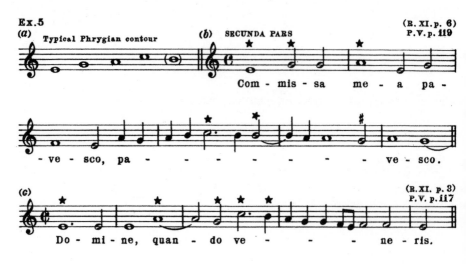

5. The Phrygian diapente and diatessaron species are notably absent
from the melodic line of all voices. This is by no means an unusual feature
of Palestrina's work in this mode. The Dorian and Aeolian species are
much better represented:

* Striking instances of the melodic use of the characteristic Phrygian formula may be found all
through Palestrina's music in this mode, whether founded on a plainsong paraphrase or not. One
instance from the well-known motet ' Super Flumina Babylonis ' may be of use in stressing this point.

Some explanation of this may be found in the note on ' Tonus Commixtus ' and the theorist's views of the modes in polyphony at the end of the chapter.

From this short survey it may be seen that the Modes as used in Sixteenth-Century Polyphony, while retaining the basis of the old Ecclesiastical or ' Monophonic' Modal System, had, of necessity, undergone a very considerable reorientation. This was inevitable as a result of the increase in the number of ' voices ' and the growing awareness of their synthesis—in other words, the vertical aspect of music. The Ecclesiastical Modes were a codification of single-line melodies; Polyphony, by its very nature, required a different system of codification.

Theorists of the Renaissance were reluctant to abandon the old premises upon which the theory of Modes was founded. Composers, on the other hand, had adapted and changed the old system to meet their needs, unhampered by theoretical considerations, working by the light of their own genius. It is inevitable that theorists' explanations of the change should be clumsy and artificial. Some further consideration of this aspect of the matter is given in the note which follows.

Palestrina's use of the ' Modes of Polyphony ' shows how the spirit, if not the letter of the old single-line system could be preserved in music for many voices, by adapting it to the new conditions without destroying its basic qualities.

Note on the characteristic diapente and diatessaron species

Some quotations from theorists of the late fifteenth and sixteenth centuries may help to throw light on deviations from the strict use of the diapente and diatessaron species of the individual mode in ' monophonic ' and ' polyphonic ' modality.

First of all, it may be useful to tabulate the diapente and diatessaron species of the modal system.

Diapente I.	D–A	Tone-Semitone-Tone-Tone	Dorian
(transposed)	A–E	Tone-Semitone-Tone-Tone	Aeolian
Diapente II.	E–B♮	Semitone-Tone-Tone-Tone	Phrygian
Diapente III.	F–C	Tone-Tone-Tone-Semitone	Lydian
Diapente IV.	G–D	Tone-Tone-Semitone-Tone	Mixolydian
(transposed)	C–G	Tone-Tone-Semitone-Tone	Ionian

Diatessaron I.	A–D	Tone-Semitone-Tone	Dorian
(transposed)	D–G	Tone-Semitone-Tone	Mixolydian
Diatessaron II.	Bᵇ–E	Semitone-Tone-Tone	Phrygian
(transposed)	E–A	Semitone-Tone-Tone	Aeolian
Diatessaron III.	C–F	Tone-Tone-Semitone	Lydian
(transposed)	G–C	Tone-Tone-Semitone	Ionian

Dorian and Hypodorian.	Diapente I	Diatessaron I
Phrygian and Hypophrygian.	Diapente II	Diatessaron II
Lydian and Hypolydian.	Diapente III	Diatessaron III
Mixolydian and Hypomixolydian.	Diapente IV	Diatessaron I
Aeolian and Hypoaeolian.	Diapente I	Diatessaron II
Ionian and Hypoionian.	Diapente IV	Diatessaron III

The key to the problem seems to lie in what the theorists term ' Tonus Commixtus '. In the case of the other classifications, Tonus Perfectus, Tonus Imperfectus, Tonus Plusquamperfectus, and Tonus Mixtus, the definitions and differences seem to be concerned with range alone. For example, Tinctoris in ' Diffinitorium Musicae ' (Coussemaker: ' Scriptores, IV ', p. 190, facsimile ed. 1931):

' *Tonus Perfectus* is that which completes the range (of its mode).

Tonus imperfectus is that which does not complete its range.

Tonus Plusquamperfectus, if it be authentic, ascends above the range of its mode; if plagal, descends below its range.

Tonus Mixtus implies that, if authentic, it makes a descent into its plagal range, if plagal, an ascent into its authentic.'

In the case of *Tonus Commixtus* another factor comes in, the mixing of the diapente and diatessaron species of one mode with those of another or others. In dealing with *Tonus Perfectus*, etc., theorists seem to take it for granted that the melodic outlines of the diapente and diatessaron species peculiar to the mode in use are prominent in the melody: in *Tonus Commixtus* diapente and diatessaron species foreign to the basic mode are interpolated and play a prominent part in the course of the melody.

Tinctoris, in his ' Liber de Natura et Proprietate Tonorum ' Cap XIII, writes (Coussemaker: Scriptores IV, p. 24):

' Concerning the mixing of tones. If indeed any of the eight tones mentioned should not have been formed from its own species of diapente and diatessaron assigned to it in the manner we have mentioned, or rather if one (tone) is mixed with another or more of this kind, it is called *tonus commixtus*. For example, if in the first tone the fourth species of diapente, normally attributed to the seventh (tone) is set up, then the result will be called a mixture of the first (Dorian) and seventh (Mixolydian) tones, thus:

Ex. 8

Mode I   DIAPENTE IV

Tinctoris goes on to discuss whether a Tonus Commixtus should be named from the authentic or plagal form of the mode, and in the course of Cap XIV gives examples of *commixti* of modes III and VII (c.f. the Phrygian motet examined on pp. 19 and 20), IV and VI, and of VII, V, and VI. For present purposes it is unnecessary to pursue his arguments in this chapter in greater detail. In Cap XV there is a passage of importance in that it throws light on the attitude of Tinctoris to the matter.

' *From which of the different species of diapente or diatessaron belonging to different tones will a Tonus Commixtus be named?*

Again, who can doubt, seeing that the mixing of a tone is due to (the presence of) different species of diapente and diatessaron belonging to other tones, from which of these in particular the tone itself is to be named? The answer is that the classification of a *Tonus Commixtus* is made according to the final species of diapente or diatessaron, however often or diversely the diapente or diatessaron species of one or another or more different tones is used; as indeed the philosopher saith, ' the matter is to be judged from its ending '; this is seen in the following case, in which the eighth tone (Mixolydian Plagal) is mixed with the fifth (Lydian) and third (Phrygian), because although it (the eighth) is mixed with the third and second species of diatessaron regularly attributed to those two tones (the fifth and third) finally it is restored by means of the fourth species of diapente assigned to it itself at the end.'

Ex. 9

Mode viii   DIATESSARON III   DIATESSARON II   DIAPENTE IV

These quotations, it must be born in mind, apply only to single-line plainchant. In Cap XXIV, however, Tinctoris turns to Polyphony:

' *The mixing of tones which may be made not only in a simple Cantus, but also in composition* (i.e. Polyphony).

Finally it must be noted that Commixtio and Mixtio of tones are made not only in the simple Cantus, but also in composition of the kind wherein, if the music is written in two, three, four, or more (parts), one part will be of one tone, another of another; one authentic, another plagal; one mixtus, another commixtus; whence, when some mass or song or any other piece of music consists of different parts in different modes, if anyone should ask to what tone the composition as a whole belongs, the answer should be, without qualification, according to the nature of the tenor, because, of the whole work, it would be the principal part and foundation of the whole relationship; and if it should be asked in particular of some one single part of such a work to which tone it might belong, the answer in particular is of such and such.'

(Author's translations.)

Pietro Aron (1490-1545) appears to be in general agreement with the theories of Tinctoris.

' The tenor being the firm and stable part, the part, that is, that holds and comprehends the whole concentus of the harmony, the singer must judge the tone by means of this part only . . . Each of the added parts will be governed by the nature of the tenor, and by means of the tenor the tone will be recognized unless the plainsong itself, which is the primary and principal to such a recognition, be in some other part.'

(Strunk: ' Source Readings ', p. 209.)

It is clear that ' Tonus Commixtus ' was accepted by theorists not only as applicable to the single strand of polyphony, but also to the diversity of mixing of modal species inherent in the overall view of the combination or these strands.   Both Tinctoris and Aron seem to have no compunction in accepting the mode of the tenor (or Cantus Firmus) as the arbiter of the mode of the whole work.

This method of modal determination was a reasonable expedient while purely linear polyphony persisted, provided that the tenor or Cantus Firmus behaved normally as to its ending.   But as the harmonic element in polyphony developed and the bass part assumed more harmonic significance, the tenor became less powerful in its defining capacity; for example its ending was often altered for harmonic cadential reasons, so that it displayed little of its former clarity as a modal ending.   A quotation from Zarlino (1517-1590) shows a modified approach and a new interpretation of overall modality in general and of *Tonus commixtus* in particular.

The following passage is translated by Strunk in his ' Source Readings ', p. 253.   Zarlino, in the edition of ' Istituzioni ' which Strunk has used for this translation (1589), has re-numbered the modes, calling those with C as the final I and II, with D, III and IV, and so forth.

' Take note, to begin with, that although we have an almost infinite number of compositions in each of the modes that have been discussed, there are many that are written, not in the simple modes, but in the mixed ones.   Thus we find the Fifth Mode (Phrygian) mixed with the Twelfth (Aeolian plagal), the Tenth (Mixolydian plagal) with the First (Ionian), and so on with the others. An examination of such compositions will make this clear, especially if we examine those of the Fifth Mode (Phrygian) that below, instead of the third species of diapente (i.e. the second of the normal classification) E-(b)♮, have the third (i.e. second) of the diatessaron, E to a, and that above, instead of the third (i.e. second) species of the diatessaron, b♮-e, have the second (i.e. first) of the diapente, a-e, so that although the species lie within the same diapason (octave), E-e, one of the modes is harmonically divided and maintains the form of the Fifth (i.e. Phrygian) while the other is arithmetically divided and maintains the form of the Twelfth (plagal Aeolian). And since the species of the Twelfth Mode are heard repeated over and over again, not only does the greater part of the composition lose all relation to the fifth mode (Phrygian) but the whole becomes subject to the twelfth (Aeolian plagal).'

He goes on to argue that such a case implies the essential diapente and diatessaron species of the Aeolian mode (in its plagal form, the diatessaron being below the diapente) and that the only Phrygian characteristics of the composition are the E-e range and the ending on E, ' which is a most deceptive thing. For although some would have us judge a composition by its final (as by its end and not by what precedes it), seeing that everything is rightly judged by or in its end, it does not follow from this that we may come to recognize the mode on which a composition is based by this alone.'

He therefore concludes that here ' we have, without a doubt, the form of the Twelfth Mode (Hypoaeolian), lying within the third species of diapason (E-e) arithmetically divided.' His general summing up is important:

' Thus in judging any composition, whatever it may be, we have to consider it most carefully from beginning to end and to determine the form in which it is written, whether in that of the First, or of the Second, or of some other mode, having an eye to the cadences, which throw a great light on this question; then we may judge it even though it concludes, not on its proper final, but on its central step or on some other that may prove to the purpose.'

Moreover, he makes it clear that this view applies not only to the single line plainsong, but also to ' figured music '.

Although this view does not tally with earlier theory (e.g. Tinctoris), and is fraught with difficulties in its practical application, it does seem to be a real attempt to face up to the problems of ' Tonus Commixtus ' in polyphony, and is, in some respects, close to the feeling for tonality of a later age. It is clear that Zarlino would have regarded Palestrina's ' Phrygian ' motets such as ' Super Flumina Babylonis ' (R. XI, p. 14) (P. V, p. 125) or the one discussed on page 19 of this book, as Aeolian or Hypoaeolian rather than truly Phrygian, and, though the accepted theoretical designation of both of these as Phrygian must be retained, it seems more acceptable to modern ears to think of them as Aeolian ending on a half-close, especially as the majority of intermediate cadences fall very definitely on A.

Glarean (Dodecachordon, 1547) also gives examples of modal mixings both in single line plainsong and in Polyphony. His attitude may be seen from his critical remarks on the works of his much admired Josquin (Glarean: ' Dodecachordon ', tr. Strunk; ' Source Readings ', p. 222):

Here, in the motet ' De Profundis ' . . . he has combined the systems of the two (Dorian and Hypodorian); at the same time, with astonishing and carefully studied elegance, he has thrown the phrase (' phrasis '; Strunk suggests = melodic idiom) into violent disorder, usurping now the leap of the Lydian, now that of the Ionian, until at length, by means of these most beautiful refinements, he glides, creeping unobserved and without offending the ear, from Dorian to Phrygian. . . . Thus, contrary to the nature of the modes, he has ended the combined systems of the Dorian and Hypodorian on E, the seat of the Phrygian. Yet there are other compositions in which he has done this also (nor is he alone in it), evidently from an immoderate love of novelty and an excessive eagerness to win a little glory for being unusual. . . .'

Bukofzer,[*] in his admirable study of the 'Caput' Masses of Dufay Okeghem and Obrecht, after pointing out that Okeghem has used a Mixolydian Cantus Firmus in a Dorian composition, says:

'In his treatise *De Natura et Proprietate Tonorum*, Tinctoris defines modes as exclusively melodic entities which apply only to single voices of a polyphonic composition. He expands his definition by what he calls mixtio and commixtio modi. . . . Quite consistently with his strictly melodic conception he determines the mode of a polyphonic piece from the tenor, and deals with the other voices, which may be in a different mode, separately. Their overall effect, which is merely another word for their simultaneous use, remains for Tinctoris a combination of melodic entities, which he expressly recognizes as a *compositio ex diversis partibus diversorum tonorum effecta*. The musical result of this *compositio* produces, however, intervallic (sic) combinations which transcend the concept of mode and lead into the realm of harmony in a large sense. Tinctoris should therefore not be accused of inconsistency or of having evaded the issue. He could not go further in modal analysis without destroying his own premises. A theory of harmony did not exist and was not yet necessary, because the combination could be explained in terms of intervals. . . .'

It is clear that by the sixteenth-century performance had outrun theory in the field of composition. What was happening in polyphony could no longer be explained in terms and theories of the mediaeval modes. The fact was that the vertical aspect of music was coming more and more into the sub-consciousness of musicians and that the harmonic factors were beginning to take charge to some extent whether composers realized it or not. The tendencies which led in the end to diatonic tonality as the only possible basis for harmonic thinking, were present in the very fact of polyphony in the stage which it had reached by the sixteenth century, and the theory of the modal system was doomed.

---

[*] Bukofzer: 'Studies in Mediaeval and Renaissance Music', p. 290.

CHAPTER II

RHYTHM AND TIME-SIGNATURES

THE whole of sixteenth-century texture is essentially an interweaving of independent rhythms, and not (as commonly said) a combination of melodies . . . Counterpoint *is* rhythm and very little else. (Morris: ' Contrapuntal Technique ', p. 72.)

IN sixteenth-century counterpoint rhythm is the mainspring of the whole mechanism; the other factors of musical thought, melody, 'harmony' and ' harmonic thinking ' in rudimentary form, structure and the rest are there, but they are mainly a by-product of the process of weaving rhythmical strands into a texture.

Duality of Rhythm

Another quotation from Morris gets to the root of the matter:
'. . . in the polyphonic music of the sixteenth century a double system of accentuation is employed. The rhythmical accentuation of each individual part is free, that is to say, the accents do not occur at strictly regular intervals, whereas the composition as a whole does conform to a fixed metrical scheme in which strong and weak accents succeed one another in a pre-determined order.' (ibid., p. 17.)

Morris goes on to show that this duality of rhythm has a close parallel in the underlying metre (quantity) in poetry, upon which a free verbal accentuation (stress) is superimposed.

' Between the rhythmical accent (accent of stress) and the metrical accent (the accent of quantity) there is continual interplay; sometimes they coincide, sometimes they are at odds, and the rhythmical problem before the poet is to strike the just balance. Too much coincidence means monotony; too much at-oddness means chaos ' (ibid., page 18).

In sixteenth-century polyphony exactly the same situation arises, but here it is vastly more complex: many voices may be singing simultaneously and each is free either to coincide in its stress accent with the basic metre or to be at odds with it; furthermore each may coincide or be at variance with any or all of the other voices.

The quantity rhythm is constant; it is the metrical basis of the work or section, definitely formulated at the beginning by a time-signature indicating the number and value and speed of the pulses in each measure. It forms a touchstone, a stable entity, against which the fluctuating and various stress rhythms of the individual voices may be measured and so achieve coherence.

The time-signature relates to the structure as a whole, and particularly to the vertical aspect of the counterpoint; *not* to the individual strand (though quantity and stress *may* coincide). Each strand is free to pursue its own rhythmic course provided that it obeys the normal aesthetic principles as regards the texture as a whole, the most important being that summarized by Morris thus: 'too much coincidence means monotony, too much at-oddness means chaos.'

A few words must be said about 'bar-lines' in sixteenth-century polyphony. It is often stated that bar-lines are nothing more than a convenient method, used by modern editors, of delineating the complete measure to help the eye in reading a score of the parts.* This is true in most vocal polyphony of the period, in so far as it was the normal practice not to bar the single voice parts, in which form most of the music has survived. There are, however, some points which must be remembered. In Italian and French keyboard music of the sixteenth century a remarkably regular system of barring is found; in England bar-lines were also used, though much more sparingly and with less regularity. Bar-lines of this irregular type appear in the 'Pars Organica' reductions of many vocal works of English polyphonists. It is a matter for serious conjecture how far bar-lines might have been used had vocal scores been the common practice of sixteenth-century polyphony.

Stress rhythm of individual strands

The stress rhythm of the individual strand in Palestrina's music is always clear, logical, and easily grasped when the factors governing accent in the normal vocal line are taken into account. These factors may be summarized thus:

1. The relative duration of a note; a longer note tends to.carry more potential accent than a shorter note preceding or following it.

2. The relative, and to some extent actual, pitch of a note; a higher note requires more tension in its production than a lower, and thereby has more prominence. In practice, however, this factor is to a great extent subservient to the others which will be considered.

---

* Apel (Notation of Polyphonic Music) in considering the advantages and disadvantages of bar lines in modern editions of sixteenth-century polyphony has a paragraph of great interest. ' It seems to us that the best device of barring is the bar-line which is drawn through each stave individually. This method avoids the sectional appearance produced by the long bar-lines of the modern score and yet allows for different barring in each part if necessary. It goes without saying that such bar-lines have only metrical significance, without necessarily implying the added modern meaning of an accentuated first beat. We say " necessarily " because a large portion of early music actually is " bar-line " music in exactly the same sense as music of Mozart and Beethoven—a fact which is usually overlooked in the discussions about the bar-line. To this field belongs the entire repertory of the thirteenth century, practically all Italian music of the fourteenth century, and the various types of sixteenth century chanson (chanson, frottola, villanella, etc.).' Compare: Morris: 'Contrapuntal Technique', p. 21. 'It is worth noticing that in secular compositions (madrigals, canzonets, and so on) the principle of irregular accentuation is not so systematically followed as in the great sacred forms of music, the Mass and the Motet. Frequently you will come across melodic sentences which resolve naturally into regular units of duple or triple measure.'

3. The method of approach to a note; a note approached by a leap, especially upward, stands out in its context more than one repeated or approached by step, though an upward step does at times create accent if other conditions are favourable.   The nature of the leap, whether upwards or downwards, is important.   The more arresting the interval, the more prominent becomes the note to which the leap is made.

4. The position of a note in a phrase; the first note of a phrase is often an *anacrusis,* and relatively unaccented, the stronger accentuation being thrown on to the following note; the *anacrusis* may consist of more than one note, in which case the note following the complete *anacrusis* figure will bear the full accent.   The anacrusis is such an instinctive rhythmic factor that description of it is almost impossible.   It is, in many cases, an over-riding force in rhythmical perception.

The highest note in a phrase, the melodic climax, may also be looked upon as a potential accent.

5. The underlaying of the words. As a rule in Palestrina's work the musical and verbal accentuation fit perfectly; on occasions where they seem at variance, the natural rhythm of the words may be an over-ruling factor in the melodic rhythm of the line.

A short example, taken completely at random from Palestrina's work, will illustrate this matter of accent in the individual strand and rhythmic duality in the texture as a whole.

Ex. 10

(R. VI. p. 67)
P. XII. p. 54
Missa Brevis. Gloria

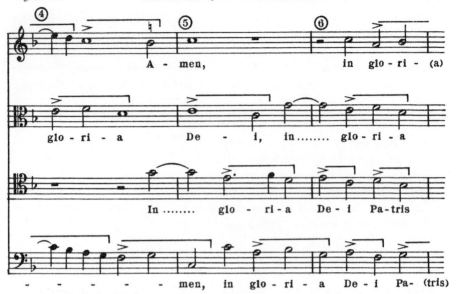

The stress rhythm of the strands is made up of irregular groups of pulses, some of two pulses, some of three, some of four. The following notes on the suggested placing of the accents may help the reader to see how they have been assessed.

Cantus. M(easure) 1. The last pulse on the word 'in' is weak, being an *anacrusis*.

The first pulse in M. 2 bears a strong post-anacrusis accent plus a verbal accent. Pulse 4 carries a verbal accent (the first syllable of 'Dei'), there being no over-riding melodic accent.

M. 3. The strong accent (the strongest in this line of the quotation) falls on the second pulse; it is a longer note, approached by leap of an octave upwards and has also a verbal accent.

M. 4. The second pulse bears a melodic accent as a longer note following a relatively short note.

In M. 6 the pattern begins again with the anacrusis, this time on the second pulse.

Altus. M. 3. The third pulse on the word 'in' is a long anacrusis and therefore without accent.

M. 4. Pulse 1 bears a strong post-anacrusis and verbal accent. Pulse 3 has a secondary longer note accent.

M. 5. Pulse 1 (semibreve) has a long note plus verbal accent. The fourth pulse, which would normally carry a strong accent (upward leap of a fifth, plus longer note) loses its accent because it is the start of a new phrase (making the interval 'dead') and an anacrusis.

M. 6. The second pulse carries a strong post-anacrusis accent.

Tenor. M. 1. The third pulse has a post-anacrusis plus verbal accent.

M. 2. The second pulse has a longer note and verbal accent; so has pulse 4.

M. 3. A secondary longer note accent occurs on pulse 3.

M. 4. The anacrusis on the fourth pulse though a semibreve in value is unaccented.

M. 5. The second pulse carries a strong post-anacrusis accent (plus verbal).

M. 6. The first and third pulses carry verbal accents strengthened by the rise to each and the drop of a third which follows.

Bassus. M. 1. Pulse 1 has a post-anacrusis and verbal accent; pulse 4, a verbal accent.

M. 2. Pulse 2 carries a verbal accent.

M. 3. There is a longer note accent on the first pulse and a strong (leap of an octave upward plus longer note) accent on the final pulse.

M. 4. Pulse 3 has a melodic accent (longer note following a series of shorter notes).

M. 5. The ' C ' on the second pulse has its melodic accent cancelled as it is the beginning of a new phrase and an anacrusis. Pulse 3 has a post-anacrusis and verbal accent.

M. 6. The second and fourth pulses carry verbal accents.

It will be seen that the only full measures in which the individual stress rhythm of any line corresponds wholly with the metrical rhythm are measure 4 Altus and measure 6 Tenor. Furthermore in no full measure, nor on any four consecutive pulses, does the individual stress rhythm of any two parts coincide. Yet the effect of the whole gives an unmistakable feeling of the four pulse metrical rhythm; there is at least one stress rhythm accent on the first pulse of every measure and on the third pulse of all save the second. It must be emphasized that this short example was chosen completely at random; on almost any page of Palestrina's work, except in definitely homophonic sections, equal or greater rhythmic complexity could be found, and equal clarity.

Time-Signatures. Proportional System

A few words must be said about ' time-signatures ' in Polyphony (the index of the metrical rhythm). The main difference between the ' proportional' system in use (c) 1400—1600 and the modern time system is that in the former variability of the speed of a particular note was controlled with mathematical accuracy by the actual time-signature; a semibreve in ¢ was of a standardized length; in the modern system the length of a semibreve in 4/2 may vary infinitely according to the speed direction which is added to the time-signature (Presto, Allegro molto, Allegro, Allegretto, Andante etc.). These speed indications were virtually unknown in vocal Polyphony.

The whole proportional system depended upon the principle of a fixed unit of time known as the *Tactus,* which may be described as a basic pulse-rate. The only method of varying the speed of a note, apart from the perfect and imperfect mensurations discussed in the next paragraph, was by applying arithmetically exact proportional diminutions or augmentations in certain ratios. These were in fact the speed indications of music from (c) 1400—1600 and were indicated by a complex set of symbols.*

Mensuration

The notes in use during the greater part of the Polyphonic Age were: The Maxima ⊏⊐, the Long ⊏⊐ , the Breve ◻, the Semibreve o, the Minima 𝅗 (𝅘), the Semi-minima (crotchet) 𝅘𝅥 (𝅘𝅥) and the Fusa (quaver) 𝅘𝅥𝅮 (𝅘𝅥𝅮). Two methods of dividing notes were used: the Perfect, which implied the division of a note into three of the next shorter values; the Imperfect, which implied division into two. Both these divisions were used in dealing with the Breve and the Semibreve. The imperfect method was chiefly used in the case of the longer notes, and exclusively in the case of the shorter.

The mensuration (division) of the Long, known as ' Mood ', had become obsolete by the sixteenth century. That of the Breve was called ' Tempus '; that of the Semibreve, ' Prolatio '. This system of mensuration gives the following four varieties of time.

	Sign	Note values	Modern signature
1. Tempus perfectum cum prolatione perfecta	☉	◻=ooo : o=𝅘𝅥𝅘𝅥𝅘𝅥	$\frac{9}{2}$
2. Tempus perfectum cum prolatione imperfecta	O̟	◻=ooo : o=𝅘𝅥𝅘𝅥	$\frac{3}{1}$
3. Tempus imperfectum cum prolatione imperfecta	C	◻=oo : o=𝅘𝅥𝅘𝅥	$\frac{4}{2}$
4. Tempus imperfectum cum prolatione perfecta	₵	◻=oo : o=𝅘𝅥𝅘𝅥𝅘𝅥	$\frac{6}{2}$

Proportions

The table given above shows what was known as the *integer valor* time signatures; in it every Semibreve was of the value of one *Tactus*. The method of shortening these basic note values was by the use of diminutions in various ratios. *Diminutio simplex* or *proportio dupla* (2/1) produced the general effect of doubling the speed, by moving the Tactus on to the Breve instead of the Semibreve. This statement is only an approximation, since *proportio dupla* called for perfect mensuration of the Breve in *prolatio perfecta*. It is probably nearer the truth to state that a passage written in *proportio dupla* is equivalent to one in the *integer valor* if the latter uses the next shorter notes throughout. An attempt to explain this complicated matter will be found in the notes on the proportional system at the end of this chapter. The signs used for simple diminution are these:

$$\Phi, \; \Theta_2 \; ; \; \Phi, O_2; \; ₵, \Im, C_2; \; ₵, \Im, ₵_2.$$

* See long note at the end of this chapter.

Proportio tripla (**C₃**, etc.) has the general effect of a three-fold increase in speed; quadrupla, fourfold, etc. These proportions all belong to the *genus multiplex* and imply fractions whose denominator is 1 $\left(\begin{smallmatrix}2 & 3 & 4\\1 & 1 & 1\end{smallmatrix}\right)$.

Other proportions of the *genus superparticulare* (fractions whose numerator is one more than the denominator, e.g. 4/3), the *genus superpartiens* (numerator 2, 3 or 4, etc. more than denominator) and combinations of these with the *multiplex* proportions, were, with the notable exception of *sesquialtera* (3/2), for the most part theoretical abstractions.

Sesquialtera (**C₂³**, etc.) implies a general quickening in the ratio 3/2; that is, three semibreves of the proportion are equal to two of the *integer valor*. This proportion belongs to the *genus superparticulare*.

Proportional augmentations (1/2, 2/3, etc.) were generally used simply as cancellations of diminutions and rarely had any reference to the *integer valor*.*

Three uses of proportional time-signatures were commonly found in polyphony. (I) Alteration of note values either by change of mensuration or diminution in all voices simultaneously. (II) Conflicting signatures in different ' voices ' of a polyphonic composition at one time. (III) The same time-signature in all voices throughout the work.

All three of these usages may be found in the works of Palestrina, though the great bulk of his music is written with the same time-signature in all voices simultaneously (III or I).

I. Simultaneous changes of time-signature are most often found in the form of short sections of **◐3** or **◐₂³** in a work or movement otherwise in **¢**.

II. Examples of conflicting signatures occur mainly in the early works, for example, the Agnus III of the Ecce Sacerdos Magnus Mass (R. I, p. 33) (P. X, pp. 29, 30) where the signatures **O O ◐ ¢** are found in conflicting combination. The five-voice Mass ' L'homme armé ', an early work, though it appears in the third book of Masses (1570), is generally taken as the *locus classicus* of proportional conflict in Palestrina. In it progressive diminutions (**¢ C ¢**) and other devices may be found. It is clear, however, that Palestrina abandoned these usages in his mature writing.

III. The use of a single time-signature simultaneously throughout a work is not, strictly speaking, proportional at all. It does not alter in any proportion another time already set. Nevertheless such a signature may well have significance as a speed indicator.

The notes which follow are offered as an attempt to explain some of the more important factors in the proportional system which have direct bearing on the technique of Palestrina.

Notes on Proportions and Proportional signatures.

1. The following table is an attempt to set out the theoretical mensuration and values of the normal signatures in *integer valor,* proportio dupla, proportio tripla, proportio sesquialtera. In proportio dupla notated *modus=* actual *tempus,* notated *tempus=* actual *prolatio;* this implies perfect mensuration of the Breve in *prolatio perfecta* (**¢ ⊙**) and perfect Longs in tempus

* See note at end of this chapter.

perfectum (**O Θ**) when these are written in simple diminution. Proportio tripla and sesquialtera call for perfect mensuration of the Breve.

INTEGER VALOR		Modus			Tempus			Prolatio		
1. Tempus Imperfectum: Prolatio Imperfecta.	C (2.2.)	4 tactus.	2t.	2t.	2t.	1t.	1t.	Tactus:	½t.	½t.
2. Tempus Perfectum: Prolatio Imperfecta.	O (3,2.)	6 tactus.	3t.	3t.	3t.	1t.1t.	1t.	Tactus:	½t.	½t.
3. Tempus Imperfectum: Prolatio Perfecta.	C (2,3.)	4 tactus.	2t.	2t.	2t.	1t.	1t.	Tactus:		
4. Tempus Perfectum: Prolatio Perfecta. (O also used as augmentation sign.)	O (3,3.)	6 tactus.	3t.	3t.	3t.	1t.1t. 1t.		Tactus:		

PROPORTIO DUPLA. (Diminutio Simplex).		Notated modus = actual Tempus			Notated Tempus = actual Prolatio					
1. Tempus Imperfectum: Prolatio Imperfecta.	¢ (Ɔ,C₂) (Π.2)	2t.	1t.	1t.	Tactus.	½t.	½t.			
2. Tempus Perfectum: Prolatio Imperfecta. (Alternative interpretation more common in Polyphony)	Φ (O₂) (Π.2)	3t. / 3t.	1t.1t. 1t. / 1½t. 1½t.		Tactus. / 1½t	½t. ½t. / ½t.½t.½t.				
3. Tempus Imperfectum: Prolatio Perfecta.	¢ Ɔ (Π.3)	2t.	1t.	1t.	Tactus	⅓t.⅓t.⅓t.				
4. Tempus Perfectum: Prolatio Perfecta.	Φ O₂ (Π.3)	3t.	1t.1t. 1t.		Tactus	⅓t.⅓t.⅓t.				

PROPORTIO TRIPLA.										
1. Tempus Imperfectum: Prolatio Imperfecta.	C₃ (¢₃)	2t.	1t.	1t.	1t.	⅓t.⅓t.⅓t.				
2. Tempus Perfectum: Prolatio Imperfecta.	O₃	3t.	1t.1t. 1t.		1t.	⅓t.⅓t.⅓t.				
3. Tempus Imperfectum: Prolatio Perfecta.	C₃	2t.	1t.	1t.	1t. NOT	⅓t.⅓t.⅓t. USED				
4. Tempus Perfectum: Prolatio Perfecta.	O₃	3t.	1t.1t.1t.		1t. NOT	⅓t.⅓t.⅓t. USED				

PROPORTIO SESQUIALTERA.										
1. Tempus Imperfectum: Prolatio Imperfecta.	C³₂	4t.	2t.	2t.	2t.	⅔t.⅔t.⅔t.				
2. Tempus Perfectum: Prolatio Imperfecta.	O³₂	4t.	2t.	2t.	2t.	⅔t.⅔t.⅔t.				
3. Tempus Imperfectum: Prolatio Perfecta.	C³₂		NOT		USED					
4. Tempus Perfectum: Prolatio Perfecta.	O³₂		NOT		USED					

¢ = C (¢ written in notes next highest in value.)
Φ = O (Φ " " " " " ")
C₃ = C (C₃ " " " " " " ")
O₃ = O (O₃ " " " " " " ")

The effect of the diminutions may be most clearly seen in the semibreves of this table in C & O.

2. *Augmentation.* In the single line augmentation was generally used merely as a cancellation of diminutions already existing. (½ *proportio subdupla*, ⅓ *sub-tripla*, etc.). In polyphony with conflicting signatures in the different voices, a more elaborate scheme of augmentation is found. From the later part of the fifteenth century the signatures denoting *prolatio perfecta* ₵ ⊙, when placed in one voice against *prolatio imperfecta* signatures C O in the other voices, lose their normal temporal significance, and imply threefold augmentation (see Apel, ' The Notation of Polyphonic Music ', pp. 163 et seq.). This is clearly the use which Palestrina implies when in the Mass ' L'homme armé ' he writes the signature ⊙ for the Cantus Firmus in the Tenor against O in the other voices in the first ' Kyrie ' and the opening of the Credo; likewise, sixfold augmentation is required by the ₵ for the Cantus Firmus against ₵ in the other voices in the Gloria.

3. *The Tactus.* The word ' Tactus ' seems to have come into general use to describe the basic pulse in polyphonic music towards the end of the fifteenth century. Sachs in ' Rhythm and Tempo ' (p. 217) dates the first appearance of the term in Ramis de Pareia's ' Tractatus de musica ' of 1482. Adam de Fulda in ' De Musica ' 1490 (Gerbert Script., III, p. 362) defines it as follows: ' Tactus est continua motio in mensura contenta rationis ' = The *tactus* is continuous movement in a measure conforming to standard plan. He recognized three tactus distributions (1) tactus = minim (augmentation); (2) tactus = semibreve (integer valor); (3) tactus = breve (diminutio simplex) or, in other words 'alla minima', 'alla semibreve' and 'alla breve'. Most authorities agree that the tactus was made up of two beats of the hand, down-up or up-down, neither being stressed more than the other, each constant and occupying the time of a pulse of ' a quietly breathing man ' (Gafori), i.e., 60-80 per minute. This suggests the standard tactus rate = M.M. 30-40, and gives the following sample speeds:

C (integer valor)   ╡ = M.M. 15-20. ο = 30-40. ♩ = 60-80.
(alla semibreve).

₵ (diminutio simplex) ╡ = M.M. 30-40. ο = 60-80. ♩ = 120-160.
(alla breve).

C½ (augmentation)   ╡ = M.M. 7½-10. ο = 15-20. ♩ = 30-40.
(alla minima).

The essential quality of the *tactus* is its unvarying pulse-rate. Apel (' The Notation of Polyphonic Music ') points out that (p. 190)

'. . . Practically every theorist gives longer or shorter explanations on the *tactus* as a unit of musical time, and although the positive information to be gained from these explanations is much less clear than we would wish, the important fact is that nowhere is a remark to be found which would give the slightest justification for the assumption that the duration of a note could be varied according to the text, the character or feeling of the piece. . . . In the sixteenth century there existed only one way of changing temporal duration of a given note, that is, by proportions. Thus the proportional signs, if used simultaneously in all parts, represent the tempo marks, nay, the metronomic marks of the fifteenth and sixteenth centuries. . . . It goes without saying that this principle does not imply stability of tempo throughout the entire early history of music, but only during certain periods, or in certain schools, or for certain ' standard ' types of music. Even in this more limited sense the term should not be interpreted too rigidly, and should be considered as the indication of a guiding idea rather than as a strict law.'

4. *The meaning of* ₵ *and* ⊕ *in sixteenth-century polyphony when used as signatures in all voices.* Curt Sachs: (' Rhythm and Tempo ', p. 222), argues that ' ₵ meant *proportio dupla* only where it clashed with ₵ in another voice part. Otherwise, its relation with ₵ was vague or nonexistent.' ' Proportional ' signatures employed in all voices lost their proportional significance. This interpretation is in conflict with Apel's view, quoted above, that proportional signs represented the tempo marks of the sixteenth century. Sachs goes on to state that ' As a rule, the non-proportional ₵ was slightly faster than ₵.' He quotes Georg Rhaw, Koswick, and Cocleus (all early sixteenth century writers) who state that ' ₵ required faster playing (*velocius tangi debent*),' and Glarean (Lib. III, cap. viii), ' . . . when musicians are afraid the audience might get tired, they hasten the *tactus* by crossing the circle or semicircle and calling it a diminution. Actually, they do not diminish the value or number of notes; they just quicken the beat, *quod tactus fiat velocior*. Thus the three sections of the Kyrie in a mass . . . are often signed O ₵ ⊕ to avoid boredom.' His comment is: ' This statement can hardly be mistaken: such a change of tempo was not a proportional diminution. It did not, as it should, affect the value of the notes and make an *alla breve* out of an *alla semibreve*. While *proportio dupla* was in fact a duplication of note values without giving the feeling of a faster tempo, this pseudo-diminution affected the tempo of beating. Instead of doubling the tempo, it was just *festinandum* and *velocior*; it speeded up.'

It must be pointed out that Sachs's interpretation of the problem is by no means completely satisfying. In the first place, if ₵ in the Altus, Tenor and Bassus against ₵ in the Cantus of the ' in nomine ' section of Palestrina's ' L'homme armé ' Mass (Benedictus) has a definite ' proportio dupla ' meaning, and hence an ' *alla breve* ' tactus speed, does the ₵ in all voices of the Crucifixus of the same mass mean something different? In the second place, when a section of a movement appears with a different signature to that used for the rest of the work (all signatures being the same in all voices) are proportional values to be disregarded? This matter will be considered later.

It is, however, clear, that a strict proportional interpretation of the signs ₵ ₡ (in all parts) cannot be upheld in the sixteenth century. Apel, ' Notation ', p. 191, points out that in the late fifteenth and early sixteenth centuries sections in ₵ in shorter note values are frequently followed by sections in ₡ in notes of double the value (roughly). If strict proportional meaning is applied to this situation it means no more than a different method of writing the same time values without any practical reason. Apel says: ' We prefer to think that it really meant a different tempo, the reduction of values being somewhat different from an exact halving '. On page 193 (op. cit.) Apel gives two extracts from the *Odhecaton* which seem to demand different interpretations of the ₡ signature.

The problem of the exact speed of the *tactus* in ₵ and ₡ as general signatures in the sixteenth century is almost certainly insoluble. Taking M.M. 36 as a ' near-mean ' *tactus* speed, the minim of ₵ and ₡= 144. This pace seems not unreasonable for some Palestrina works, but on the whole it is too fast. If, however, it is too fast for the majority of Palestrina works written under a common signature in all parts (? non-proportional) it is equally unsuitable for a work in which conflicting proportional signatures are used (e.g. ' L'homme armé ' Mass), since in these the note values are generally much the same as in the common signature works. It may be suggested that a slower tactus rate for sixteenth-century polyphony would solve some of the difficulties.

Apel (op. cit., p. 192) suggests that during and after the period of Josquin the semibreve under ₵ had approximately the same value as it had formerly under ₵. The general adoption of the signs ₵ and ₡ in the sixteenth century (except perhaps in England) as the normal signatures for duple and triple times, together with the undoubted fact of the lengthening of all note values from 1200 onwards (see Thurston Dart: ' The Interpretation of Music ', p. 152) seems to strengthen this hypothesis. It may be that ₵ and ₡ came to be regarded as the *integer valor* signs of the Palestrina period, and this contention seems to be borne out by the considerations set out in the next paragraph.

5. *Proportional Signatures in Palestrina's music.* By far the greater part of Palestrina's sacred music is written under the sign ₵ in all voices. Sometimes a section under the sign ₡ followed by some proportional connotation (or more rarely O_1^3 or $₵_3$) is interpolated into an otherwise ₵ movement. In a few works the signs ₡ and $₡_2^3$, $₡_3$ are used in all voices throughout a movement. In the early works the signs ₵ and O (uncrossed) may be found.

It seems clear that ₵ and ₡ as common time signatures throughout a complete work or movement imply the same minim and semibreve speeds.

(R.III.p.108)
P.V. p.86
'Quam pulchri sunt'

Ex. 11

(a)

R.III. p.109
P.V. p. 87
'Tollite jugum meum'

(b)

In both the motets from which the above extracts are taken, the time-signatures, common to all voices, are unchanged throughout the work. The disposition of the suspended discords, as well as of the note values, unessential notes, etc., leaves little doubt in the mind that the speed of both is basically the same. ₵ implies four minims to the measure, each able to carry a change of vertical interval combination (which will be referred to as ' harmonic' pulse in future to save space). ₵ implies six minim harmonic pulses. If the proportio dupla interpretation of the signs is taken ₵ means that the measure consists of one *tactus*=an imperfect Breve=four minim harmonic pulses each of ¼ of a *tactus*. The ₵ sign means that the measure consists of one perfect Breve (1½ *tactus*)=3 semibreves (each ½ *tactus*)= 6 minim harmonic pulses each of ¼ tactus.

The signatures ₵$^3_2$ O₃, ₵₃, ₵₃ are found from time to time throughout Palestrina's church music, though the actual amount of triple time in his output is surprisingly small. (Curt Sachs, op. cit., puts it at less than 1 per cent, though he is probably referring to complete movements in triple time.) The ₵$^3_2$ and ₵₃ signs are used occasionally throughout an entire motet or movement of a Mass in all voices (for example, the motets for double choir 'Lauda Zion'(P. VII, p. 91), ' Veni Sancte Spiritus ' (P.VII, p. 117), ' Gaude, Barbara' (P. VII, p. 70).). More frequently, and with apparently the same temporal significance, they appear in sections, sometimes short, sometimes relatively long, of works beginning and ending with the signature ₵. The signs ₵₃ and O₃ are merely another method of writing ₵$^3_2$, as may be seen from the table given on page 34. They are very rarely encountered, and then (in the mature works, at least) only for sections in ₵ works.

The strict *proportional* meaning of ₵$^3_2$ implies a measure of three (or six) semibreves each of one-third of a tactus, and each a potential ' harmonic' pulse, the group of three semibreves equalling one perfect breve of one tactus (diminution 6/2). ₵₃ implies a measure of three (or sometimes six) semibreves each of one-sixth of a tactus, and each a potential harmonic pulse, the three semibreves equalling 1 perfect breve of half a tactus (diminution 6/1). This theoretical interpretation, which makes the semibreve of ₵3 twice as fast as that of ₵$^3_2$, is clearly untenable; when music written under the two signatures is examined and compared it soon becomes obvious that in Palestrina's work there is little difference ·between the speed of ₵$^3_2$ and ₵3. This is completely borne out by the passage which Sachs quotes (op. cit., p. 230) from Martin Agricola (*Musica figuralis deudsch*, Wittenberg, 1532):

. . . Agricola says expressly that the *sesquialtera* is used ' in *proportione tripla*/*hemiola*/when all voice parts have it/and thus they always sing a semibreve instead of a minim.'

Sachs points out that ' *Hemiola*—not to be confused with the name for the exchange of 3/4 and 6/8—was a frequent misnomer for *sesquialtera.*' He prefaces the Agricola quotation by stating that ' In one of the confusing inconsistencies of the time, *proportio tripla* was actually only *sesquialtera* whenever the signature 3 appeared in all voice parts.'

This means that all the signatures ₵3, ₵$^3_2$, O3, ₵3 have the same temporal significance. What Agricola means by ' and thus they always sing a semi-breve instead of a minim ' is less clear. From the example which Sachs examines in his next paragraph (Josquin: ' Stabat Mater ') it is obvious that sesquialtera 3/2 and not proportio dupla 2/1 which semibreve=minim would imply, is intended. It is possible that Agricola meant that the semi-breve harmonic pulse replaced the minim.

It may be asked why, if the figure 3 implies not *tripla* but *sesquialtera* in 𝇋3 (following 𝄴), should it not have the same implication in O3 (following 𝄴)? The reason may be that the sesquialtera is already implied by the proportio dupla diminution in 𝇋₃.

The following examples should demonstrate these points.

Ex. 12   (R.VIII. p.148)
                                  P.III. p.114

Haec dies

Gaude Barbara   (R.VII. p. 81)
                                  P.II. p. 61
                (Time signature incorrect in Haberl)

The note values and technical features (passing notes, suspensions, etc.) in the above examples are so similar as to suggest that the various triple-time signatures employed are, in reality and practice, synonymous, when used in all voices for a section of a movement otherwise in duple time (₵). The examples which follow, taken from complete movements in a triple-time, force the same conclusion; despite Sachs's statement, there seems to be no reason, on internal evidence at any rate, for suggesting a different speed for triple-time complete movements from that of sectional triple-time passages.

Ex. 13

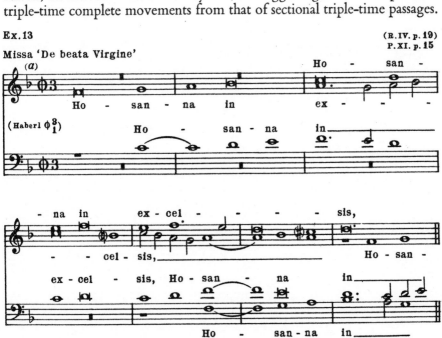

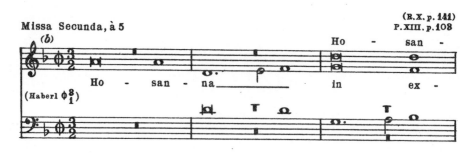

A comparison of the following passages, one with the signature $\oint_2^3$ and the other $O3$ in four of the voices, the fifth voice having a 'conflicting' signature, with the passages already quoted will show little evidence to support the view that $\oint_2^3$ (or O_3) with a conflicting signature demands a different basic tempo to that required by the signature in all the voices.

Two examples from the same work of passages in ¢, the first with one voice signed ¢, the second ¢ in all voices, do not suggest any essential difference of speed.

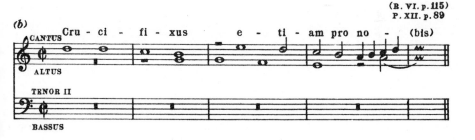

If the arguments set out above are accepted, the following conclusions may be drawn.

1. The actual speed values of the semibreve, minim, crotchet, and quaver in ◐ and ¢ are the same.

2. The signatures ◐³₂, ◐3, ◐³₁, O3 and ¢ 3 are synonymous, and imply a *sesquialtera* × *proportio dupla* diminution of the *integer valor*.

Three semibreves of $\mathbf{0}^{3}_{2}$, etc., equal to two semibreves of $\mathbb{C}$.*

3. The musical and technical evidence suggests that the signatures $\mathbf{0}^{3}_{2}$, etc., and $\mathbb{C}$ and $\mathbf{0}$ have the same meaning when used as 'total' signatures (that is, in all voices simultaneously) throughout a whole work or movement as they have when used sectionally (following or preceding another total signature) within a work or movement.

---

* Perhaps the most convincing proof of the theory that three semibreves of $\mathbf{0}^{3}_{2}$, etc. are equal to two semibreves of $\mathbb{C}$ is to be found in the Hymn 'Vexilla Regis'. Here (in verse VI) Palestrina writes a short passage of triple rhythm in a verse beginning and ending in $\mathbb{C}$. Instead of following his customary practice of changing the signature to $\mathbf{0}^{3}_{2}$ he uses blackened notation (c.f. Missa: Aeterna Christi Munera, 'Et in Spiritum'. R. xv., p. 10). The generally accepted ruling is that '(1) a blackened note loses one-third of its value; (2) blackened notes are always imperfect' (Apel: 'The Notation of Polyphonic Music', p. 127). That means that ▉ ▉ ▉ = ◖◗ : ● ● ● = ○ ○ etc. The passage using coloration, therefore, implies a sesquialtera diminution of the note values of $\mathbb{C}$, and is thus another way of writing $\mathbf{0}^{3}_{2}$, etc. In this case the ratio of diminution is certain, and furthermore the example given below shows no discrepancy with the examples of $\mathbf{0}^{3}_{2}$, etc., quoted above in the disposition of note values from a technical point of view.

(R. XIV. p. 95)
P. VIII. p. 72

(c)

u - ni - ca, _____ in hoc pas - cha - li

tem - po - re   au - ge

(d)   (Haberl)   ibid

4. These signatures, when used as total signatures, imply the same tempo as when they are used with conflicting signatures in one or more parts.

5. If proportional signatures when used in conflict have real meaning of tempo, there is no evidence to suggest that they lose this significance when they are used as total signatures.

CHAPTER III

THE RHYTHMIC MELODIC LINE

THE individual strands which made up the texture of polyphony consisted of two closely interconnected elements, one rhythmic, the other melodic. The shaping of these strands became in the sixteenth century a highly organized artistic achievement, and Palestrina's art in this sphere may well be regarded as the culmination of the process of refining and perfecting the pure vocal line, a process which had been maturing throughout the polyphonic period, having its roots in the melodic shapes of the older art of plainsong.

Melodic Line

The characteristic feature of Palestrina's line in its melodic aspect has been described as ' curvilinear movement '—that is, a series of carefully proportioned curves in which ascending movement is balanced by descending. This balancing of upward and downward progress is as characteristic of the rise and fall of the extended phrase as it is of the smaller undulations which combine to make up that phrase.

Jerkiness of any kind is foreign to the nature of this curvilinear line, so, in general, it will be found that the melodic leaps are relatively small, though marked enough to form a contrast to the more general stepwise movement. Moreover the leaps themselves are usually smoothed over and balanced by being preceded and followed by progress, often stepwise, in the opposite direction. An example of an almost perfect curvilinear line will make this clear.

Ex. 16

(B. VI. p. 74)
P. XII. p. 59
Missa Brevis

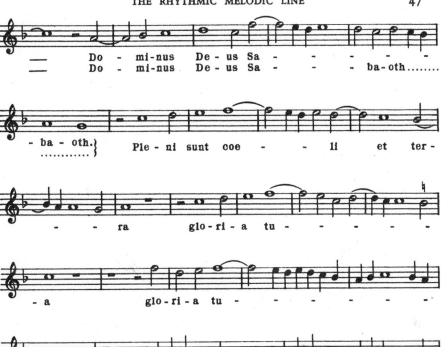

Melodic Intervals

The purely melodic aspect of the line is so closely bound up with rhythmical considerations that it can scarcely be examined apart from these. Nevertheless, it may be useful to list the melodic interval progressions normally found before describing their use in a rhythmical context.

Stepwise progressions of a tone or *diatonic* semitone, ascending or descending (major and minor seconds) are the common practice of the style. The chromatic semitone (C–C sharp, etc.) ascending *is* found in Palestrina's work as a 'real' melodic interval,★ especially in the Third Book of Motets (1575), but always without change of ' chord '; that is to say, the chromatic change, usually a minor to a major third above the bass, takes place while the bass remains fixed and the intervals made by the other parts are not altered except by interchange. Jeppesen gives a list of instances† but argues against their authenticity, and disposes of many of them convincingly. It is probably wise to regard this progression as outside the normal practice of Palestrina.

★ The matter of ' real ' and ' dead ' intervals is dealt with below. It may be noted that chromatic semitones as ' dead ' intervals are more often found.

† The Style of Palestrina, pp. 34 et seq. Jeppesen gives examples from Ingegneri of much more definite chromatic alterations.

Leaps of a minor or major third, perfect fourth, and perfect fifth are common both upwards and downwards. The minor sixth is found ascending only. The ascending octave is frequently used; the descending octave rather less often.

The ascending major sixth is so rarely found (Jeppesen quotes only two instances, P. IV, 116, P. XXIX, 157) that it must be excluded. All augmented and diminished intervals, sevenths, and intervals larger than an octave, as well as descending sixths are outside the scope of Palestrina's melodic line as ' real ' intervals.

' Dead ' Intervals

A distinction must be drawn between real melodic intervals and what are generally termed ' dead ' intervals. A real melodic interval is one which occurs in the course of a phrase. A ' dead ' interval is the interval between the end of one phrase and the beginning of the next; a rest of any duration may intervene in such cases, or the new phrase may begin without rest. ' Dead ' intervals between phrases include all the normally used real intervals, and also most of the ' forbidden ' leaps which are never found in the course of a phrase.

Approach and quitting of Leaps

The larger melodic leaps (minor sixths and octaves) are almost invariably preceded and followed by movement in the opposite direction, generally stepwise. The same method is most often found in the case of the smaller intervals, though these are also used approached and/or quitted by movement in the same direction; this is especially true of major and minor thirds.

Compound Leaps

Sometimes two leaps in the same direction are found. In ascending passages of this kind the larger leap is generally taken first, followed by the smaller; 〔▞〕 is the characteristic shape of the curve rather than 〔▞〕 : in downward progressions the shorter leap generally comes first, making the pattern 〔▞〕 rather than 〔▞〕. The same principle applies to leaps followed or preceded by steps in the same direction. A few examples will make this clear.

Ex. 17

(a)
CANTUS   Maj.3rd. Mi.3rd   P. XXII. p. 72

qui tol - lis   pec - ca - ta   mun -   -   - di

(b)   Perf. 5th   Mi. 3rd   P. XIX. p. 66

Et   in   ter - ra   pax.

Rhythmic Considerations

Palestrina's rhythmic-melodic line is influenced in the behaviour of its interval progressions, not only by strictly rhythmical considerations, but also by the actual values of the notes employed in forming the intervals of the melody. It may be wise to stress once again the leading premise that the line is a product of rhythm and melody in about equal proportions; it is the variation and balance of note lengths and rhythmic shapes just as much as of melodic contours which give the line its character. It is, therefore, not surprising to find that actual note values play a large part in governing the melodic behaviour of the line.

The treatment of the various note values, especially in the case of the shorter notes (crotchets and quavers), varies to a considerable degree with the time signature employed. The difficult problems arising out of the ' proportional ' time signatures of the sixteenth century have been mooted in the note at the end of Chapter II. It was there shown how uncertain the real meanings of these signs must remain. In practice, however, various factors relevant to the matter under consideration emerge quite clearly. The chief of these seems to be the value of the basic ' harmonic pulse ' (i.e. the shortest note values on which changes of interval combination from the vertical point of view occur) in the measure, under the various time signatures used. This, in turn, is largely dependent upon the actual temporal value of the notes in question.

Under the signs ₵ and 𝇈 the minim is clearly the normal (shortest) rate of ' harmonic ' change.* ₵ implies 4 minim harmonic pulses to the breve (imperfect) of 1 *tactus* which occupies the measure (or bar, in modern terms). 𝇈 means 6 minim ' harmonic ' pulses of the same value (¼ tactus) to the perfect Breve (1½ tactus) of the measure.

In the case of the signatures 𝇈$\frac{3}{2}$ and 𝇈3 the semibreve becomes the ' harmonic ' unit.† 𝇈$\frac{3}{2}$ (sesquialtera diminuta) implies three semibreve harmonic units each one-third of a tactus to the Breve (perfect but diminished by sesquialtera: 1 tactus), the measure consisting normally of one such perfect breve (three semibreves) and occasionally of two. 𝇈3 has been shown to be another method of writing 𝇈$\frac{3}{2}$ (see note at the end of previous chapter). ₵3 and O3 (very rare) have the same meaning.

The uncrossed C and O$\frac{3}{2}$ signs are only found in the sacred works in the earliest period of Palestrina's music. There C seems to imply sometimes a measure consisting of four crotchet harmonic pulses each of ¼ tactus=one semibreve of 1 tactus (tactus alla semibreve), at other times four minim pulses. O$\frac{3}{2}$ (following C) has a meaning similar to the ₵ . . . 𝇈$\frac{3}{2}$ contrast: that is three minim pulses=1 tactus=1 measure.

From the above calculations it becomes obvious that the ' harmonic ' pulse values of notes under the various time signatures may be summed up as follows:

The *minim* ♩ of ₵ and 𝇈 or O$\frac{3}{2}$ is represented by the *semibreve* o of 𝇈$\frac{3}{2}$ 𝇈3 ₵ 3 and O3 (and the *crotchet* of C or O if used in the proportional sense). The *crotchet* ♩ of ₵ and 𝇈 is represented by the *minim* ♩ of 𝇈$\frac{3}{2}$ and 𝇈3, etc. (and the quaver of C).

This simply means that minims and crotchets in 𝇈$\frac{3}{2}$ 𝇈3 ₵ 3 and O3 must receive approximately the same treatment as crotchets and quavers in ₵ and 𝇈 and so forth (even though the 𝇈$\frac{3}{2}$ ♩ equals 1½ crotchets of ₵).

Quavers

Quavers are the shortest note values found in the sacred music of Palestrina. They are not used in signatures where the ' harmonic ' pulse falls on the semibreve (𝇈3 𝇈$\frac{3}{2}$ O3 ₵3). Under the signs ₵ and 𝇈 they are normally found in pairs on the weak second half of the minim. Occasionally a four-quaver group appears, in which case it occupies a complete minim; groups of four quavers beginning on the weak half of the minim, or pairs of quavers on the first half are outside the normal style of Palestrina's music.

* See examples 11a, 11b, page 38.
† See examples 12a, b, c, pages 40, 41.

Pairs of Quavers

Stepwise movement is almost the invariable rule where quavers are concerned. Pairs of quavers always seem to be introduced by step following a crotchet or dotted minim: the melodic interval between the two quavers is invariably either a major or minor second: a pair of quavers is usually followed by another step. The various formulae of stepwise movements normally found may be seen in the following set of examples.

Three other figures, theoretically possible, not included in the list given above, are so rare that they cannot be considered as a normal part of Palestrina's technique.

Ex. 19

Pairs of Quavers quitted by Leap

When the second of a pair of quavers is consonant, and the movement is downward, an upward leap is quite often used as a continuation of the melodic line.   The following patterns are found.

Ex.20

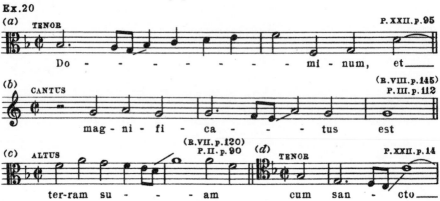

So far as the present writer knows, leaps downward or upward from the second of an ascending pair of quavers are not a part of Palestrina's technique. The continuation by leap from the second of two quavers seems to be confined entirely to the formulae given above, that is, to the upward leap of a third, fourth, fifth, or octave from a pair of descending quavers approached by step from above.

Four-quaver groups

Groups of four quavers occupying one complete minim are found sporadically throughout Palestrina's works, but their appearance is comparatively rare.★ They generally occur as isolated instances in a movement, but occasionally they are used in imitation; the pattern shown in Ex. 21a below is used fourteen times in some twenty consecutive measures.   The four-quaver group is most often introduced by stepwise movement, though

* A very rare instance of a group of three quavers following a dotted crotchet is worth citing, even though its authenticity may be doubtful.   This is really equivalent to a four-quaver group, the first quaver being represented by the dot of the crotchet.

Ex. 23   P.VI. p.152

sometimes the first quaver is approached from a stationary note or by leap:
the continuation of the figure and the quitting of it always demand conjunct
movement.   The four-quaver group may be used on any minim (complete)
of the measure.   It is very rare in the top voice.

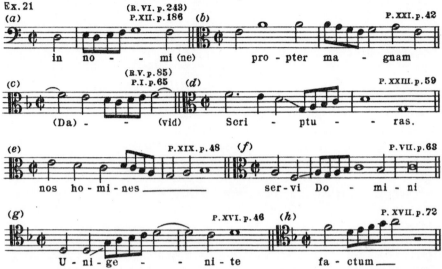

Ex. 21
(a)   (R. VI. p. 243)
        P. XII. p. 186   (b)   P. XXI. p. 42

in no - - mi (ne)   pro - pter ma - gnam

(c)   (R. V. p. 85)
        P. I. p. 65   (d)   P. XXIII. p. 59

(Da) - - (vid)   Scri - ptu - - ras.

(e)   P. XIX. p. 48   (f)   P. VII. p. 63

nos ho - mi - nes____   ser - vi Do - mi - ni

(g)   P. XVI. p. 46   (h)   P. XVII. p. 72

U - ni - ge - - ni - te   fa - ctum____

The single quaver following a dotted crotchet, equivalent to a crotchet
tied to the first of a pair of quavers, is occasionally found in Palestrina's
work.   In some cases it is no more than a verbal-rhythmic device; in others
it has melodic importance, and at times some significance in the vertical
interval technique.   A few examples will show its melodic function.

Ex. 22
(a) ALTUS   (R. VII. p. 155)
                 P. II. p. 116   (b)   (R. X. p. 164)
                                                               P. XIII. p. 120
TENOR quam - di - u sum,   (De) - i Pa - - (tris)

(c) (ALTUS)   P. VII. p. 11, 13

(TENOR)

Under the signatures $\mathbb{C}\frac{3}{2}$ and $\mathbb{C}3$ (or $\mathbb{C}3$) crotchets replace the quaver
values of $\mathbb{C}$ and $\mathbb{O}$.   They occur usually in pairs.   A few examples must
suffice to illustrate this.

Ex. 24
    (a)   (R. VIII. p. 63)
                                                     P. III. p. 49

trans - for - ma - - - - - tum.

(b)   ibid.   (c)   (R. VIII. p. 167)
                                                     P. III. p. 128

(transfor) - ma - - - tum   A - - men.

The rule of stepwise movement seems to be even more rigidly enforced; upward leaps from the second of a pair of crotchets ($\mathbb{C}_2^3$) appear to be avoided, and four-crotchet groups do not occur so far as the present writer knows.

Crotchets in ₵ and ⊘

Crotchets are used very frequently in ₵ and ⊘ in pairs or in groups of four, six, eight, ten, or even twelve. Groups of more than twelve consecutive crotchets are seldom found. The dot of a dotted minim is equivalent to one crotchet, and may be followed by a single crotchet or odd number. Crotchet groups may begin on any pulse of the measure.

Stepwise movement is used to a large extent where crotchets are concerned. When leaps between two crotchets occur they are generally small, and governed by definite restrictions, which will be considered later. The suggestions concerning the contours of leaps given earlier in this chapter apply with special force to movement in these short note values.

Groups of crotchets may be approached from a longer note by a leap in either direction. If the leap be larger than a third, the crotchets almost always proceed by movement in the opposite direction to the leap.

A downward leap from the first of a pair of crotchets (or from the third, fifth, etc., notes of a group) is commonly found. On the other hand, an upward leap from an accented crotchet (first, third, fifth, etc., occurring on the pulse beat) is very rare. Possibly the accent produced by an upward leap on a normally very weak part of the measure accounts for this; even the upward auxiliary (returning) note on the second of two crotchets is not very common.

From the even crotchets of a group (provided they are consonant) leaps in either direction are commonly found. If such leaps are larger than a third they are preceded and followed by movement (step or leap) in the opposite direction; this general principle applies equally to leaps (downward) from accented crotchets.

Ex. 25

Further restrictions in the melodic contours used in crotchet movement must be observed. Two successive leaps in the same direction are outside the style. Jeppesen* points out that '. . . while the Gregorian chant abounds in pentatonic figures such as the following:

Ex. 26

the Palestrina style avoids such figures because the succession of intervals is contrary to its basic principles.' (See above, p. 48.)

Groups of crotchets may be quitted in general in the same way as a second (unaccented) note of a pair; that is, by step or leap, provided that the rules of contrary progress after a leap and general contour are observed.

Jeppesen† stresses the fact that crotchet movement most often begins on a second or fourth minim harmonic pulse (weak) in ₵, and suggests that an isolated pair of crotchets should not occur on the first and third minims unless the note following the second crotchet is a minim tied over to the next pulse, or the preceding minim is tied to the first of the pair of crotchets. Palestrina's music shows that the first of these stipulations is no more than a tendency; a better case can be made out for the second, but, though isolated pairs of crotchets on 'strong' pulses are most often either followed by a note longer than a minim (e.g., a tied or dotted minim) or preceded by a minim tied to the first of the pair, many instances like the following may be found.

Ex. 27

The rhythmic figure produced by a single crotchet on a minim pulse of the measure followed by a minim and then another crotchet is rarely used in Palestrina's work, and then generally in conjunction with the ' Consonant Fourth' idiom. A few examples of this and kindred uses are given below. The first, from the Marcellus Mass, shows a ' consonant fourth' idiom in crotchet-minim-crotchet values preceded by a minim. The second, a series

---

* Jeppesen: ' Counterpoint', p. 88.
† Jeppesen: ' Counterpoint', pp. 139, 140.

of ' tied crotchets ' following a larger crotchet group. The third, a consonant fourth idiom (as in the first), preceded by two crotchets. The fourth,
which is of very doubtful authenticity (? by Ruggiero Giovanelli) shows a
usage as far removed from Palestrina's normal style as it is common in the
music of Byrd and his compatriots.

The dotted crotchet has already been mentioned above (see page 53).
Under the signatures ()3 and ()³₂, etc., the minim replaces the crotchet
of ₵ and ().

So far it has been chiefly the melodic and rhythmic aspect of quavers
and crotchets that has been considered. The vertical aspect will be dealt
with in the next chapter.

White Notes

In the case of white notes (minims, semibreves, and breves) there is much
less restriction in both melodic and rhythmic usage, though the general
tendencies of contour and rhythm are normally followed; the larger leaps
will usually be preceded and followed by movement (stepwise or leap) in
the opposite direction; if a leap is approached or quitted by movement in
the same direction, the larger movement will come first ascending and in
the reverse order descending. (In ()3 and ()³₂ when the ' harmonic ' pulse
is on the semibreve, minims must be treated as crotchets of the normal ₵.)

Except in the case of Cantus Firmus compositions, it is uncommon to find
a large number of white notes of the same kind in unbroken succession.
Rhythmic variety is the very essence of the style. Twelve successive minims,
eight semibreves, and four or five breves may be regarded as the maximum
numbers in ₵ and ().

Ties and Dotted Notes

Ties are a modern notational method of representing dotted or ' synco-
pated ' notes. They are the result of conceptions of bars and bar lines of a
later age. It is scarcely necessary to point out that such conceptions did not
exist in the minds of musicians of the sixteenth century, when bar lines and
ties in the later sense were unknown. Modern editions of sixteenth-
century music, however, use bars as a convenient method of defining the
extent of the measure, and most of them, quite logically, use ties to a greater

or lesser extent. Some editors attempt a compromise, using modern barring and the older form of notation. This method is a clumsy and anachronistic compromise and it seems only sensible to employ modern notation with modern barring.

The rules for ties may be summarized briefly, as follows:

1. A white note may be tied to another note of equal value.

2. A white note may be tied to a note of half its value.

3. No note can be tied to a note of less than half its value.

4. Semibreves are sometimes found tied to breves, but this is generally confined to the end of a composition.

5. Crotchets are rarely tied in ₵ and ₵.

6. In ₵3 and ₵³₂ dotted breves tied to semibreves and semibreves (on the second pulse) tied to dotted breves in the next measure are sometimes found.

When the signature is ₵ the dotted semibreve or semibreve tied to a minim only occurs on the first or third pulses (minims) of the measure. Such rhythms as ₵ ♩♩. | ♩♩ ♩ | ♩ are outside the style. A dotted minim or minim tied to a crotchet may be found on any of the four pulses. A breve, occupying a full measure, is often tied to a semibreve in the next measure (= a dotted breve). The other rhythmic form of a dotted breve, a semibreve on the third 'pulse' of one measure tied to a breve occupying the whole of the next measure, is sometimes used, generally at the end of a section or movement.

When the signature is ₵, dotted (or tied) semibreves fall normally on the odd minim pulses. Dotted (or tied) breves may fall on the odd or even pulses, appearing as (1) ₵ ○. | (2) ₵ ○ ○ ○ ○ ○ | (3) ₵ ○ ○ ○ ○ ○ |. Dotted minims occur on any minim pulse.

Under the signatures ₵3 and ₵³₂ dotted (or tied) semibreves are used freely, beginning on any of the three semibreve harmonic pulses of the measure. Dotted breves fall on the first pulses only (occupying a complete measure). Dotted minims do not seem to form a part of the rhythmic style in ₵3 and ₵³₂ (= dotted crotchets of ₵).*

Beginnings and Endings of Phrases

The opening voice (or voices if they enter simultaneously) of a movement or major section almost always starts with one of the longer white note values, most often on the first pulse of the measure. In ₵ and ₵ semibreves and breves are the commonest initial leads: next come dotted semibreves; dotted minims are rare. With the signatures ₵3 and ₵³₂ the first note is usually a breve or dotted breve, though dotted semibreves and semibreves are also found. Openings in these signatures are generally for several voices simultaneously and homophonic in character. These rulings apply to the first lead or the simultaneous entry of several voices at the very beginning

---

* The passage containing dotted minims and crotchets P. XIII, p. 79, is a case of faulty transcription. See, however, Ex. 169f.

of a movement; subsequent entries of voices, though the first appearance of the particular voice in the movement, may have the initial note shortened to a minim or dotted minim in ₵ and ₵. Leads in short sections where the time changes from ₵ to ₵3 or ₵³₂ are best thought of as intermediate (see below).

The final note in all the voices at the end of a movement or separate section is always a breve or longer note.

Intermediate phrases, whether preceded by rests or not, may start with a minim or any longer note in ₵ or ₵. Leads beginning with crotchets (generally a group of four) on the even pulses of the measure (anacruses) are also often found.*

Ex.29

(R. XVI. p. 69)
P. XXVII. p. 70

(a) E - su - ri en - tes im _____

(R. XVI. p. 161-162)
P. XXVII. p. 124

(b) su - i cor - - - (dis)

(R.V. p. 53)
P.I. p. 42

(C) (bea)- ta Tri _____ (nitas)

Intermediate phrases in ₵ and ₵ normally end on a semibreve or longer note. Phrases ending on an even minim (second, fourth, or sixth in ₵) are also found; of these the fourth (or sixth) minim (last pulse of the measure) is the most usual. Minim endings on the odd pulses appear to be foreign to the rhythmic style, except where a new phrase begins immediately without intervening rests.

Ex. 30

(R. VI. p. 83)
P. XII. p. 65

(a) (pa) -cem do - na no - bis, do - na no-bis, do- (na)

(R.VI. p. 81-82)
ibid. p. 64

(b) mun - - - - di, qui tol - lis

(R.XVI. p. 236)
P. XXVII. p. 185

(c) (im) ple - vit bo - - nis, e su - ri - en - tes,

* It may be noted that these anacrusic crotchet entries nearly always take the form of a rising scale passage of four notes followed by a white note value. This is consistent with Jeppesen's observations ('Counterpoint', p. 138) that 'Though it is best in descending movement to have the longer note values come before the shorter ones, it is quite correct in ascending movement to begin with the quicker notes.' This is indeed (as Jeppesen seems to imply) the rhythmic corollary of the melodic contours of two leaps or continued movement in the same direction as a leap considered on page 48 of this book. The ascending melodic contour of larger interval followed by smaller finds its counterpart in quicker rhythmic movement (=the larger melodic interval) followed by slower note values (= shorter melodic space covered). A similar situation is found conversely in descending movement rhythmic and melodic.

Under the signatures 𝄵3 and 𝄵³₂, etc., intermediate phrases, whether anacruses or not, frequently begin with a semibreve on any of the three semibreve pulses of the measure; longer notes are equally common. Minim intermediate leads do not seem to be used as a normal part of the technique. Endings of phrases on semibreves on any pulse are common when the phrase is not followed by a rest; otherwise a breve or longer note is generally found.

Special treatment of the Bass

The behaviour of the Bass often differs from the characteristic melodic and rhythmic shape of the upper parts. The Bass may, on occasions, progress with normal imitation like any other voice. It may, however, acquire a particular character of its own, and become much more akin to the typical bass line of the harmonic age. Here may be seen one of the earlier signs of the growing preoccupation with the synthetic or vertical aspect of the texture. In order to make possible a clear and satisfactory interval synthesis with the movement of the upper parts, and to allow those parts the maximum freedom of movement, the advantages of a relatively static, less melodic bass become apparent, especially where many voices are singing simultaneously.

Ex.31 (R.V. p. 42) P.I. p. 84

(a)

qui in - fer-num con - fre - git.

(R.V. p. 211) P.I. p. 157

(b)

e - le - cta ut sol e -

- le - - cta. ut sol, ut sol.

The two short examples quoted above, the first from near the beginning of a five-voice motet, the second the concluding ten measures of a seven-voice setting of 'Virgo Prudentissima' in which there is a continued canon *in diapente et in subdiatessaron*, show some of the special characteristics of the bass line: (*a*) the predominance of the longer white note values; (*b*) the disjunct character of the melodic line; (*c*) the almost harmonic movement of the part, 'Tonic, Dominant, Subdominant root relationships' as a later age might have defined it. It is noteworthy that, despite the slow moving note values, the rhythmic interest of the line remains beautifully varied and balanced; so does the melodic progression, leaps being followed by movement in the opposite direction, and disjunct general progress being broken from time to time by stepwise interpolations. Palestrina's basses, however slow moving and disjunct, still preserve the essential character of the pure polyphonic line.

Range of the Individual Voices

R. O. Morris gives the following practical summary of the problem of compass of the individual voices:★
' Every melody must be conceived as being in a definite mode, and as being definitely either in the Authentic or Plagal form of that mode. The strict compass of each of these forms has already been given; it may now be added that in practice a certain extension of compass, upwards and downwards is usually conceded. The extent of the concession varies slightly amongst different authorities; but it is substantially defined in these two rules:

1. That such extension must never exceed a major third in any one direction.

2. That the total extension (upwards and downwards) must never exceed that of a perfect fourth.'

This statement is, in practice, very near the truth, though some modification of the definition of mode and its plagality or authenticity must be made in the light of the note at the end of the first chapter of this book. The average voice part of Palestrina would probably have to be described as '*x Mode, Authenticus* (or *Plagalis*) *Plusquamperfectus* (or *Mixtus*) and *Commixtus.*' Nevertheless Morris's ruling as to extension of the particular octave species used is practical and sets limits to which, as he says, ' the practice of the Palestrina school conforms very closely '.

★ Morris: ' Contrapuntal Technique in the Sixteenth Century ', p. 28.

CHAPTER IV

VERTICAL INTERVAL TECHNIQUE
CONSONANCES

Approach to the Problem

THE vertical interval technique of Palestrina is the product of a process of refining the methods of preceding periods of polyphony. The general tendency throughout the fifteenth century to give increasing attention to the synthesis resulting from the combination of the individual lines so that a reasonably euphonious whole should be attained, had been very evident from the time of Dunstable onwards.

The cause of this awareness of the vertical aspect of polyphony has been accounted for by various theories: the best explanation seems to be found in the remark made by R. O. Morris in his article on Polyphony (Grove's Dictionary of Music; fourth edition):

' To attend to two melodies simultaneously requires intense concentration: to attend to three is beyond even the most expert capacity, so far as the writer, searching carefully, has been able to discover.'

The listener to polyphony in more than two parts is aware, not of three or more individual strands moving simultaneously together in the horizontal plane, but the synthesis of the parts at points of time, generally occurring at regular intervals.

This process of vertical listening, in the normal course of its development, must eventually lead to a point where harmonic thinking and harmonic progression should become either the dominating factor in music or at least a matter of importance equal to that of the horizontal progress of the individual lines and the interval and rhythmic relationship between pairs of these lines; but it is clearly wrong to approach Palestrina's technique from the viewpoint of the harmonic age. Linear counterpoint, that is, the combination of one melodic and rhythmic line with another line or lines of the same kind in such a way as to produce a reasonably euphonious whole, is the foundation of Palestrina's technique. Growing awareness of the vertical aspect of polyphony may have produced a need for a high degree of euphony; it was by scrupulous refinement of the interval technique of his predecessors that Palestrina achieved a vertical synthesis of the greatest clearness and subtlety; yet the horizontal element is the driving force of the whole mechanism—that horizontal element implying the rhythmic and melodic behaviour of each individual line and its rhythmic and interval relationship with the other lines which make up the texture.

Harmonic Thought

Harmonic thought had been developing in rudimentary form for at least a hundred years before Palestrina, though it had not progressed much beyond cadence formations. The cadences of polyphony, contrapuntal in origin, had probably become fixed and standardized in their vertical aspect before Palestrina's time; but a system of logical harmonic progressions covering the relationship of each ' chord ' to a ' tonic ' and to every other chord was as yet unknown; it was not until diatonic tonality had become firmly established a century or so later that anything like a comprehensive harmonic system could exist.

It is, therefore, necessary to approach Palestrina's technique from the linear view-point, and to regard the synthesis of the lines not as a preconceived harmonic basis for the counterpoint but as the outcome of the linear weaving of the strands.

Interval Technique

The interval technique has two closely interconnected facets: (1) the interval relationship of each voice with every other voice, and particularly of each upper voice with the lowest; (2) the vertical syntheses of the interval combinations made by all the voices on the ' pulse beats ' of the measure.

The voices must be thought of in pairs. A three-part composition for Cantus, Altus, and Bassus, for example, consists of three two-part combinations, Cantus-Altus, Cantus-Bassus, and Altus-Bassus. A four-part work consists of six two-part combinations; a five-part, of ten; a six-part, of fifteen, and so forth.

The technique of the interval relationships used in these pairs of voices is complicated by the fact that a slightly different system is applied when one of the voices is the bass or lowest part. The bass controls, to a large extent, the interval structure of the whole texture.

The interval combinations on the harmonic pulse beats of the measure are the vertical landmarks of the texture. These combinations are normally consonant; if a dissonance occurs on the harmonic pulse it demands special treatment which will be described later. On the second half of a harmonic pulse (for example, the second of a pair of crotchets in ₵) a consonance or dissonance may be found, but again the dissonance is subject to definite rules.

Consonant Intervals

The consonant intervals between the bass and any upper voice are these: perfect unisons, fifths, and octaves; major and minor thirds; major and minor sixths; the compounds of all these. Perfect fourths and all augmented and diminished intervals as well as all seconds and sevenths and their compounds are dissonant against the bass.

Between two upper parts the list of ' consonant ' intervals given above holds good; to these may be added perfect fourths, and rather less commonly the technical dissonances, augmented fourths and diminished fifths. The other

augmented and diminished intervals and seconds and sevenths are dissonant.[*]
Consonant intervals on harmonic pulses may be approached and quitted freely, by step or leap, provided that the rules of melodic progression and part writing (see below) are observed. The combinations of intervals normally found on the pulses are $\frac{5}{3}^{(8)}$ and $\frac{6}{3}^{(8)}$, though Palestrina seems to favour the former on the more important pulses.

Part Writing. Treatment of Perfect Intervals

Direct consecutive perfect fifths and octaves or unisons between any two voices were rigidly prohibited in sixteenth-century polyphony.[†] It does not matter on what pulses or fractions of pulses of the measure they occur, nor how many voices may make up the tale of the parts; nor will

[*] Rare cases of the augmented fifth and its inversion, the diminished fourth, occurring between two upper parts can be found in Palestrina. Jeppesen ('Palestrina and the Dissonance', p. 164) says: 'the use of the augmented fifth makes possible the chord called in modern times "the augmented triad in its first inversion". As the occurrence of this chord in the pure style is seldom mentioned . . . examples are appended here, taken from Palestrina's works, showing that the sixth chord was understood as a full consonance.' He then gives one example in music type and twenty-two references followed by 'etc'. In the present writer's opinion, the use of the 'chord' as a 'full consonance' is not nearly so firmly established as Jeppesen suggests. Some of the cases he quotes may be regarded differently: for example, P. XXVII, p. 43, 2, + 2, the diminished fourth between the upper voices is caused by a suspension plus a consonant fourth; P. XXVI, 38. 4, + 2, may be accounted for by the fact that the F in the second Tenor can be regarded as a minim passing note; the same applies to P. XI, 101, 2, 1. etc. Even more disquieting is the fact that many of these instances which Jeppesen cites depend on the interpretation of *Musica Ficta*. For example P. XIV. 33, 1, 1; in the Haberl edition the F sharp-B flat interval appears, but in Casimiri's new edition (Roma) a B natural is suggested, cancelling the diminished fourth. Even such apparently sound examples as P. XIII. 45, 4, + 2, doubts may arise as to the validity of the first G sharp (see below). R. O. Morris ('Contrapuntal Technique', p. 43) was probably right in stressing that the various augmented and diminished intervals available by means of Musica Ficta alterations, such as Eb-C♯, Fb-G♯, Bb-Eb, etc., were 'not in the style of the period'.

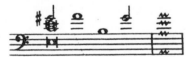

[†] It must be admitted that on very rare occasions direct consecutives, both fifths and octaves, are found in Palestrina. These may be instances of 'dormitat Homerus', or they may be deliberate deviations from normal procedure (see also Ex. 96).

Ex. 34

consecutives be saved by the fact that one of the notes making the progression may be an unessential note.

The interpolation of another *concordant* note in either voice between the consecutive intervals does away with the effect of the consecutives. So does a rest and the beginning of a new phrase in either part. Three short examples from the Missa Brevis may suffice to demonstrate these points.

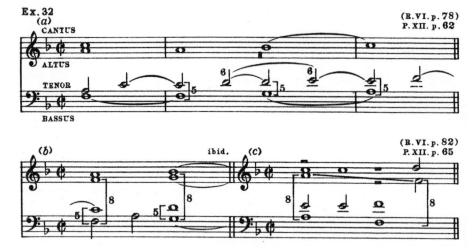

Ex.32
(a)
(B.VI.p.78)
P.XII.p.62

(b) ibid. (c)
(B.VI.p.82)
P.XII.p.65

The note interpolated *must* be a concord in the synthesis in being at the time. A passing note will not suffice to break the effect of consecutives. The following hypothetical cases are all incorrect technique.

Ex.33

Morris remarks: 'A suspension may be said to temper the wind to the shorn consecutive. The scholastic rule that "Passages which would be incorrect without suspensions are equally incorrect with them" is demonstrably out of all relation to the facts'. The example given below shows a case which cannot be explained with complete conviction by the intermediate consonance rule given above.

Ex. 35
(B.VI.p.81)
P.XII.p.64
Missa Brevis

'Sound' fifths and octaves in succession are unobjectionable, since the consecutives do not occur between the same voices.

Ex. 36

(R.VI. p. 68)
P. XII. p. 55
Missa Brevis

CANTUS
ALTUS

sounding

TENOR
BASSUS

Consecutive perfect fourths between upper parts are, again, a matter of some controversy. Jeppesen: 'It is not desirable for two or more fourths to follow each other in similar motion. The only exception is . . . the progression which, in modern terminology, would be called a series of parallel chords of the sixth.'★

Morris: 'Consecutive bare fourths are of frequent occurrence between upper parts; once again one can only remark that the rule forbidding them is out of all relation to sixteenth-century practice. Occasionally you find even a sequence of 6/4s' (i.e. upper parts forming 6/4s between themselves) 'but this is exceptional. . . .'†

A study of Palestrina's use of fourths between the upper voices shows that Morris is right: perfect fourths may be freely used consecutively in pairs or greater numbers within reason.

Contrary Movement

Consecutive 'octaves' by contrary movement, or more precisely the octave-unison-fifteenth variants, are rarely found in Palestrina's polyphony for fewer than five voices, and then seldom, if ever, between the outside parts; usually they seem to occur between the bass and an inner part. Contrary movement consecutive fifths are rather more frequent in work for four or more voices. Here again most cases occur between the bass and one of the middle parts. Morris is probably too restrictive when he states:

'Consecutive octaves are best avoided even by contrary motion. Consecutive fifths by contrary motion are also best avoided between the extreme parts, and in any case when writing for four voices or less. In writing for five or more parts consecutive fifths by contrary motion are not seldom found between two of the inner parts, or even between one outer and one inner part. The reason is not that such progressions are harder to avoid in five-part than in four-part writing, but that they are less likely to be heard.'

The last part of this quotation is particularly worth noting. In eight-part work, especially for double choir, strings of contrary movement consecutives

★ Jeppesen: 'Counterpoint', p. 99.
† R. O. Morris: 'Contrapuntal Technique', p. 42.

E

are often found between the two bass parts as well as between other parts.

Ex.37

Ex.38

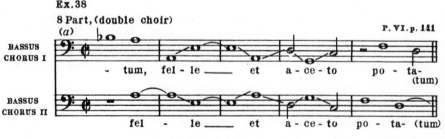

' Hidden' Fifths and Octaves

The approach by similar motion to perfect fifths and octaves between two parts is subject to a certain amount of restriction. The ruling usually given is that perfect fifths and octaves may be approached by similar motion provided that *one* of the parts moves by step; this holds good for the two extreme parts as well as any other pair. This ruling requires some modification and extension.

Morris is probably right when he states that ' Hidden consecutives need not be feared except between the extreme parts' but his continuation, ' There it is best to avoid them unless one part proceeds by step' must be qualified by at least two exceptions.

If a perfect fifth is approached by the drop of a third in the upper part and of a fifth in the lower, the ' hidden fifth' resulting is, apparently, acceptable, even in two-part writing.

Jeppesen, in an interesting Appendix to his ' Style of Palestrina' points out that progressions of a sixth to a perfect fifth do not occur in Palestrina's music in two-part writing. He quotes Artusi's ' L'arte del contraponto' explanation that it is 'forbidden because it is too much like consecutive fifths.'*

* Jeppesen: ' The Style of Palestrina', p. 299.

As Jeppesen points out, the progression is found in four-part writing between middle or middle and outer voices. Nevertheless, although it satisfies the clause which insists that one part should move by step, it does not seem to be used in Palestrina between the extreme parts.

Consecutive thirds or sixths may be used freely between voices provided that the successions are not too long. In crotchet values eight in succession may be considered reasonable, about six in minims, and rather fewer in semibreves. The theorists' rule that consecutive major thirds should be avoided, especially in two-part writing, because of their 'tritonal' effect if they stand a tone apart, is a ghostly legacy from 'strict counterpoint' which has already been laid by R. O. Morris.

It is natural, perhaps, to speculate on the fact that mature polyphony rejects a succession of perfect consonances while accepting imperfect. Many theories have been advanced to account for the abandonment of the strings of Unisons, Octaves, Fourths, and Fifths of early *organum*. Morris gives a good answer to the problem in the Grove article cited above. It may be briefly summarized thus: When two notes are sounded together, what is heard is, to a large extent, their synthesis; they tend either to merge into a single sound, or to stand apart, according to the nature of the interval which separates them. The tendency to merge implies a greater or less degree of consonance; to stand apart, dissonance. Fifths and Octaves, etc., merge almost completely if perfectly tuned; dissonances such as seconds and sevenths stand apart in violent contrast; thirds and sixths, relatively consonant, are the perfect compromise. They stand apart in a polyphonic texture enough to allow the individual voices to retain their individuality, and coalesce enough to make a reasonably euphonious synthesis.

CHAPTER V

PASSING AND AUXILIARY DISSONANCES

PASSING and auxiliary dissonances may be defined as dissonant notes, not forming part of the essential interval structure of the pulse, used in conjunct movement on unaccented or relatively unaccented parts of the measure. The passing dissonance is a note used to fill in the melodic interval of a third: the auxiliary or returning-note dissonance is a decoration of a consonance; a dissonant note, either a tone or a semitone above or below, interpolated between two statements of the same consonance.

When the time signature is ₵ or ₵ the second of a pair of crotchets occupying any minim of the measure is regarded as *unaccented;* so is the second of any pair of quavers: the even minims, if the 'harmonic' pulse is a semibreve, may also be looked upon as *unaccented.* The first of a pair of crotchets occupying an *even* (weak) minim is regarded as *relatively unaccented;* so is the first of any pair of quavers (on the second half of a minim pulse).

When the time signature is the sesquialtera diminution of ₵ (₵³₂, etc.) and the semibreve becomes the normal harmonic pulse, the second of any pair of minims occupying a semibreve pulse is regarded as *unaccented;* so is the second of any pair of crotchets. The accentual value of the semibreve is more difficult to assess. The signature ₵³₂, etc., may imply a measure of three semibreves or a (double) measure of three breves; Palestrina seems to use both interpretations indifferently, and the standard editions, disregarding this, employ three semibreve measures with equal impartiality. This sets the student of Palestrina's style a difficult problem. In the case of three breves to the measure the even semibreves are unaccented when the breve represents the harmonic pulse, and the measures must be thought of as 'double'; the first of a pair of minims occupying a weak (even) semibreve may be classified as *relatively unaccented;* so may the first of any pair of crotchets. The matter will be dealt with more fully later.

A detailed investigation of Palestrina's treatment of passing and auxiliary dissonances may best be undertaken under five general headings. For the sake of brevity the terms 'passing notes' and 'auxiliary notes' will be taken to mean *dissonant* passing notes, etc., unless the contrary is stated.

1. Unaccented passing notes, filling in the melodic interval of a third.
2. Unaccented auxiliary (returning) notes.
3. Relatively unaccented passing and returning notes.
4. Unaccented and relatively unaccented passing notes in combination (four crotchet groups of which the third is a passing dissonance).

5. Quaver passing and auxiliary note groups.

1. *Unaccented Passing Notes*

Unaccented Passing Notes in Crotchets (¢ *and* ₵)

Unaccented passing notes of crotchet value are used almost without restriction on the even crotchets. Such restrictions as seem to exist are concerned with the situations which arise when crotchet passing notes are combined with crotchet movement in another voice. Simultaneous crotchet movement in two or more parts is most commonly found when the parts are moving in thirds or sixths, or are progressing in contrary movement in alternating 'harmony' and 'passing' notes.

Ex.41

(B.XVI. p.111)
P. XXVII. p. 88

(a)

(b) (First Choir)

P.VI. p.122

More rarely simultaneous passing notes in fourths are used, sometimes combined with another part in sixths or thirds.

Ex.42

(a)

(B.XIV. p.10)
P.VIII. p. 9

(b)

(B.XIV. p. 87)
P. VIII. p. 29

When two parts are moving together in crotchets a situation frequently arises in which the second of a pair of crotchets in one part is a consonant 'harmony' note sounded against a passing dissonance. In most cases where this occurs the interval between these two unaccented crotchets is a consonance. (Third, perfect fifth, sixth, or perfect fourth sounded between the upper parts.)

More rarely, dissonant combinations of passing and 'harmony' notes are sounded together on the unaccented crotchet. Such instances as the following appear often enough to allow of their inclusion in the technique; nevertheless, they must be looked upon as exceptional.

(d) Vulnerasti, m.29

(R.XI. p. 125)
P.IV. p. 29

dim. 5th

Palestrina seems to go to considerable trouble to avoid the percussion of a second or ninth between two unaccented crotchets. Such passages as the following are rare (Ex. 45a). Sometimes the clash is apparently avoided by the unusual expedient of using a dotted crotchet (Ex. 45b).

Ex.45

(a)   P. XXIII. p. 138   (b)   P. VII. p. 12

Clashes between unaccented crotchets where the Cambiata figure, anticipations, etc., are part of the process will be considered under those headings.

Unaccented Passing Notes in Minims ¢ *and* ¢

Unaccented passing note dissonances also occur in ¢ on the second and fourth minims of the measure. In these cases the 'harmonic' pulse is, of necessity, a semibreve. Such unaccented dissonant minims must be preceded either by another minim, or by a longer note.

Ex.46

(a)   P.VI. p. 27

(R.III. p. 39)
P.V. p. 33

(b)

One of the basic principles of Palestrina's treatment of passing dissonance is that it should be given as little rhythmic prominence as possible. Whereas the shorter notes (crotchets and quavers) are treated with considerable freedom, minims are used with much more caution. Minim passing notes are not employed with anything like the same frequency as crotchets. Furthermore, they are nearly always sounded either alone or in consonance with other second and fourth minims (also usually passing notes) of the measure.

Very occasionally the simultaneous percussion of an unaccented minim dissonance with a harmony note occurs. This situation is treated with much more restriction than in the case of crotchets. Dissonant clashes are very rare. The following may give some idea of the procedure.

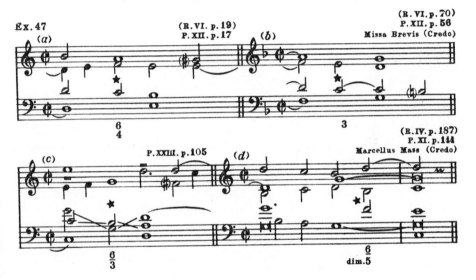

On rare occasions a minim unaccented passing dissonance is found against crotchet movement in another part. In these cases the first crotchet of the pair heard against the minim is consonant with it. Two examples may be cited:

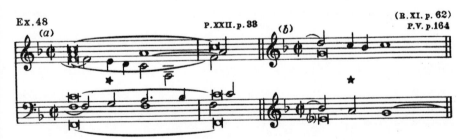

In the first of these examples both the E and the D crotchets are dissonant against the sustained ' chord ', the E against the F, and the D against the C. They are, however, consonant in relationship to the minim G, which itself is dissonant with the sustained parts. If the methods of linear analysis suggested below are employed the explanation of the passage becomes clear. One example of considerable complexity may be given.

Ex.49

(R.VI.p.61)
P.XII.p.51

This example is of interest, since it illustrates particularly well the essentially linear nature of Palestrina's interval technique. In order to explain the synthesis marked★ linear analysis of the voices in pairs must be used. If the bassus and tenor of the second measure are taken together, the bassus E is a minim passing note against the tenor B flat, and the progression normal in the style. The bassus and altus form consonances on the pulse beats, the E in this case being a 'harmony' note. The bassus and cantus are consonant on the first two pulses and a normal 9-8 suspension is used between them on the last two pulses. Between the tenor and altus the situation is rather more complicated; the first pulse is a consonance, the crotchet E an accented passing note resolving on the D, the last two pulses consonant. In the case of the tenor and cantus the first pulse is a suspended seventh which has an exceptional ornamental resolution on to a sixth, followed by another 7-6 suspension. The altus and cantus relationship is perfectly normal. Each pair of voices behaves regularly (with the possible exception of the ornamental resolution mentioned; this will be spoken of in more detail in the section on suspensions) and therefore the sum of the pairs of voices is correct technique.

It is worth noting that several notes have a dual personality in their technical status. The E in the bassus is a minim passing note vis-à-vis the tenor B flat, and a 'harmony' note consonance with the other two parts; the altus E is an accented passing note in relationship to the tenor B flat, but a concord with the cantus and bassus; the tied A in the cantus is a suspended dissonance to the tenor B flat, but a consonance when considered against the altus and bassus. The situation at ★ is in reality a complex of six two-part progressions each of which is individually correct. This linear analysis is a safe and sufficient guide to the correctness of the passage as a whole in the Palestrina style.

An interesting passage from the Mass 'Assumpta est Maria' also demands linear analysis for its explanation:

Ex.50

P.XXIII.p.120

The second minim in the first measure of this example is, from the point of view of a later harmonic technique, ' the second inversion of a dominant seventh '. Such an explanation is quite out of the picture in dealing with Palestrina's technique. The dotted semibreve G is the crux of the matter. Against it the minims D, F, and F are unaccented dissonant passing notes, while the B is a ' harmony ' note. Without the G the progression of the other parts is perfectly regular.

In $\mathbb{O}$ passing notes of minim value on the even minims are very rare. When they are used, the same carefully unobtrusive methods of introduction as in $\mathbb{C}$ are noticeable.

Ex. 51 (a)　　(R.III. p.112)　P.V. p.89　(b)　ibid.

Unaccented Passing Notes in $\mathbb{O}_2^3$

In the sesquialtera diminution of $\mathbb{O}$ ($\mathbb{O}_2^3$, etc.) the minim replaces the crotchet of $\mathbb{C}$ and $\mathbb{O}$ as the most common passing note value; likewise the semibreve and crotchet of $\mathbb{O}_2^3$ replace the minim and quaver of $\mathbb{C}$ and $\mathbb{O}$. It is important to note that under the signature $\mathbb{O}_2^3$ the passing note minim is used with less freedom than its crotchet counterpart in $\mathbb{C}$ and $\mathbb{O}$ and the semibreve is practically never found as a passing dissonance. This observation has considerable theoretical importance.　It has been pointed out that Palestrina's treatment of secondary dissonance insists, as a general principle, on the giving of the minimum of prominence to the discordant note: therefore dissonances occurring on shorter note values and weaker accents are treated with greater freedom than those on longer note values and more conspicuous accentual positions; for example, crotchet passing dissonances in $\mathbb{C}$ are treated more freely than those of minim value, and quavers, as will be shown later, are yet freer in the matter of dissonance; this will become even more obvious when the treatment of relatively unaccented discords is considered.

If the actual speed of a $\mathbb{O}_2^3$ minim equalled that of a crotchet in $\mathbb{C}$ or $\mathbb{O}$ it would be reasonable to expect exactly the same treatment for both, and so for the other equivalent values. If a proportional reading of the meaning of $\mathbb{O}_2^3$ is accepted the minim under that signature is not the same speed as the $\mathbb{C}$ crotchet, but one and half times longer. This would account, to some extent, for the undoubted fact that the $\mathbb{O}_2^3$ semibreves and minims when used as discords are treated with greater caution than their $\mathbb{C}$ and $\mathbb{O}$ counterparts, minims and crotchets.

In $\mathbb{O}_2^3$, etc., minim passing notes on unaccented minims occur fairly often individually, or in prolonged minim movement alternating with concordant minims, against longer note movement in the other voices. When minim passing notes are used against minim movement in other voices, the progress in thirds or sixths or contrary movement described on page 70 is usually followed.

Ex. 52
                                                            P.VI.p.29-30

The discordant simultaneous percussion of minim passing and 'harmony' notes is exceedingly rare. (Compare the equivalent situation in crotchets in 𝄴 and 𝄵, page 71.)

Ex. 53   P. XXII. p. 153

The use of a passing dissonance of semibreve value (replacing the minim of 𝄴 and 𝄵) is so rare as to place it outside the normal technique. The instance quoted below must be considered as doubtful.

Ex. 54   P. XXII. p. 71

2. *Auxiliary Notes*

Unaccented Auxiliary (or Returning) Dissonances in 𝄴 *and* 𝄵.

Auxiliary or, as they are more properly called, 'returning' dissonances on the unaccented crotchets or half pulses of the measure are among the most common devices of Palestrina's technique. These 'ornamental' dissonances may be found in considerable numbers on almost any page of his work.

The lower returning note forms, amongst other uses, a characteristic part of a favourite extended resolution of suspensions. The upper is rather less common, though it is frequently found.

In 𝄴 and 𝄵 both upper and lower forms are used (sometimes simultaneously) on any unaccented crotchet, either alone, or combined and moving in consonance with other passing or auxiliary notes.

The percussion of unaccented dissonant returning notes with other crotchets which are 'harmony' notes is not nearly so frequent as in the case of passing note dissonances described above. The more dissonant clashes are seldom found.

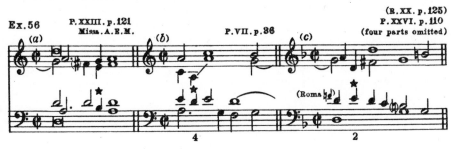

Auxiliary dissonances on the weak minims of 𝄴 are extremely rare in Palestrina's work, if the cases of returning minims used in conjunction with the 'consonant fourth' (see below) are excluded. This formula is given in the first example below (Ex. 57a); its implications must be considered in a later chapter.

The cadential decorative idiom which forms the second example is much less common. It sometimes occurs in an even more dissonant form which may be expressed as $\frac{5}{3} \frac{\bar{4}}{4} \frac{\bar{3}}{3}$

The third example, quoted by Jeppesen, is one of the very few instances of a real auxiliary minim dissonance in the course of a work.

Unaccented Returning Notes in $\mathbf{O}_2^3$

Under the signature $\mathbf{O}_2^3$ minim unaccented returning notes (replacing the crotchets of $\mathbf{C}$) seem to be confined to the semitone or tone *below* the ' harmony ' note decorated. They most often appear without other simultaneous minim movement, but when sounded against another minim, consonance between the two is normally found. An instance of a mildly dissonant percussion is given below (Ex. 58c).

Ex. 58   (B.VIII.p. 93)   (B.X. p. 83)
          P.III. p. 72   P. XIII. p. 25
(a)   (b)

(c)   (B.VI.p. 126)
       P.XII.p. 97

The present writer knows of no cases of semibreve ($\mathbf{O}_2^3$) dissonant returning notes in Palestrina's authentic work.

3. *Relatively Unaccented Dissonant Passing Notes*

Relatively unaccented dissonant passing notes are frequently used by Palestrina on the first of a pair of crotchets occupying the even (weak) minims of the $\mathbf{C}$ (or $\mathbf{O}$) measure. These dissonant notes (when of crotchet value) are only used in a downward progression in Palestrina's music, though his immediate predecessors also used them ascending. Being strictly passing notes they must be introduced and quitted by downward stepwise movement. Palestrina does not allow them to occur on the odd (strong) minim pulses (i.e. as fully accented passing notes).

They may be preceded by a consonant minim or note of greater value, or by a pair of crotchets which may be either both consonant, or the first consonant and the second dissonant (see below).

The ' second ' crotchet which follows the relatively unaccented dissonant passing note must be a consonance with the interval combination in being.* As it is the note of resolution of a dissonance its further progress is of importance, especially in the case of the four crotchet descending figure in which the relatively accented dissonance (the third crotchet of the group) is itself often preceded by an unaccented crotchet dissonance (the second crotchet of the group). This almost idiomatic process will be considered in the next section of this chapter.

When the relatively unaccented dissonant crotchet is preceded by a minim or longer note, the consonant second crotchet on which it resolves may continue downwards by step, or it may return by step upwards. It may also proceed upward by leap of a third (common), fourth (fairly common), fifth (less common), or octave (rare). The upward leap of a minor sixth, though technically possible, is not found, so far as the writer knows, nor are downward leaps. The note following the second crotchet (consonance) is almost always of minim value (or longer) though occasionally continuation in crotchet values does occur.

The set of examples which follows will illustrate these points.

Ex. 60
(a)
(R.X.p.7)
P.XIII.p.6
(b)
(R.VI.p.65)
P.XII.p.52
Missa Brevis. Gloria

* Jeppesen: ' The Style of Palestrina and the Dissonance ', pp. 182, 183, cites two very exceptional cases of pairs of crotchets, in which the first is a relatively unaccented dissonant passing note and the second an unaccented dissonant auxiliary note (Ex. 59 a, b). From a purely theoretical point of view, these seem rather less irregular than he suggests; if linear analysis is applied, both cases seem to be technically possible. The formula is, however, so rare that it cannot be accepted in the normal style. An even rarer occurrence is shown in Ex. 59c. It consists of two dissonant crotchets filling in the gap of a fourth. This cannot be explained by linear analysis, since both the C and B flat are obstinately dissonant against the F sharp.

Ex. 59
(a)
(R.I.p.8)
P.X.p.4
(b)
(R.I.p.61)
P.X.p.54
(c)
P.XXII.p.119

(A) and (B) show the returning upward step from the note of resolution,
(A) being in a two-voice context; (C) has the descending step: in (D) and
(E) the upward leaps of a minor and a major third are found; in (F) the
upward leap of a fourth is combined with a returning upward step in the
simultaneous use of the figure by two voices; (G) and (H) illustrate the less
common leap of a fifth; (I) (quoted by Jeppesen) is an instance of the rather
rare octave leap, together with some very harsh note-against-note clashes.
All these cases have the common factor that the crotchet dissonance and its
resolution are flanked by white note values.   In (J) the progress continues

in crotchet values; this is much less usual, and does not seem to be found in conjunction with a leap.

The percussion of the dissonant crotchet against other crotchets or longer notes is of interest, bearing in mind the fact that such percussion occurs on a pulse of the measure. These simultaneous soundings may be consonant, as in (C, E, H, and J), or they may form dissonances of sevenths (A, B, D, F), fourths with the bass (B), or seconds (I). The simultaneous use of relatively unaccented passing notes in different voices is well seen in (F).

Relatively Unaccented Minims not possible

'Relatively unaccented' minim passing note dissonances are impossible in ₵ and ₵. By implication these would fall on the odd minim harmonic pulses, a position in which only prepared (suspended) dissonances are possible; they would, in fact, be fully accented unprepared discords, completely foreign to the style of Palestrina, as well as contemporary theory.[*] Jeppesen disposes of the few apparent examples of accented passing dissonances in Palestrina's music (P. X, 30; P. V, 9; P. XVI, 53; P. XXI, 89) showing that they are faulty transcriptions, misprints, or misinterpretations.[†]

For the same reason, dissonant relatively unaccented passing notes cannot occur on the first crotchet of a pair on the odd minims of the measure.[‡]

Relatively Unaccented Passing Notes in $\mathbb{O}_2^3$

In $\mathbb{O}_2^3$ time where the minim replaces the crotchet of ₵, minim relatively unaccented passing dissonances on the unaccented semibreves are very rare indeed.

Four examples may be offered with some reservations as to the authenticity of the second.

Ex.61   (B.X.p.105)   P.XIII.p.79   (B.XVI.p.226)   P.XXVII.p.176

(a)   (b)

[*] Jeppesen: 'The Style of Palestrina', pp. 101 et seq., explores the views of theorists on the subject of dissonance in general and passing dissonance in particular. His summing-up is valuable (op. cit., p. 108):
'. . . as it (dissonance) was unavoidable, the point at issue was to conceal or muffle it as far as possible. The methods of doing this were:
1. To place dissonance only on unaccented beats.
2. To allow dissonance only on comparatively small note-values.
3. To use dissonance only when introduced and continued in conjunct movement, or treated as a suspension.
4. To allow dissonance only when introduced in such a manner that the mutually dissonant voices do not simultaneously proceed to the discord . . .' Jeppesen, op. cit, pp. 101 et seq.
(This last cannot be applied to unaccented crotchets in ₵ and ₵).

[†] His disposal of Casimiri's amended version of P. XXV. 54, 3, plus 2 (Jeppesen, op. cit., p. 114) does not carry quite the same conviction.

[‡] See Jeppesen: op. cit., p. 144 et seq.

F

The first of these instances seems to be straightforward. In the others, the dissonant passing note apparently occurs on the first pulse of the measure. It has been shown that the signature Φ_2^3 can imply a measure of three imperfect breves, each containing two semibreves, as an alternative to the perfect breve (= three semibreves); and Palestrina seems to use these two interpretations as interchangeable. (See p. 34 and p. 136.) This means that these two measures are in reality a single measure of three imperfect breves, and so the relatively unaccented dissonant passing note falls on the fourth (weak) semibreve of the measure.

Relatively Unaccented Returning Notes

Most authorities agree that relatively unaccented returning notes are found only in quaver values (in $\mathcal{C}$ and Φ) in Palestrina's music. (In Φ_2^3 quavers are replaced by crotchets.)

4. *Relatively Unaccented Crotchet Passing Dissonances preceded by crotchet movement.*

One of the most characteristic idioms of Palestrina's style is the four crotchet descending scale passage starting on an odd minim of the $\mathcal{C}$ or Φ measure, with a relatively unaccented passing note dissonance on the third crotchet of the group. The first two crotchets of this figure may by either a consonance followed by an unaccented passing dissonance, or two consonances (6.5. above the bass).

Two very important factors directly connected with the use of this formula must be noted. Firstly, the note which the third (dissonant) crotchet decorates, that is, its note of resolution (fourth crotchet of the group) is, in ninety-nine cases out of a hundred, present in another part together with the dissonant note, and is there prolonged and treated as a suspended discord

on the following pulse.   Secondly, the further progress from the fourth
crotchet of the group is *always* by an upward step.*
The following examples will demonstrate the formula.

The first four examples cited above show the idiom complete with the
suspension of the note of resolution in another part and the upward returning
step from the fourth crotchet.†   In all these cases both the second and third

* This book is concerned primarily with an investigation of what Palestrina did, rather than why he
did it.   Jeppesen: ‘ The Style of Palestrina and the dissonance ’, pp. 119, et seq., gives a long survey
of possible reasons for these restrictions in the use of the four crotchet formula, viewing the problem as a
“ musico-psychologic ” one (p. 128).   Those readers who are interested in such explanations will find
Jeppesen's discussion extremely instructive both in method and content.

† Jeppesen: ‘ Style of Palestrina ’, pp. 128 et seq., examines two cases of apparent continuation downwards of the four note descending figure under discussion (P. XXII. 50.   P. XV. 21).   He shows that
both are faulty readings.

crotchets are dissonant, and the way in which the clash between third crotchet and its note of resolution in another voice is introduced should be noted; most often the latter is approached by step or remains stationary, but sometimes, as in B, a leap is used. In E the first two crotchets of the figure are consonant (6-5); otherwise it follows the same pattern.

Examples F and G appear to be very irregular in that the second, third, and fourth crotchets of the figure are all dissonant with one or other of the ' harmony ' notes above them. In each case the first crotchet is a concordant tie-over from the previous pulse and the second a normal unaccented passing dissonance; the third and fourth have each to do a double duty. In example F the B in the Bassus (third crotchet) is consonant with the Altus and Tenor, but a relatively unaccented dissonant passing note against the Cantus; the A (fourth crotchet) is a concord with the Cantus and Altus but a dissonant unaccented returning note in relation to the Tenor. The voice pairs are regular in progression. In example G the Bassus and Tenor voices show the accepted use of the dissonant third crotchet; between the Bassus and top part a normal progression of consonances on the minim pulses and passing dissonance and returning note on the unaccented even crotchets is found; the two upper parts progress normally. Once more the method of linear analysis employed earlier in this book provides the complete explanation of two passages which are inexplicable by harmonic means.

The last quotation (H) is one of the comparatively rare cases of the idiom used without the suspension of the resolution note in another voice. All these examples are taken from the same volume of Masses in the Haberl edition; this may show, to some extent, the frequency with which the idiom is used. In $\emptyset_2^3$ the four minim group is an extreme rarity.

5. Quaver Groups in ₵ and ◐

Palestrina uses quavers normally in isolated pairs on the weak (second) half of any minim pulse in the ₵ and ◐ measures. These are invariably introduced by step of a second from a crotchet or tied crotchet (dotted minim), and the interval between the quavers is always a second; normally the second quaver is quitted by further conjunct movement, but exceptionally, when the second of the pair is a consonance and the movement has been in a downward direction, an upward leap is possible (cf. page 52).

In the vertical aspect, either or both of the quavers may be consonant or dissonant, passing note or returning note. The movement may be upward or downward or turning backward, according to the circumstances, and the only restriction seems to be that the upward dissonant returning note on the

second of a pair of quavers does not occur in Palestrina's work.★
The following examples will demonstrate most of the common usages.
Examples A to F give instances of a fourth filled in by quavers both in
the upward and downward direction. Either or both of the quavers may be
dissonant, according to the needs of the particular circumstance. Example D
also contains an instance of an upward leap of a fifth from the second quaver
of a pair, this quaver being a consonance. In the cases G to J, quaver returning notes are seen used freely; in G and J both quavers are consonant.
Examples K and L have dissonant lower returning notes in a relatively
unaccented position; M and N provide examples of contrary movement

Ex. 63

Note. ✗ Dissonance. ○ Consonance

* Such figures as the following are virtually outside the normal technique of Palestrina.

simultaneous quavers, in the former case both dissonant with the longer notes and clashing with each other. When the first of the pair of quavers is a relatively unaccented dissonant passing note, clashes against crotchets in other parts may often occur with apparently complete freedom, and the same is true of cases where the first quaver is consonant with the essential notes of the interval structure on the harmonic pulse.

It is important to notice that much greater freedom is used in the treatment of relatively unaccented quaver dissonances than in the case of crotchets. Examples D, F, K, L, M and N would not be tolerated in crotchet values since they contain upward-going relatively unaccented passing dissonances and returning notes.

Four-Quaver Groups

Four-quaver groups are found occasionally in Palestrina's works on any (complete) pulse of the ₵ measure. The first note of the group is always consonant and approached by step or leap (see page 53); normally the third is also consonant, the second and fourth being passing notes or returning notes, dissonant or consonant as the case may be. Occasionally the third quaver is dissonant, and the figure conforms to the pattern of the descending four-crotchet idiom described on page 83, the fourth quaver turning back on its tracks and being heard in conjunction with a suspension of that note in another part on the following pulse: the figure in quavers without the attendant suspension is also found, though it is very rare (example E below). Conjunct movement between the four quavers and following the last of the group is essential, even where the last is a consonance.

Ex. 64

Single Quavers after a Dotted Crotchet

A single quaver following a dotted crotchet, the equivalent of a pair of quavers the first of which is tied, is a rather rare occurrence in Palestrina's sacred work, though it is common in ₵ in the madrigals.* Apart from the

* In the Madrigals Palestrina treats quavers much more freely in ₵. Cases will be found of four quaver ascending figures in which the third quaver is dissonant, of simultaneous four-quaver groups in different voices, of two groups of four quavers in succession, and of six and even ten (nine plus a dotted crotchet) together. It may be suggested that such passages as B and C below imply a crotchet pulse even though the time is ₵, yet they occur in the course of what is clearly a minim-pulse work.

Ex. 66

See also examples on p. 53 of this book, and P. V. 129, 170; P. VI. 123, 125, 143, 152, 107; P. VII. 126; P. VIII. 26, 59; P. XI. 135, etc.

comparative rarity of the figure, it offers no partieular problems.† The single quaver is always introduced and quitted by step.

Ex. 65

See also P.XIII. p. 120

Crotchets in $\mathbf{C}^3_2$

In the sesquialtera diminution of triple time ($\mathbf{C}^3_2$) the crotchet replacement of the quaver of $\mathbf{C}$ is used with much less freedom. Crotchets appear only in pairs‡, the first or second being dissonant, the other consonant in strictly conjunct movement. When the first of the pair is sounded against a minim in another voice it is generally consonant with it, though a dissonance is sometimes found (ex. c below).

Ex. 67

On rare occasions relatively unaccented dissonant crotchet returning notes and ascending passing notes are used.

Ex. 68

---

† See also examples on p. 53 of this book, and P. XXVI. 114, 116, 117, 128, 130, etc.

‡ On very rare occasions a single crotchet following a dotted minim occurs (equivalent to a pair of crotchets of which the first is ' tied '). An example may be found in P. XXIV., p. 92 (Ex. 169f.).

CHAPTER VI

THE 'NOTA CAMBIATA', ANTICIPATIONS,
IRREGULAR UNACCENTED DISSONANCES

THE Cambiata is a common idiom in polyphony, whose salient characteristic is the leap of a third downwards from a dissonant unaccented
crotchet (in 𝄵 and 𝄵) introduced by step from above, to a concord.

This figure dates back to the early days of polyphony; a troped ' Sanctus '
from ' Worcester Mediaeval Harmony ' (c. 1300) shows two forms of the
idiom, one a three-note group in which the melody after its leap from the
dissonant unaccented note to the consonance a third below seems free to
move as it will; the other a four-note combination in which a stepwise
return to the note omitted in the leap is made.

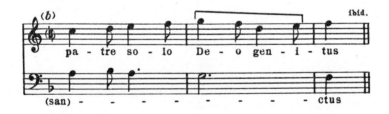

Both these forms of Cambiata were the common practice of polyphony
until the end of the first half of the sixteenth century.* In the mature music
of Palestrina the ' three-note ' figure seems to have dropped out of favour,
and it is the four-note Cambiata which must be regarded as the norm in his
music.

* The ascending Cambiata figure was also in use in the fifteenth and early sixteenth centuries, but it
is, so far as the writer knows, never found in Palestrina's authentic writing. Jeppesen gives some
examples from the earlier schools on page 218 of ' The Style of Palestrina and the Dissonance '.

The most generally found Cambiata patterns in Palestrina's work may be tabulated thus:

Ex. 70

Of these the first and second forms are by far the most common. No. 1 is the normal four-note figure in which the first note is a dotted minim, the second a crotchet dissonance, and the third a consonant minim; the fourth note, a tone or semitone above the third, may be of any length (from

a crotchet upward) and the further progress of the melody, though most
often continuing upward by step, is quite free within the normal rules of
melodic progression.   Whatever its length and further mode of progress
the fourth note must be a concord.   The figure may begin on any pulse
of the measure.

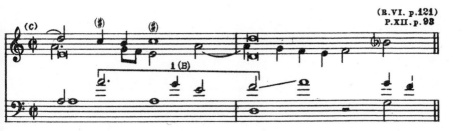

The second pattern may be found on almost any page of Palestrina's
music. Often groups of the figure occur in quick succession, simultaneously

or overlapping.   In practice it is a *five*-note idiom,* for, with very few
exceptions, the melody proceeds by step upwards from the fourth note. The
first note is a dotted minim; the second (the discord) a crotchet; the third
note (a consonance) a crotchet; the fourth (either a passing dissonance or
a consonance) is also a crotchet; the fifth note is of any duration (from a
crotchet upward) and is, of necessity (since it falls on a pulse) a consonance.
The figure may begin on any minim of the measure.

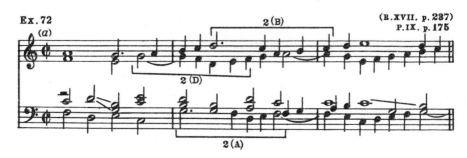

* Jeppesen cites two examples of the second pattern where the melody progresses by leap downwards
(a third) from the fourth note of the figure, (b and c below), stating that these are the only cases he
knows.   The present writer offers one further instance (a).

The third form given above is less commonly found than the two already discussed; it is, nevertheless, met with often enough for it to be ranked as a normal part of Palestrina's technique. As in the case of the second pattern, it is a five-note figure, the first four notes being crotchets, and the fifth, a tone or semitone above the fourth, of any value from a crotchet upward. The inception of the figure is most often on the odd beats of the ₵ measure, though it may also start on the even pulses.

The fourth pattern is generally considered to be of rare occurrence in Palestrina's work. In the present writer's observation it seems to have much the same standing as the third type. It is, again, a five-note figure, starting on any pulse of the measure, the first note being a dotted minim consonance, the second a dissonant unaccented crotchet quitted by leap of a third downwards to a dotted minim consonance; the fourth note is of crotchet value and is nearly always a dissonant passing note, proceeding upward by step to the fifth note, a consonance of crotchet value or upwards.*

---

* A decorated version of this fourth pattern is quoted by Jeppesen (op. cit. p. 216). The crotchets C-D (second D) in the Altus part in measure 2 may be regarded as decoration of a dotted minim D on the first pulse. As far as the writer's knowledge goes this is a ἅπαξ λεγόμενον in Palestrina's work.

A form of Cambiata which, though it does not rank with the more ortho-
dox kinds given above as a normal part of Palestrina's technique, occurs
often enough to merit careful consideration is this:

Ex. 77

Jeppesen regards it as an 'amplified cambiata' and remarks that 'the
amplified cambiata in Palestrina's time was a phrase which was undoubtedly
becoming obsolete'. He goes on to comment that it is only in the early
works that it is encountered with any frequency. This view does not seem
to be completely substantiated by the list of instances which Jeppesen
himself quotes, and it is hardly tenable that the phrase was becoming obsolete in Palestrina's time in view of its popularity in England during the
latter part of the polyphonic age.

This form of the Cambiata may, perhaps, be regarded as a modification
of the three-note figure; that is, the three-note figure, plus an obliga-
tory further procedure for two more notes. In practice it may be
codified thus: first note a dotted minim consonance, falling by step to the
second note, a dissonant crotchet; from this unaccented crotchet dissonance
there follows the characteristic leap of a third downwards to the third note,
a minim consonance; the fourth note is the same note as the second, but
this time a consonance and generally of minim or dotted minim value; this
descends by step to a fifth note, of crotchet value or upwards which may be
consonant or dissonant according to the circumstances. Series of such
Cambiata forms are found in Palestrina's work, though not nearly so

frequently as in the later Elizabethans.*‡ The figure may begin on any pulse of the measure.†

Ex. 78

(R.IV. p.66)
P.XI. p.51

* The following shows a curious example of this type of Cambiata in crotchet values:

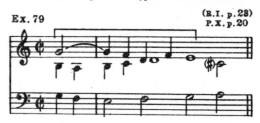

Ex. 79

(R.I. p.28)
P.X. p.20

† See also P. X., pp. 12, 79, 91, 119.

‡ It seems strange that one type of Cambiata which was so strikingly used by the English School of the sixteenth century is very rare (if, indeed, it occurs at all) in Palestrina's work.

Ex. 82   'Hosanna' Gibbons

In the name of the Lord

The nearest approach to this figure, which seems so acceptable in its method of introducing the dissonance and in its rhythm, seems to be the following, in which the actual dissonance of the second note of the Cambiata is uncertain.

Ex. 83   P.XVIII. p.141

Another irregular form of the Cambiata in ₵ is worth mentioning, though it is extremely rare.

Ex. 84

(R.XII. p.3)
P.IV. p.92

The occurrence of the real three-note type of Cambiata in the works of Palestrina is infrequent and mostly confined to the early period. Jeppesen gives an admirable list (op. cit., p. 215) of which two characteristic examples given below may serve to show how the figure was used.

Two further examples not mentioned by Jeppesen may be quoted.

Cambiata in 𝇋³₂

In 𝇋³₂ (where the harmonic pulse is the semibreve), the first and second forms of Cambiata are found fairly often in double-length note values, though they are not nearly so common as in the ₡ measure.

G

The third form is extremely rare. The first of the examples given below (and a fair number of these can be found) is clearly more akin to form 2 than 3. The other two examples, taken from the same work, are good instances.

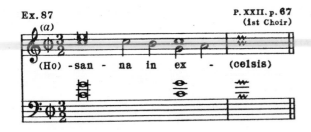

The fourth type of figure is even more exceptional in $\bigcirc^3_2$. An example

in a semi-consonant conjunction is given below, and also a curious rhythmical alteration of the idiom.*

A number of cases of type 5 appear from time to time under the $\mathbb{C}^{3}_{2}$
signature.

The three-note Cambiata is encountered on rare occasions. The two
cases quoted below show that it is by no means confined to early or imma-
ture works. The Veni Creator Mass (1570 ?) is one of Palestrina's finest
works, and the Hymns belong to his full maturity.

* " Auctor, loco signi temporis, usus est notatione nigra".

The freedom with which the discordant second note of the figure is
allowed to clash with other notes sounded against it is remarkable; even in
the case of sesquialtera minims, though consonant percussions with the
Cambiata dissonance are the general rule in the other parts, clashes are also
found. (See examples 85b, 86.) It seems as if the formula had come to be

* The suspension processes in Ex. 88b are of unusual interest and rhythmic complexity. The E in the
Bass against the D in the Altus (measure 2 pulse 1) has to do double duty as a consonant bass for the
Cantus voice, and as a suspended discord at the same time. The passage can only be explained by
horizontal analysis.

regarded as an entity capable of standing in its own right against the movement of another voice. This self-sufficiency of decorative figures and formulae was to play a very important part in later contrapuntal technique of the harmonic age; in Palestrina's technique it is evidence of the survival of a linear melodic formula which could be absorbed into a generally euphonious vertical texture without disturbing its character.

The Portamento Dissonance

The so-called ' Portamento ' note, that is, (in ₵) an unaccented crotchet introduced by step from above, and anticipating the next consonance on the subsequent pulse of the measure, is, in its consonant form, one of the most frequently found procedures in Palestrina's music. It is, for example, one of the most commonly used ornamental resolutions of a suspended discord.

In its dissonant form it is found widely enough for it to be ranked as a normal facet of Palestrina's technique. Three common uses may, perhaps, be classified:

1. Where the note preceding the portamento dissonance is of dotted minim value★ and the note following is of the value of a minim or upwards. In these cases the preceding note is sometimes a suspended discord (in its dotted part), and about equally often a consonance; the note following the portamento dissonance is, however, in the majority of cases, the preparation of a suspension, though as the fifth example (which Jeppesen quotes) shows this is by no means a hard and fast rule.

★ Occasionally the preceding note may be a crotchet. See Ex. 93a (altius).

P. XVIII. p. 82

2. Where the portamento dissonance forms part of the characteristic figure.

Ex.92

This is probably the most frequently found usage of the portamento note in dissonant form. The preceding note may be a plain crotchet (a, c, below) or a dotted minim (tied) (b, d, below); it may be a consonance (a, c, d) or a suspended dissonance (b). The note following the portamento dissonance is always a concordant crotchet.

Ex.93

3. Where the portamento dissonance forms part of the old cadential formula which was already becoming obsolete.

Ex.94

This use is rare in Palestrina. Jeppesen quotes two instances (P. XVIII, p. 9; P. XII, p. 106) one of which is given below (Ex. 95b), saying that they are the only cases he has found. A further example is given (P. **XX**, p. 27) (Ex. 95a).

Ex. 95

Palestrina's treatment of the portamento dissonance shows a notable refinement of technique, compared with that of his predecessors who used upward stepwise dissonant portamento notes, anticipations approached by leap (thirds and fifths), and even minim forms of these. None of these archaic idioms forms a part of Palestrina's normal technique; it can be said with some degree of safety that authentic examples do not occur in his music. This process of refinement of existing practice may be taken as an indication of growing awareness of the vertical aspect of the contrapuntal texture.

Portamento notes in $\mathbf{\mathbb{C}}^3_2$

The portamento dissonance in $\mathbf{\mathbb{C}}^3_2$ is extremely rare. One instance is quoted below.

Ex. 96

It may be noted that in all these cases where a dissonant portamento note is sounded against another crotchet (or minim in $\mathbf{\mathbb{C}}^3_2$) the percussion is consonant.

Other uses of unessential dissonance

Some further cases of irregular treatment of unessential crotchet dissonances in $\mathbf{\mathbb{C}}$ must be mentioned for the sake of completeness, and on account of their interest as further illustration of Palestrina's methods of dealing with the dissonant forms of an earlier period. None of the usages mentioned below can be regarded as the normal practice of Palestrina's style,★ yet their sporadic appearance shows that he had not discarded them altogether.

(I) The upward leap of a third from a dissonant unaccented crotchet introduced by the step of a second from above.

Ex. 97

★ Jeppesen: ' Style of Palestrina ', p. 189.

Jeppesen points out that this melodic figure was a favourite one in the period, and was freely used by Palestrina in consonant conjunction. Of the dissonant form he says that it is 'extremely rare, and principally found in the composer's earlier works'. He quotes one example (P. XII, p. 71) and cites eight others, three from doubtful works, and one at least (P. XIII, p. 112) which is corrected in the Roma edition. Two examples given below are not included in his list.

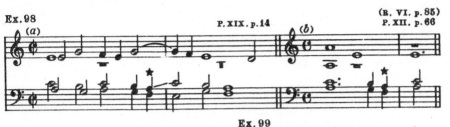

(II) The well-worn fifteenth-century cadential formula:

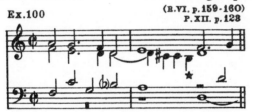

survived in occasional appearances in Palestrina's work. Jeppesen can find only one instance in which the last crotchet of the group is dissonant.*

(III) Slightly less rare is the upward leap of a fourth from a dissonant unaccented crotchet.†

* Jeppesen: op. cit., p. 194 et seq. The following apparent examples are obviously due to Haberl's *musica ficta* interpretations.

† Jeppesen (op. cit., p. 203) cites some twenty-nine instances, to which these two may be added.

It is, perhaps, worth noting that in most of the above cases of a leap of a third from a dissonant crotchet, the dissonant crotchet is not only itself unaccented, but is the second half of a weak pulse of the measure; when the leap is a fourth, the dissonant crotchet falls more commonly on the second half of an odd pulse.

(IV) Of extreme rarity is the leap of an octave from a dissonant crotchet. Here it may be noted that the dissonance falls on the second half of the odd (strong) pulses. The treatment is nearly related to the dissonant anticipatory notes considered above, and seems to suggest that the octave leap was regarded in a different light from other leaps, and almost as a repetition of the same note.*

Palestrina appears to have discarded the other upward leaps (fifths and sixths) which are occasionally met with in the Netherland Schools; neither does he use the leap away from the unaccented minim dissonance in ₵.

(V) The reverse process, an unaccented dissonance approached by step from below and quitted by a downward leap, was used occasionally by the Netherlanders. In Palestrina's work Jeppesen can only find this single instance.

(VI) It remains to consider the rare cases in which a dissonant unaccented crotchet in ₵ is approached by leap. In Palestrina's music this procedure seems to be used exceptionally in connection with two melodic figures which were common in the earlier part of the century.

Ex.105

* Jeppesen (op. cit., p. 209) cites six examples, of which these are two.

Jeppesen cites some four instances of the first (A), of which the following may be taken as fair samples:*

Of the second type (B) Jeppesen's quoted example, together with about eight of his citations, seem to invite a different explanation. In the first case quoted below it is possible to regard the E in the highest part (Cantus 2) as a minim passing note, in which case the crotchet figure in the Altus becomes normal. Yet enough instances where the unaccented crotchet is clearly dissonant exist to make the idiom worthy of note. Some examples from Jeppesen's admirable list are quoted (Ex. 107b, c).†

On very rare occasions the retrograde inversion of the figure given in Ex. 105b is found in a dissonant context.

These irregular unaccented dissonant forms do not seem to occur in $\mathbb{C}_2^3$ time. This further strengthens the theory that the $\mathbb{C}_2^3$ minim is a longer note requiring more careful dissonance treatment than the crotchet of $\mathbb{C}$.

NOTE AGAINST NOTE DISSONANCE

The problem of the percussion of dissonances in Palestrina's work has caused a lot of complicated explanation by modern writers on the subject.

* Jeppesen: 'Style of Palestrina', p. 220. Jeppesen's fourth example (P. XVII. 20) is possibly a misprint in Haberl. It seems that the last note in the Cantus part should be a tied minim A, not another G.

† Jeppesen: op. cit., p. 220.

Sixteenth-century theory, as Jeppesen points out, does not help much. Rockstro's ruling that ' These notes (crotchet dissonances) must always be irreproachable in their relation to the Bass ' does not fit in completely with Palestrina's practice.

In the present writer's view, the matter becomes clear if the interval structure of the ' harmonic ' pulse is taken as the touchstone by which dissonance is to be assessed. Then suspended and unessential dissonances fall into their proper perspective, and complications such as Jeppesen argues about on pages 176 and 177 of ' The Style of Palestrina and the Dissonance ' do not arise.

The theory may be stated thus. In the case of unaccented (second) crotchets in the ₵ and ₵ measure the sounding of a note dissonant with the interval structure of the pulse against another note, consonant or dissonant with the prevailing ' harmony ', is permissible whatever clash may occur, provided that both parts causing the clash are treated correctly in relationship to the interval structure of the pulse. In the case of first crotchet dissonances falling on the relatively unaccented minim pulses (even), clashes may occur against a note of any value, being a part of the ' harmonic structure ' of the pulse, or a suspended discord, provided that the dissonant note obeys the laws applicable to it. In the case of minim unaccented passing dissonances where the ' harmonic ' pulse is a semibreve, clashes are usually avoided.

In ₵$_2^3$ time, unaccented (even) minim clashes do occur, but with much less freedom than do crotchets in ₵. In the relatively unaccented position (first minims of a pair on the weak semibreve pulses) clashes are very rare indeed.

CHAPTER VII

SUSPENDED DISCORDS

THE term 'Suspended Discord' or 'Suspension' is a post-sixteenth-century method of describing a dissonance occurring between two voices on a pulse beat when the discordant note has been prepared, that is, heard as a concord immediately before. Whereas the passing note dissonances and other allied forms described in the preceding chapters may be classified as 'incidental' or 'unessential', suspended discords must be regarded as primary phenomena in the interval structure of the music.

Two approaches to the nature and use of suspended discords are possible; the first, rhythmic; the second, 'harmonic' or vertical. R. O. Morris advocates the first of these, and his illustration is worth quoting:*

'Imagine four people walking abreast; one of them stops for an instant, and then has to run to catch the others up; or possibly one of them waits for him, and then the two run together till they have got into line again with the other two. The sixteenth-century view of discord (and it is a mistake to assume without consideration that this view is permanently obsolete) is that of a similar breaking of line. Instead of all the parts moving together to a new concord, one of them gets left behind (suspended) for a moment and then the others wait for him to rejoin them, concord being restored as he does so; . . . Strictly speaking, the discord itself is merely a method of preparing a fresh concord, and the object of such preparation (not in itself necessary) is to obtain variety of texture, and to enable the different voices to maintain their rhythmic independence.

'At the same time there is no doubt that the sixteenth-century composers, by constantly employing such procedure, became increasingly sensitive to the emotional effect of discord, and to the possibilities of employing it for a harmonic, and not a purely rhythmical purpose.'

Jeppesen's view of the matter is essentially harmonic or vertical. For him the suspended dissonance is used *because it is a dissonance*.†

'It is true of all the forms of dissonance treatment which have been discussed up to this point, that the melodic phrase introducing the dissonance may just as often (and in most cases, oftener) be used in consonant as in dissonant conjunction. Here for the first time we encounter a dissonance which is not the accidental result of a melodic progression, but which is used just because it is dissonance, and because it is desired that dissonance—and dissonance only—should be heard at the point where it is placed.'

---

* R. O. Morris: 'Contrapuntal Technique,' p. 33.
† Jeppesen: 'The Style of Palestrina', pp. 224, 225.

Jeppesen goes on to suggest that English composers were the first to use suspended discords, about the beginning of the fifteenth century, and quotes an interesting passage from the theoretical writings of Monk William, which seems to imply an aesthetic justification of their use; the consonance following the dissonance gains added ' sweetness ' from the juxtaposition.*

The complete suspension process consists of three factors; preparation of the suspended note on a consonance, the (suspended) discord itself, and the resolution of the discord upon a consonance, by the downward step of a second.   Normally the preparation takes place upon a relatively unaccented pulse of the measure; it remains stationary upon the next accented pulse making the dissonance; it resolves upon the following relatively unaccented pulse.

Suspensions in ¢

When the time signature is ¢, three speeds of the suspension sequence are found: (A) in minims; (B) in semibreves; and (C) in crotchet values.

(A) Minim Suspension Sequences

Suspension sequences in minim values are by far the most common. The normal requirements are: preparation on a relatively unaccented (second or fourth) minim of the measure, the taking of the discord on the following accented minim (third, or first of the next measure) and the resolution on the next (relatively unaccented) minim.   The whole process thus takes up three minim pulses of which one is accented (the discord) and the other two relatively unaccented.

(B. VI. p. 66)
P. XII. p. 58
Missa Brevis

Ex. 109

Sometimes the note of preparation is lengthened to a semibreve in an otherwise normal minim suspension sequence.   This procedure, if semibreve preparation is on the first pulse, gives rise to the apparent irregularity of the discord falling on a weaker pulse of the measure than the preparation. It seems probable, however, that in the sixteenth century there was not much difference in accentual importance between the first and third pulses as ' harmonic ' accents; even so the equality of preparation and discord in these cases is worthy of note.

---

* Coussemaker: ' Scriptores III ', p. 291, ' secundum usum modernum consonantie dissonantes aliquoties nobis serviunt, sicut dissonantia secunde dat dulcedinem tertie basse; dissonantia vero septime dat dulcedinem sexte . . . '
For Jeppesen's interpretation of the passage, see op. cit., pp. 225 and 226.

Note of resolution

Except in the case of ornamental resolutions, which will be considered later, the note of resolution in the minim suspension sequence is generally of minim or greater value.

One common exception to this rule is the practice which may be termed the extended resolution, in which the minim preparation and discord proceed by a downward step of a second to a crotchet (concord), which is followed by a returning note crotchet a step below, the process being completed by the return to the note of resolution. This very common figure may be regarded as an extension of ornamental resolution I (see below).

On rare occasions the resolution of the minim suspension sequence is upon a crotchet which proceeds downwards by two further step progressions.

So far as the present writer's knowledge goes, Palestrina's treatment of the minim discord resolving on a crotchet does not allow either upward

stepwise movement from that crotchet or any kind of leap.   Such hypothetical cases as the following seem to be outside the style.

Ex.113

Ornamental Resolution of Suspensions.   The device commonly known as
an 'ornamental resolution' is to be found on almost every page of Palestrina's music.   The term is rather misleading, since it is the dissonant note
itself which is decorated rather than the note of resolution, if the process is
regarded from a rhythmical viewpoint.

Two ornamental patterns seem to have become almost standard procedures in the style:

Ex.114

Ex.115

Ex.116

The first of these is simply an anticipation of the note of resolution on the
second half of the pulse which contains the dissonance.   The fact that the
actual dissonance is only of crotchet value, and that the resolution on the
third minim of the sequence is anticipated, seems to allow a freer treatment
of the real note of resolution, which in this case is often of crotchet value followed by a pair of quavers or another non-returning crotchet.   Conjunct
movement as far as the note of resolution and its next step, is still necessary.

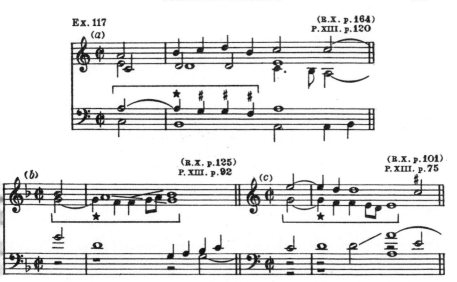

In the second pattern, which consists of a quaver anticipation of the note of resolution followed by a quaver lower returning note, on the second half of the dissonant pulse, the real note of resolution (third pulse of the sequence) is almost invariably of minim value or upwards.

A variant of (I) which is occasionally encountered may, perhaps, be classified as an 'ornamental resolution,' though it is, strictly, no more than the repetition of the dissonance within the pulse belonging to that factor of the suspension process. The quotation given below shows the process quite clearly.

Other Ornamental Resolutions rarely found in Palestrina's work

Of the ornamental resolution forms employing disjunct movement from the dissonance, which were so greatly favoured by the Netherland Schools before Palestrina and by his English contemporaries and their successors, only one seems to have found occasional acceptance in the technique of the Roman master. It consists of a downward leap of a third from the dissonance, followed by an upward step to the note of resolution. Both dissonance and ornament are of crotchet value, occupying the minim pulse belonging to the discord, and the ornamental note is usually concordant with the prevailing interval structure. Jeppesen cites about three dozen instances of this formula.*

In the Missa Brevis the figure  is a characteristic part of the

melodic material, and it is not surprising to find quite a number of instances in this work where it is used in the resolution of suspensions. The note of resolution is generally a minim or note of greater value.

Ex. 119

Note: the musical examples Ex. 119 (a), (b), (c) are part of image 2.

It will be seen that in the third example above the suspended discordant crotchet in the Altus part (second measure) leaps down a third to another *discordant* crotchet before resolving. Jeppesen† cites some six examples of this procedure and points to its extreme rarity. Two of his instances are given below. In the case of the first the B in the Altus (second measure) though apparently dissonant against the A in the Cantus, is consonant with the prevailing interval structure, and the A is, in fact, the (suspended) dissonance.

Ex. 120

Of the other ornamental resolutions of the period which contain leaps of more than a third downward from the discord before the resolution, Jeppesen

* Jeppesen, op. cit., p. 266.
† ibid., p. 267.

can only find one instance in the whole collection of Palestrina's works.

Ex. 121

(R.X. p.2)
P.XIII. p.1

Ornamental resolutions using ascent from the dissonant note, either in conjunct or disjunct movement, are outside the style. Such hypothetical resolutions as those given below, though they occur in other schools of the sixteenth century, may be ruled out of Palestrina's technique with a reasonable degree of certainty.

Ex. 122

(B) *Semibreve Suspension Sequences*

In ¢ time suspension sequences in semibreves are found fairly often, usually, but not invariably, when the rate of change of the interval structure is the semibreve. The normal requirements are: preparation on the second semibreve of the measure, the discord on the first semibreve of the next measure, and resolution on the following semibreve.

Ex. 123

(R. VI. p.77)
P.XII. p.61
Missa Brevis.

Ho - san-na   (ROMA)

★ The 'Roma' edition reads a breve 'G' in the Altus, measure 3 of the quotation.

On rare occasions the note of preparation is lengthened to a breve; this gives rise to the same situation which has already been discussed on page 108, in which the preparation and discord have equal accentual importance.

Ex. 124

(R.XIII. p.200)
P.XXV. p.175

H

When the discord is of full semibreve duration, that is when it is not decorated, the note of resolution is always, so far as the present writer's investigation goes, of semibreve or greater value. The extended form of resolution described in the section on minim suspension sequences (page 109) does not seem to be used.

Ornamental Resolutions in semibreve sequences

The two common 'ornamental resolution' patterns described on page 110 are very often found in notes of twice the value in semibreve suspension sequences.

As in the case of ornamental resolutions in minim sequences, the note of resolution is much more freely treated when the dissonant pulse contains decoration. After either of the normal ornaments the note of resolution is often of minim value, and its further progress may be made either by step or by leap, upwards or downwards. It will be seen that this treatment is considerably freer than in the shorter value sequences, both in the matter of leaping from the half value note of resolution, and in the fact that half note resolution is used in conjunction with the second form of ornament.

A considerable number of instances occur in which the preparation takes place on the first semibreve of a measure, the discord and one or other of the regular ornamental attachments on the second semibreve, and the resolution on the first semibreve of the next measure. So far as the writer knows this rhythmic arrangement is not used with the undecorated form of the semibreve sequence. It apparently runs counter to the leading principle of rhythm in suspensions, in that the preparation and resolution are each as strong or stronger in accent than the dissonance. It is just possible to regard these cases as examples of minim sequences with extended preparation and resolution, but the following examples show that this theory is improbable.*

It seems unlikely that Palestrina ever uses the forms of ornamental resolution which are based on disjunct movement in the semibreve suspension sequence. The present writer knows of no such instances. The other irregular forms of decoration are even more remote from the style.

(C) *Suspension Sequences in crotchets*

Except in the case of the so-called 'consonant fourth' idioms, which will be considered on page 122, the suspension process in crotchet values (𝄞) is a rare occurrence. Nevertheless, it does appear often enough to justify its inclusion as part of Palestrina's technique. The preparation take place on an unaccented second crotchet of any minim pulse; the discord follows on the succeeding pulse crotchet, and the resolution is completed within that pulse. Conjunct movement from the note of preparation onwards persists as far as the resolution in all cases, and usually one note further. The following instances will show the process.

Lengthened preparation of the crotchet suspension is also found:

* In the 'Roma' Edition, Ex. 128b appears with altered 'barring', placing the suspension preparation on the second semibreve of the measure, and the discord on the first pulse of the next measure.

In crotchet suspension sequences the note resolution sometimes remains stationary on the next pulse.   When this occurs in combination with a lengthened preparation, the process may bear a superficial resemblance to the minim sequence with a portamento note ornamental resolution, as in the first suspension sequence of the above example (Altus).   The process in this case is clearly a crotchet sequence with lengthened preparation: the discord is of crotchet value, resolving on the second crotchet of pulse one of measure two in the quotation (C).   The note of resolution then becomes the preparation of another crotchet suspension sequence.   Were it an ornamental resolution of a minim sequence, the D would resolve on the C at the second pulse of measure two; by this time the C has become a dissonance.

Two examples of crotchet sequences with lengthened note of preparation, in which the note of resolution is quitted by leap, leave no doubt about the correctness of the explanation of the formula.

The counterpart in simple diminution of the extended resolution discussed on page 109, is, possibly, the commonest form of the crotchet sequence.

Ornamental resolutions in crotchet sequences

Diminution of the ornamental resolutions commonly found in minim suspension sequences (page 110) is not available in Palestrina's style.   The first of these ornaments would imply the use of a pair of quavers on the first half of a minim pulse; the second would require semiquaver values; neither of these forms a part of the technique.

Vertical aspect of suspensions

Thus far, consideration of suspensions has been directed mainly towards the rhythmic and melodic aspects of the matter, though a certain amount of attention had, of necessity, to be given to the consonance or dissonance of the various notes forming the suspension sequences.

Suspensions above the bass

Turning now to the vertical aspect, the most commonly found suspended dissonances above the bass (that is, the actual lowest note), may be described in figuring, provided the figuring is understood to imply no more than the interval relationships of the upper voices with the lowest voice, thus:

7 6 *and* 4 3

    (*a*) $\begin{smallmatrix}7\\3\end{smallmatrix}\begin{smallmatrix}6\\-\end{smallmatrix}$ (*b*) $\begin{smallmatrix}5\\4\\3\end{smallmatrix}$ or $\begin{smallmatrix}6\\4\\3\end{smallmatrix}\begin{smallmatrix}5\\3\end{smallmatrix}$ or $\begin{smallmatrix}5\\4\\3\end{smallmatrix}\begin{smallmatrix}6\\3\end{smallmatrix}$

It should be observed that, though the 4 3 suspension is often accompanied by a 6 5 or 5 6, the $\begin{smallmatrix}6\\4\\3\end{smallmatrix}$ combination is very rare indeed.* In the case of the 7 6 the seventh may be minor or major.

Ex.133   (R.X. p.80)   (R.XV. p.14)
(*a*) In two parts   P.XIII. p.60   (*b*)   P.XIV. p.10

                7   6   4   3

* A very interesting example, albeit from a doubtful work, of a so-called 'English Cadence'—a 4-♯3 suspension accompanied by a ♭3 in another voice against the 4—is worth quoting (Litaniae Domini 28. m. 116-117). The Haberl Edition omits this : see Ex. 56c.

    (*e*)   R.XX.p.125 (3 Voices omitted)

                                   5 ——
                                   4 —— ♯3
                                 ♮3   2   8

Ex. 133 (continued)

9 8 *and* 2 1

Much less common is the 9 8 or 2 1 suspension. Both forms are extremely rare in two-part writing. Of the 2 1 kind Jeppesen† cites one instance only (example 134a), and of the 9 8 the four cases which he quotes, are, as he points out, scarcely in real two-part writing. The extreme emptiness of the resolution into the bare unison or octave may account for the rarity of these forms. In the examples given the portamento-note ornamental resolution is used, perhaps to compensate for the lack of fullness.

Ex. 134

In three or more parts the 2 1 suspension remains rare. When found it is usually embellished with the portamento-note ornamental resolution $\frac{5}{3}\ \frac{-}{2\ 1\ 1}$ The 9 8 is fairly common in writing for more than two voices. Again the portamento decoration is generally, though by no means invariably used. The $\frac{9\ 8}{3\ -}$ formula is the most usual, though $\frac{9\ 8}{6\ -}{3\ -}$ and $\frac{9\ 8}{6\ 5}{3\ -}$ do occur; instances of these may be seen in examples 135c and 139b. The other usages described are illustrated below.

Ex. 135

Augmented and Diminished intervals as suspensions

The augmented fourth is fairly common as a suspended discord. Here the question of *musica ficta* accidentals becomes something of a problem and

† Jeppesen: ' Style of Palestrina ', p. 252.

many doubtful cases exist. The diminished fourth does not seem to be used in this connection. The instance in P.V. p. 133 appears to be a misreading, and is corrected in the Roma edition (R. XI. p. 23).

Ex. 136
Aug. 4th
P. XIX. p. 27

The diminished fifth is found as a suspended dissonance over a bass which moves to another note at the point of resolution. (See below for a discussion of this process.) In such cases it is found even in two-part writing. In similar circumstances the diminished seventh is also used, though this is rare.

Ex. 137
(a)
(R. XV. p. 12)
P. XIV. p. 8
(b)
P. XIX. p. 75

The Sixth and Fifth as suspended dissonances

Occasionally the sixth is used as a suspended dissonance in the combination $\begin{smallmatrix}6&5\\5&-\\3&-\end{smallmatrix}$ It is also found with the 4 3 suspension, (example 138a).

The fifth against the sixth with change of interval at the point of resolution is far more common (example 138b). It may also resolve on a consonant fourth without change of interval structure (example 148b).

Ex. 138 (a)
(R. VI. p. 96)
P. XII. p. 74
(b)
P. XXIII. p. 88

Double Suspensions

Double suspensions are freely used by Palestrina. The following examples will give some idea of the combinations available.

Triple Suspensions

Jeppesen cites three examples of triple suspended dissonance in Palestrina, pointing out that these, though much used by the earlier schools, are extremely rare in the Roman school.

SUSPENSIONS IN THE BASS

Normal use of suspensions in the bass

Suspended discords in the bass (lowest part) are a regular part of Palestrina's technique; they are not, however, nearly as commonly found as suspended discords above the bass.

The possible interval combinations above a suspension are (a) $\begin{smallmatrix}(7)\\5\\2\end{smallmatrix}$ and (much more rarely) (b) $\begin{smallmatrix}(7)\\4\\2\end{smallmatrix}$; in the case of suspensions where some of the parts move at the resolution making a new combination of intervals, the $\genfrac{}{}{0pt}{}{6}{\genfrac{}{}{0pt}{}{(4)}{2}}$ combination is also available (see below).

The examples given below will suffice to show the normal usages.

Ex. 141
(a)
(B.XV. p. 22)
P. XIV. p. 16

(b)
(B.XV. p. 69)
P. XIV. p. 52

(c)
P. XVII. p. 17

In two-part writing the only suspension commonly used in the bass is the 2-3 progression.

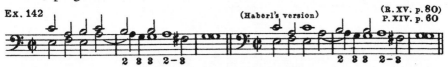

Ex. 142
(Haberl's version)
(B.XV. p. 80)
P. XIV. p. 60

Jeppesen points out the reluctance of Palestrina and his school to resolve a suspended dissonance into a bare perfect interval in two parts. He knows of no instance of the 7-8 suspension. He cites three instances of the 4-5

Ex. 143
(a)
(B.VI. p.129)
P. XII. p.100

(b)
(B.XVI. p. 86)
P. XXVII. p. 67

(c)
(B.XVI. p.11)
P. XXVII. p. 9

progression ; these are of considerable interest and are worth quoting.*

(*a*) has a portamento-note ornamental resolution, but is otherwise a clear-cut instance of the 4-5.

(*b*) is an example of the second part moving to a new note at the moment when the resolution is completed (see p. 129).

(*c*) is a crotchet value sequence with prolonged preparation, according to the Breitkopf (Haberl) edition.   The Roma edition, however, reads a B flat crotchet on the first pulse of the full measure, making the preceding A an untied minim, thus doing away with the suspended dissonance.

Double Suspensions one of which is in the Bass

Double suspensions of discords, where one appears in the lowest voice, are occasionally found.   The interval combinations seem to be:
$\begin{smallmatrix} (7) \\ 4, \\ 3 \end{smallmatrix}$ $\begin{smallmatrix} (5 \text{ or } 4) \\ 3, \\ 2 \end{smallmatrix}$ $\begin{smallmatrix} (7) \\ 6. \\ 2. \end{smallmatrix}$
The following examples will show some of the possibilities.

Ex.144
(a)   P.XVI.p.85   (b)   (B.III.p.74)
                                                                                                      P.V.p.59

(c)   (B.XI. p.44)   (d)   (B.XI. p.49)
                    P.V.p.150   P.V.p.154

Augmented and diminished intervals as suspensions in the bass are very infrequent in Palestrina's music.

PREPARATION OF SUSPENSIONS

The ' Consonant Fourth ' idiom

The ruling that every suspended dissonance must be prepared by a consonance in Palestrina's style has one important exception which must now be considered.   The idiom known generally, but for no very good reason which the present writer can see, as the ' Consonant Fourth ' implies the preparation of a suspended discord by a fourth over a static bass.   The most usual forms of this idiom, which is very common indeed throughout

* Jeppesen: ' The Style of Palestrina ', p. 247.   In Ex. 143c the Roma edition emends the lowest voice, doing away with the suspension.

Palestrina's music, are the two given in the examples below: (*a*) where the fourth, occurring on a relatively unaccented even minim, is approached by step from below; (*b*) where it is approached by step from above in the same accentual situation.

* [Roma Signature: O]

Normal usages

Three factors remain constant in the normal usages: (1) the stationary bass; (2) the introduction of the fourth by step upon an even minim; (3) the consonance of the fourth with every other part except the bass at its point of introduction, and the immediate production of a more acute dissonance on the succeeding pulse in the form of treating it as a suspension. The idiom is most often, but not exclusively, used in cadences.

Exceptional usages

The first of these factors, that the bass remain static throughout the whole process, is obviously a necessary feature of the idiom; so is the introduction by conjunct movement. The third condition, however, is often not observed in entirety. Passages such as the following, and they are by no means rare, do not fulfil either of the requirements laid down in (3). Here the fourth from the bass is introduced against the fifth, making the dissonance of a second at its point of introduction, and this persists till the resolution.

In the next two examples, though the introduction of the fourth does not form an additional discord with any other part than the bass, there is no stronger dissonance on the following beat to distract the attention from the fourth from the bass. In the second instance the fourth is introduced against an accented passing note in the treble (measure 1); this however does not add to its dissonance, since it is the top part and not the tenor which is responsible for this clash. The first pulse of the second measure shows the resolution of a suspended discord (fifth) on the 'consonant fourth'; see page 133.

'Consonant fourth' in Crotchet Suspension Sequence

Quite often the 'consonant fourth' formula is found in the form of a crotchet suspension sequence, both in the normal idiom and the stationary accompaniment variation.

Inversion of the 'Consonant fourth' formula

An interesting inversion of the formula is given below.★ It must be regarded as a distinguished rarity in the style. By *musica ficta* usage it may well be another example of resolution on a diminished fifth (see below; page 132).

★ Jeppesen (op. cit., 241) quotes an interesting variation of the static form of the consonant fourth where two of the accompanying parts have minim returning notes at the point of introduction.

Other Dissonant Preparations

Jeppesen quotes an instance in which the seventh from the bass is used as a dissonant suspension preparation in the same way as the consonant fourth with the accompanying parts remaining stationary. This case must be taken into account when possible explanations of these dissonances are sought.

The *Agnus Dei* (I) of the *Hexachord* Mass has some interesting examples of dissonant suspension preparation. This early, but very important work shows considerable influence of the Netherland style, and it may be argued that some of the dissonance treatment found in it is foreign to Palestrina's mature technique. Nevertheless, the cases quoted by Jeppesen must be weighed carefully in any full consideration of the matter. Three of them are given below.

These instances, and the almost note-for-note repetition of the third, nine measures later, are variants of one formula. This dissonant note (A) in the first two cases is introduced by step from below, and in the third by leap of a fourth upwards; in all it remains as a suspension normally resolved, and at the point of introduction it is consonant with all the parts except the static note (B). The interval combination at the point of preparation of the suspension is $\frac{6}{5}$.
$\ \ _3$

This formula is by no means peculiar to the *Hexachord* Mass.

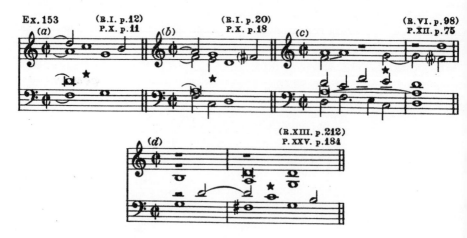

In considering these examples of dissonances and trying to discover some rational explanation of them, it must be borne in mind that most of the more irregular forms are found only in Palestrina's earlier works, though they were generally the common practice of the preceding period. Only the consonant fourth in its normal usages became, or rather, survived as a real part of his mature technique.

It is possible to make out a case for the theory that the 'pedal' point, which became such an important technical feature in the next period of musical history, had some close connection with the 'consonant fourth' type of dissonance. Such an example as 151 seems to imply that a stationary note in the bass allowed considerable freedom of movement to the parts above it. Passages like the following seem to bear out the idea.

(The fourth from the bass falling on the odd beat cannot be dismissed as a minim passing note*.)

Whether the pedal-point theory can be accepted or not as an explanation in some degree of the normal consonant fourth formulae, it would be pressing the theoretical practice of later times too far to suggest that an inverted pedal gives much help in dealing with the other examples cited. It should, however, be noted in passing that in all these cases the dissonance is introduced unobtrusively by step and that in each instance it is dissonant against a stationary note which continues till the final resolution has taken place, thus minimizing the discord produced.

There is something to be said for the theory that the $^6_5$ interval combination above the bass was treated with considerable freedom in the sixteenth century. The $^6_5$ with the 5 as a suspended discord over a moving bass was a perfectly normal procedure. The 5-6 and 6-5 crotchet figure was also treated quite freely.

The following examples may show something of the freedom of treatment which Palestrina occasionally uses.†

* Jeppesen, quoting the second and third and citing the first of these passages from the Lamentations, accepts them as foreshadowing the pedal point. He rejects this theory in the following case on the ground that the stationary bass has only just begun when the dissonance occurs, and further, that while the other examples occur at the end of a section, this one is introduced while the movement is in full course.

On the first count there seems little to choose between this case and the first or third of those quoted above; on the second, though this is in the course of a movement it is strongly cadential. However Jeppesen classes it as a unique (as far as he knows) example of an " expressive " dissonance. (Op. cit. pp. 280. 281.)

Ex. 155

(B.XII.p. 97-98)
P.IV. p.158

† Some exceedingly irregular passages in which $^6_5$ (and even a $^7_3$) combinations are treated with complete freedom, may be found in the five-part ' Litania de Beata Virgine Maria '. This work is of doubtful authenticity, and it is fairly clear that the text used by Haberl was either faulty or wrongly transcribed. They are interesting in so far as they indicate the free attitude to the 6/5 dissonance sometimes found during the sixteenth century. (The Roma Edition emends Ex. a by reading a G (in brackets) for B in the top voice m. 2., and Ex. b by reading Altus : m. 1. A semibreve, B minim, D minim.)

Ex. 157   (B.XX. p.75)   (b)   (B.XX. p.76)
(a)   P.XXVI.p.69   P.XXVI.p.70

(a) is a case of a 'short' $^6_5$ ^{5} suspension; (b) a curious instance of a dissonant 6 introduced by leap against a 5 which then leaps upward a fourth; (c) shows a leap from a dissonant 6 (against a stationary 5).

THE RESOLUTION

The melodic resolution of a suspended discord is always effected by the fall of a second, either major or minor, in Palestrina's music. The rarely used ornamental forms described on page 112 are no exception to this rule, since the leap of a third (or fifth) from the dissonance is no more than an embellishment of that note, the real resolution being a tone or semitone below the discord. The few apparent instances of upward resolution of suspensions which occur in the Haberl edition of the works have been shown by Jeppesen to be incorrect transcriptions of the text.* The instance of an apparently unresolved suspended discord given in the footnote on page 133 need not be taken very seriously; it is also, probably, a textual misreading, and is emended in the Roma edition.

Vertical aspect of the resolution

The vertical aspect of the resolution is much more complicated, and of far greater interest, since it demonstrates more clearly, perhaps, than any other factor in Palestrina's technique, the essentially linear, as opposed to harmonic, outlook.

The notes accompanying the discord in the other voices may, as commonly in the harmonic practice of a later age, remain stationary while the

---

* Jeppesen: 'Style of Palestrina', p. 260.

discord resolves, or move to other notes of the 'chord' which creates the dissonance, at the moment of resolution.

Change of interval structure at point of resolution

Just as often, however, some of the parts accompanying the dissonance and responsible for it, move to other notes forming a new set of interval relationships on the point of resolution. Such 'changes of harmony' on the resolution, as the process might be called in the harmonic age, could be produced either by moving the bass or any other voice. By this means the possibilities of suspensions were greatly increased. Any attempt at purely harmonic explanation of some of the examples given below should satisfy the reader of the futility of trying to understand Palestrina's technique in terms of common chords and their inversions. Linear analysis is often the only reasonable explanation.

The one almost constant requisite of resolution in its vertical aspect is that the note of resolution should be consonant with all the other parts at the point of resolution. Exceptions even to this fundamental practice may be found and will be considered later.

Some examples of change of interval combination at the point of resolution must now be considered in some detail.

I

These, with the possible exception of G, may be regarded as perfectly normal and regular in the style.

(A) shows a suspended seventh with a (dissonant) portamento-note ornamental resolution: at the point of resolution (second minim pulse, measure 2) all the other parts move making a new ' chord ' of resolution on a bass a third lower: on the third pulse of the measure another suspended seventh accompanied by a fifth and third is formed; this resolves normally on a sixth over a stationary bass, while the fifth descends to the third.

In (B) a suspended seventh plus a third resolves ornamentally, while the bass moves up by step and the third down a step, making a new interval combination on a bass a tone higher.

(C) contains two examples of the fifth from the bass as a suspended dissonance, accompanied by a sixth.   Linear analysis will make the process which goes to the formation of successions of $^6_5$ suspensions over a moving bass clear.   Between the Cantus and Bassus voices in this case there is no dissonance at all; the same is true of the Altus and Bassus; between the Cantus and Altus appear a series of normal 7-6 suspensions.

(D) is a slightly more complicated instance of the same process.   The ' chord ' of resolution from a harmonic point of view appears to be a discord (Diminished fifth).   Again linear analysis shows that each two-part combination is satisfactory; the B natural which is the apparent trouble maker is merely a minim passing note in relation to the F.   (See R. O. Morris's analysis of this passage, op. cit., p. 37.)

(E) is a straightforward example of a suspended $^5_4\ ^-_3$ in which the accompanying 5 is replaced by a 6 at the point of resolution, producing $^5_4\ ^6_3$ progression over a stationary bass.

(F) gives two instances of the process with the suspension in the bass. The sixth above the suspended dissonance is consonant with both the other parts, but would be dissonant against the note of resolution of the suspension; it is ' cleared ' by moving down a third at the point of resolution.

(G) is a less normal usage. There is what appears to be a $^6_4$ interval combination on the third pulse of the measure. By linear analysis it will be seen that the top part progresses quite normally with each of the lower parts. Between the lower parts there is the (discordant) interval of a fourth, which is prepared and resolved by downward step in the bass while the middle part proceeds upward by step. The only irregularity here is the rather unusual treatment of the fourth from the bass; in this context the G sounds like the dissonance rather than the D in the bass.

Problematic types of resolution

Three examples of the rather more problematic types of resolution which are occasionally met with are given below.

Ex. 160

(B.VI. p.78)
P. XII. p.62
Missa. Brevis

(B.XIV. p.158)
P. VIII. p.115

P.XXIII. p.4

(A) shows a diminished fifth suspended dissonance in a semibreve suspension sequence with an ornamental resolution. The problem here is rather rhythmic than vertical; the preparation and resolution are both on first semibreves of the measure, the discord on the relatively weaker second semibreve. The matter has been touched upon on page 115. The vertical interest lies in the change of bass at the real point of resolution, and the fact that the first crotchet of the decoration is dissonant with the bass, in a semibreve sequence.

(B) at first sight appears to be a straightforward minim sequence with an extended resolution. In these cases, however, the note of resolution is the first crotchet of the third minim pulse of the sequence (see page 109). Here this crotchet (marked †) is a discord (fourth from the bass), and the real resolution is *delayed* till the following minim pulse, where the bass part moves up to D and the E in the altus drops out, thus forming a consonant interval structure. This process must be regarded as one of delayed rather than extended resolution.

(C) is a very similar case. A much more satisfactory explanation is obtainable by linear analysis than by harmonic means. If the C crotchet on the second minim pulse of measure 1 in the top voice be regarded as a normally used relatively unaccented passing note, the progress of the two outside parts is regular; *vis-à-vis* the middle voice, the top part is also quite normal, the minim suspension sequence having standard preparation and extended resolution; between the middle and lowest voices, the situation is again quite regular, the crotchet F sharp on the last minim pulse of the Altus voice being a relatively unaccented passing note. The same process of analysis may be applied to example B.

Resolutions on diminished fifth

The resolution of a suspended fourth in the bass into a diminished fifth (dissonance) was commended by theorists of the sixteenth century, provided that the bass after resolving returned to the note which had been suspended, that is, moved up a semitone. Zarlino and Artusi both give their approval to this procedure.* Morley also deals with the matter with that penetrating common sense which is so characteristic of his writing.†

' MA.   As for the discord it is taken in binding manner, and as for the sharp in the bass for the flat in the treble, the bass being a cadence the nature thereof requireth a sharp, and let your ears (or whoever else) be judge, sing it, and you will like the sharp much better than the flat in my opinion; yet this you must mark by the way, that though this be good in half a note (as here you see) (i.e. *as a minim*) yet it is intolerable in whole semibreves.'

The ' example ' under discussion contains this passage:

Ex. 161

Backed up by this theoretical evidence, it is clear that the examples of the usage in Palestrina must be taken seriously, even though they depend upon a *musica ficta* sharpening in most cases. The *sine qua non* of this resolution

---

* Zarlino: Opere I, p. 242.   The relevant passage is quoted by Jeppesen: ' Style of Palestrina ', p. 248. Artusi: ' L'arte del contraponto ', p. 50 (a precis is given by Jeppesen, ibid.).

† Morley: ' A Plain and Easy Introduction to Practical Music ', ed. Harman (Dent), pp. 174-175.

of a suspended dissonance is the return of the bass note of the diminished fifth upward by a semitone.

Resolution on Consonant Fourth

Occasionally a dissonant suspended fifth is found resolving on a 'consonant fourth'. This constitutes, theoretically at any rate, the resolution of a dissonance on another dissonance.* (Ex. 148)

SUSPENSIONS IN TRIPLE TIMES

Suspensions in ◐ time

When the time signature is ◐, implying six minim harmonic pulses to the measure, suspension sequences are found apparently in minim values only. The preparation may be on any 'weak' (even) minim of the measure, the discord on the following strong minim, and the resolution on the next (weak) pulse. The normal 'ornamental resolutions' are freely used, and change of interval structure at the point of resolution is commonly found.

* A very unusual instance of what appears to be an unresolved suspended discord occurs in the Haberl edition of the four-part Magnificat on the First Tome (P. XXVII., p. 2). It is clearly a misreading of the text.

The 'Roma' edition emends the Altus part by making the A (pulse 2) a plain minim and the third pulse G F crotchets.

Ex. 165

(B. III. p. 110)
P. V. p. 87

(B. III. p. 109)
P. V. p. 87

(B. XVI. p. 236)
P. XXVII. p. 185

(B. XVI. p. 237)
P. XXVII. p. 185

Extended preparation sometimes occurs, bringing the note of preparation into a relatively strong accentual position (see page 108).

Ex. 166

(B. III. p. 110)
P. V. p. 87

(B. III. p. 110)
P. V. p. 88

Extended resolutions are also found, following the normal procedure discussed on page 109 (see Ex. 165b, measure 1, Bassus).

Ex. 167 (B.XVI.p.238) P.XXVII.p.186

The more exceptional variations of suspension treatment noted and discussed in ₵ time do not seem to be used in the few ₵ works which occur in the corpus of Palestrina's Church music.

Suspensions in ₵³₂ ₵3 *etc.*

When the time signature is ₵³₂ (or ₵3, etc.) the suspension process occurs, so far as the writer's observations show, only in semibreve values. Here a rhythmic difficulty arises. Morris says:[*]

'. . . if the tempo is fairly fast, ³₁ time is considered as having three accents only in each measure, discords being prepared on the first beat, taken on the second, and resolved on the third.'

This ruling is unsatisfactory. In the first place it is contrary to the fundamental principle that, with the exception of the extended preparation discussed earlier in this chapter, a suspended discord is prepared on a weak pulse, the dissonance taken on a strong pulse, and the resolution on the ensuing weak position. In the second, a more thorough investigation of suspensions in ₵³₂ will show that, apparently, the suspension process may begin on any semibreve of the three semibreve measure.

Jeppesen goes further towards explaining the situation.[†]

'With respect to the syncope dissonance (in triple rhythm) it appears that it occurs more frequently upon the second minim than—as it would be natural to expect—upon the first. This is due to the syncope dissonance being most often used in forming conclusions; consequently in triple time (in which the conclusion falls customarily upon the first note of the measure in cadences) it is desirable to hear the leading note immediately before the end (that is, on the third unit), and the result is that the suspension (preceding the leading-note) falls upon the second unit. Occasionally Palestrina placed the syncope dissonance upon the third unit in triple time . . . it is only possible for us to understand places like this as an accentual alteration, since it is the nature of suspension to be resolved on unaccented beats. . . . Instead of two bars of ³₁ we get one bar of three breves, by which change (the semibreve being still the unit), the syncope dissonance falls upon an accented unit, and is prepared and resolved upon unaccented units.'

[*] R. O. Morris: 'Contrapuntal Technique', p. 39.

[†] Jeppesen: 'The Style of Palestrina', pp. 273 et seq.

The first part of this explanation seems just as unsatisfactory as Morris's ruling. Suspended discords are by no means confined to endings in $\mathbf{C}^3_2$ or any other time, nor are they a necessary prelude to the 'leading-note'. The second part of Jeppesen's argument, however, does seem to point to the real explanation, not only of suspended discords on the 'third unit', but to the whole rhythmic aspect of suspensions in $\mathbf{C}^3_2$.

If the table of proportions given on page 34 of this book is examined it will be seen that the *proportio dupla* diminution of *Tempus Perfectum, Prolatio Imperfecta* may imply two quite distinct rhythmic patterns.

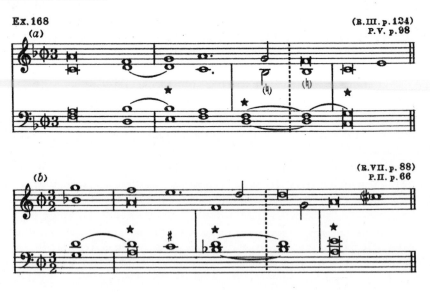

The semibreve in each interpretation is of the half tactus value. The additional diminution of sesquialtera in the $\mathbf{C}3$, $\mathbf{C}^3_2$, etc signatures does not in any way alter this duality of meaning.

It seems that Palestrina regarded these two interpretations as interchangeable, though in most cases where the semibreve suspension process is used the first appears to hold sway. The following examples will show how, if two three-semibreve measures are read as a single measure of three breves, the normal rhythm of the suspension process is observed, whether the sequence begins on the apparent first, second, or third semibreve of the three-semibreve measure.

Ex. 168 (a)   (R.III. p. 124) P.V. p. 98

(b)   (R.VII. p. 88) P.II. p. 66

If this rhythmic interpretation of $\mathbf{C}^3_2$ is accepted, the semibreve suspension sequence under this time signature is the exact counterpart of the minim process in $\mathbf{C}$. Preparation takes place upon an even semibreve of the six-semibreve measure, the discord on the following strong semibreve, the resolution on next weak pulse.

Ornamental resolutions of the returning and portamento-note types are often found, and even the rare decoration of a downward leap of a third before the discord resolves occurs (C and F below). Change of interval combination at the point of resolution is used, but less frequently than in the corresponding situation in ₵ (Ex. D and F). The resolution on a minim (= crotchet in ₵) treated freely, that is, proceeding by step downward to another minim which is not a returning note, is a very rare occurrence (Ex. E).

Resolution on Consonant Fourth in ₵$^3_2$

The ' consonant fourth ' is found as the note of resolution of a suspended discord, and also as the note of preparation in a following suspension sequence:

Ex. 170   (R.VI. p. 55)
P. XII. p. 44   P. XXIII. p. 44

The suspension process in augmentation (Breves) or diminution (Minims) does not seem to be part of Palestrina's normal practice in $\textbf{C}3$, $\textbf{C}_2^3$ time. A very doubtful case of the minim sequence with extended preparation is given with due reservations.

Ex. 171   P. VII. p. 13

CHAPTER VIII

CONTRAPUNTAL TECHNIQUES
FUGUE, CANON, INVERSION

Fugue

PERHAPS the most important of the technical processes of Palestrina's art is what is known as 'fugue', 'imitation', or 'lead work'. Of these terms, fugue is probably the best to use for the imitative entry technique, provided that it is clearly understood that in the sixteenth century it did not signify the fully developed formal structure which is generally, though erroneously, associated with the term when it is applied to the works of Bach and later composers. Tovey's corrective dictum that fugue is a texture rather than a form gives the right idea of its function in Palestrina's music. The definition ' Fugue is a contrapuntal process which produces a particular kind of musical texture ' comes near to meeting the case.

The fugal process of the sixteenth century consists of the imitation of a phrase or ' subject ' announced by one of the voices, by some or all of the other voices taking part in the composition. The imitation may be strict and extended, in which case the result is known as Canon (*fuga per canonem*), or free and of comparatively short duration ; in the latter, the process has strong affinity to the close 'fugal exposition' of a later age; the original phrase is treated with imitation in other parts until the composer has made whatever use he wishes to make of it; it is then abandoned, and a fresh set of fugal entries or a different form of texture succeeds it.

Leaving on one side the Canon, which will be considered later, there are three main varieties of fugal procedure which may be briefly described as follows:

1. *The single-subject imitation*, in which one voice enters, generally alone if it is at the beginning of a movement, or accompanied by other voices if in the course of the composition, with a ' subject ', ' point ' or ' lead '; this subject is imitated by entries of the other voices taking part in the composition at various distances of time and interval.

2. *The two-subject type of imitation*, in which two ' points ' are announced, either simultaneously, or one starting hard on the heels of the other, or separated by quite a long interval of time. The two subjects are imitated by the other voices, often in pairs.

3. *Fugal imitation used in conjunction with a Cantus Firmus*, in which the Cantus Firmus appears in one voice in long note values, while the other voices weave a fugal texture founded upon either a completely independent subject or one derived from the Cantus Firmus with rhythmic and melodic alterations.

These three varieties of the fugal process must now be examined in greater detail, together with some intermediate types.

1. Single Subject Imitation

The subject, in the single-subject variety of fugue, is usually a melodic phrase of moderate length with some well-defined character of melody, or rhythm, or both, rarely extending in compass beyond the strict limits of either the authentic or plagal form of the mode, though often much more restricted in compass. In the case of the opening 'lead' at the beginning of a movement, the first note is almost always of semibreve duration or longer in ₵; leads which occur in the course of a movement may begin with a minim or (more rarely) a crotchet. In theory, the subject is supposed to begin only on one of the specified notes of the particular mode in use, known as an 'Initial'; in practice, however, almost any note of the mode is found in this position. Morris* points out that the Final and Fifth degrees of any and every mode are the most common notes at the start of a subject, even though the fifth degree of the Phrygian mode, for example, is not a recognized and legitimate 'Initial'.

The subject phrase may end on any note of the mode; there is often no very clearly defined 'end' of a point of imitation, though in some cases the complete subject phrase ends with a rest.

The subject is often founded on a plainsong theme treated freely both rhythmically and melodically, but equally often it is an original piece of melodic invention.

The imitations

The imitations of the subject may be at any interval; most commonly they are introduced at the unison, or the octave, fourth or fifth above or below the pitch of the previous entry. Sometimes the whole of the subject is reproduced in the imitation; sometimes only the first few measures or even notes of the initial subject phrase are so treated. The imitation, if at the octave or unison, is generally 'strict as to interval', that is, the melodic interval progression is reproduced exactly, a minor third being answered by a minor third, a major by a major, and so forth; if it is at some other interval it is usually 'free', major and minor melodic intervals being interchangeable.

In the case of imitation at the fourth or fifth, certain more important modifications of the subject are often found. If, for example, an 'authentic' subject starts with an upward leap of a fifth (D to A in the Dorian mode) it is frequently (but not always) represented in 'plagal' imitation a fifth higher or fourth lower by an upward fourth leap (A to D), the pentachord of the authentic being answered by the plagal tetrachord. This method of answer requires some further alteration to the succeeding part of the subject. In it is clearly seen the process which led to the 'tonal answer' of later fugues.

* R. O. Morris: 'Contrapuntal Technique', p. 46.

Other alterations of a melodic character are frequently found. They are of considerable interest in that, when they are not directly due to the authentic-plagal influence, they show a harmonic awareness growing up in what is basically a linear technique.

Alterations in note lengths in the imitation are also used. The most general is the shortening of the first note of the subject, but other rhythmic changes occur, sometimes apparently for harmonic reasons.

No definite order or position of entries appears to be thought an essential part of the process. The imitations usually overlap, a new voice entering before the previous voice has completed the ' subject '; on some occasions, (after the initial statement of the subject and its imitation by one or more voices) an imitative entry may get delayed till some time after the previous statement of the subject has been completed. The interval of time which separates the entries is apparently completely free, and is governed to a great extent by vertical considerations, such as the desire for sonority at the entry of a third part, the three voices forming a complete 5/3 or 6/3 ' harmony ', as well as by the considerations of how the lead may be fitted in from a rhythmical and linear standpoint. It will be seen from the examples which follow that Palestrina had an almost uncanny knack for devising subjects which would work in imitation, and also for seizing exactly the right moment for introducing his imitations. Sometimes the entries are regularly spaced; sometimes they come in close pairs. The whole process, in Palestrina's hands is so spontaneous and so beautifully contrived that the technical problem of the introduction of voices in imitation is almost unnoticed in the texture which it creates.

In normal cases each voice, after the initial voice has entered, comes in with at least the opening notes of the subject; (' free parts ' are occasionally found in otherwise fugal passages). After singing the whole or part of the subject, the voice may continue in a free contrapuntal line, or rest, or repeat the subject; a second statement of the complete subject by a voice which, at its initial entry, has only sung a part of the subject is by no means uncommon. The process of imitation of a single subject may be confined to a single entry by each voice employed or may be extended to considerable lengths until the text demands a new ' point ' or change of texture.

The first imitative entry generally begins by forming a perfect consonance with the voice which has had the initial lead, especially in the opening section of a movement where two parts alone will be singing at this point. The major or minor third, however, is very often found. Sixths, major or minor, are rarer. Dissonant entries (that is, the new entry causing the part which is singing to become a suspended dissonance) also occur.

Some examples illustrating these points may now be examined.

Ex. 172

(R. XI. p. 11)
P. V. p. 123

This example is the opening of the ' Secunda Pars ' of the Motet *Heu mihi Domine*. It is of extremely penitential character and is in the Phrygian Mode. The first three leads are at regular intervals (Altus, Bassus, Cantus) and each has the complete subject starting a measure and a half after its antecedent. The Tenor entry is delayed by one pulse and its first note shortened; this is quite a normal alteration; it completes three and three-quarter measures of the subject (though the reproduction is not strict as to interval, the minor second of the original statement, between the second and third notes, becoming a major second in this statement) and then becomes free for two measures; after this the ending of the original subject is completed in measures 11 and 12. It is interesting to note that, immediately following this entry, the tenor repeats the whole subject, again with the shortened first note. Other restatements of the subject in part by the Cantus, Altus and Bassus, show how the fugal process continues. This whole passage, too long to quote here, deserves careful analysis.

The initial lead begins on the fifth degree of the mode (Altus) and is of restricted compass in the plagal division of the mode. The Bassus and Cantus entries begin on the final and reproduce the subject strictly as to interval, although they stand to it in the relationship of a fifth below (or fourth above). This happens naturally with a subject restricted to these particular notes of this mode. The Tenor lead on the fourth degree of the mode (a fifth below the preceding entry) is, of necessity, free as to interval.

The bass entry forms an octave against the subject; the Cantus enters with a fifth above the Bassus and makes the dissonance of a major second against the suspended discord in the Altus; it should be noted that the third entry makes full ' harmony ' in three parts.

The second example (Ex. 173) shows a much less regular series of entries. It is the opening of the first part of the motet quoted above.

Ex. 173

(B. XI. p. 8)
P.V. p. 121

The subject is again of small compass and shorter than in the previous
instance. It is imitated in full and strictly by every voice. The Bassus
imitates the tenor at the distance of a semibreve a fifth below, with absolute
strictness as to interval. The Altus entry is delayed till four and a half
measures after the Bassus, that is, until both Tenor and Bassus have completed the subject and sung a free measure. The Cantus entry comes two
measures later.

The initial lead (Tenor) begins on the fifth degree of the Phrygian mode;
it is in the Authentic position. The Bassus begins on the final of the mode
making a fifth with the Tenor; it is in the Plagal position.   The Altus enters
on the final, and makes (as in the previous case) a fifth with the Bassus and
a discord against the suspension in the Tenor at this point.   The Cantus
entry copies the Tenor.

Ex. 174   R.VII. p. 81
                                                 P. II. p. 26

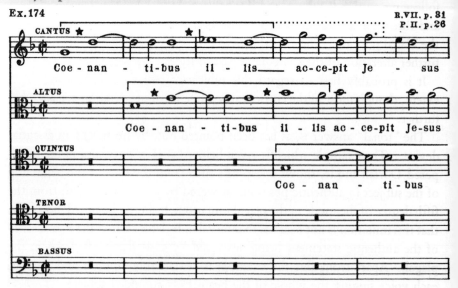

Tonal alterations in imitations

The third example (above, Ex. 174) shows the modifications often found in what may be termed the ' tonal ' answer of later times. The motet is in the transposed Dorian mode. The subject (Cantus) is Authentic, beginning with a fifth leap upwards from the final; the Altus imitates it at a measure's distance in the Plagal range (beginning on the fifth degree of the mode); in doing this the pentachord of the Authentic is replaced by the tetrachord of the Plagal form, i.e., the leap of a fifth is answered by a fourth. The two following entries (Quintus and Tenor) are Authentic at a distance of two and three measures respectively. The Bassus lead, one measure later, is in the Plagal position. The ' tonal ' answer, it will be noticed, makes necessary further alteration of the subsequent part of the subject in the imitation.

It is probably best to regard this subject as being of three measures in extent, though most of the entries carry a free form of imitation considerably further.

The ' tonal ' answer is, as has been pointed out, by no means an essential device. The example which is given below (4) (Ex. 175), also in the transposed Dorian mode, shows a leap of a fifth from the final at the beginning of the subject in authentic position, answered by the leap of a fifth from the fifth degree of the mode in the plagal imitation. It should be noted, however, that this imitation is not exact as to interval in its later course, the F-E-C-E-D of the authentic statement being answered by C-B *flat* -G-B *flat*-A in the plagal. Apart from this the example is remarkably smooth and regular, each voice singing the whole of the beautifully moulded subject.

K

Ex. 175   (B.VII.p. 1)
                                                                                                          P. II. p. 3

Rhythmic alteration of the subject in the imitations is shown in extreme
form in the fifth example (Ex. 176). Here all the initial leads differ in note
lengths; the closeness and irregular spacings of the entries are interesting
points. The mode is Mixolydian; after the first note of the 'point' in
Bassus II the Tenor enters at the fourth, making a minor third with the
bass; the third entry, unusually, fails to complete a three note 'chord': this
is remedied on the next pulse. The imitations are not 'strict as to interval';
they could scarcely be so as one is on the fourth degree of the mode and
another (the Altus) on the fifth. The effectiveness of the varied rhythmic
presentation of the subject is remarkable.

A few examples of second entries making intervals other than octaves, unisons, perfect fifths, and thirds with the initial lead, are given below.

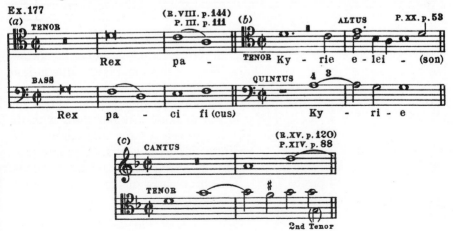

2. *Two-subject imitation*

The two-subject type of fugal imitation is very often used by Palestrina, and a great variety of methods of treatment is found in his work. The two subjects are often announced close together in time or even simultaneously in pairs, though sometimes the second is delayed even until the first has been imitated. In construction they are generally similar to the single subject type; in some cases they are rhythmically contrasted, while in others they may approach rhythmic identity.

It is unwise to make any attempt to regard the process as one of 'subject' and 'countersubject' as in later fugal practice. In Palestrina's style the two subjects are rarely even apparently bound together in such a relationship. They are indeed independent units in the fugal structure, though they may be used together.

Palestrina makes use of a large amount of device in this kind of fugal imitation. The two subjects may be in invertible counterpoint (see below), or the second may be a melodic inversion of the first, in which case the process is in reality a variety of the single-subject type, rather than a distinct two-subject example.

Much variety may be seen in the timing and order of the two-subject imitations; these may appear regularly in pairs, or one of the subjects may receive more attention in imitation than the other; sometimes one or other of the subjects may be abandoned after a single imitation and attention focussed entirely on the other.

Most of the technical details examined in the case of the single-subject fugue are equally applicable to the two-subject variety. Imitations may be strict or free as to interval; rhythmic alterations of one or both subjects are commonly found; melodic variation of the 'tonal answer' kind is frequently used, and so forth. A favourite device is to let the voice which has sung the first of the subjects proceed to the second either immediately or a few measures later, and vice-versa.

The illustrations which follow will demonstrate most of these points.

Ex. 178 (B.VII. p. 47)
P. II. p. 87

E - go ro-ga-bo Pa - - - - - -

E - go ro-ga-bo Pa - - - - - -

E - go........ ro-ga-bo Pa - - -

Ex. 179

P. XXIII. p. 44

These two examples show the close type of announcement of the two subjects, the first at a semibreve distance, the second simultaneously. In both cases the subjects are worked in pairs, though in the first there are additional entries of A without B. In the first case the two subjects are rhythmically identical save for the shortening of the first note in B; in the second case they are rhythmically strongly contrasted.

The next example (Ex. 180) shows a delayed entry of the second point. The Cantus part completes its imitation of A which has been announced by the Tenor and taken up at a semibreve distance, before subject B is announced by the Altus; B in its turn has to wait for four measures before it is imitated by the Bassus; at this point the Altus sings a modified version of A, after which A is dropped and the discussion kept to B and a new point C which makes its appearance in the twelfth measure.

Ex.180

(R.XV. p. 45)
P.XIV. p. 34

The next quotation (Ex. 181) gives a fine instance of two subjects in invertible counterpoint at the octave. The two themes enter in the Cantus and Altus at a semibreve distance; the reply is by Bassus and Tenor, the themes being inverted. Modified entries of both subjects (both rhythmic and melodic alterations are seen) then follow in the Cantus, Altus, and Bassus (A, B). The whole process is of extreme interest, and shows remarkable economy of material and almost thematic development.

One further example, this time of melodic inversion, must suffice to illustrate the two-subject type of fugue. In this case subject B is a melodic inversion of subject A, free as to interval (if the E flat and F natural are accepted) but otherwise an exact mirroring, at the fifth above and fourth below. It is of interest to observe that the first entry of the inversion is at a measure and a half distance while the second (Tenor I and Bassus) is at one measure. This type of imitation may equally well be regarded as a special variety of single-subject fugue, as has been suggested above. Cases do occur (e.g. P. XXV, p. 127) where one of the subjects is modified in the course of imitation in such a way as to suggest that it is a real second subject. This present example (Ex. 182) also shows harmonic inversion.

(R.XVI. p. 11)
P. XXVII. p. 9

Ex. 182

3. *Fugal entries woven round a Cantus Firmus*

The simplest, and at the same time the oldest and stiffest form of fugal technique, is that in which imitative entries of a point are used against a long note *Cantus Firmus* in one of the voices. The ' point ' in these cases is generally independent of the C.F., though occasionally it has some melodic connection. The fugal leads may begin simultaneously with, or before or after, the C.F. This treatment is found in Palestrina, mostly in the very early works, and the examples given below show something of the rigid, almost mechanical process, in contrast to the later type of C.F. decoration. Both come from the ' Ecce Sacerdos Magnus ' Mass. The first shows the C.F. in the top voice with an independent subject treated fugally and beginning immediately after it; in the second the fugal point is based on a diminution of the Cantus Firmus, which enters after the three fugal parts; a second ' free ' point is introduced in the sixth measure.

Ex. 183

(R.I. p. 1)
P.X. p. 3

Ex. 184

(R.I. p. 28)
P.X. p. 25

Even in his earliest works, Palestrina rarely used the long note Cantus Firmus in a single voice throughout a movement. Much more often he employed the technique of a partially decorated Cantus Firmus, often moving from one part to another (migrant C. F.) and sometimes itself treated fugally or in canon, while fugal entries on independent subjects were given to the other voices, and subsequently taken up by the part which had been singing the C.F. The C.F. in these cases is often fragmentary, and the 'subjects' either free or suggested by it. A short 'opening' extract from the Sanctus of the masterly 'O Sacrum Convivium' Mass (? 1586) illustrates this type of treatment.

Ex. 185   P. XXIII. p. 88
                                                'O Sacrum Convivium'

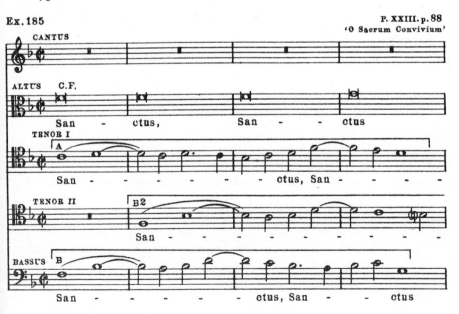

One more example, in which both the C.F. and independent point are treated fugally, will show the artistic heights which Palestrina could attain when treating a more or less undecorated plainsong C.F.

Ex. 186   (R. XV. p. 17)
                                                              P. XIV. p. 13

CANON

Canon, 'Fuga per canonem', implies the extended imitation of a leading part without any alteration, rhythmic or melodic, save that major melodic intervals may be answered by minor and vice versa when the imitation is at an interval other than the octave or unison.

The subject of the canon is given out by the *Vox antecedens* and each phrase of it and its continuation is imitated by the *Vox consequens*. The *Vox consequens* may be at any interval above or below its antecedent, and at any distance in time. More than one 'resolution' (as the *Vox consequens* is sometimes called) is often found, that is, more than two of the parts may be in 'canon'; the other parts may proceed in free fugal imitation.

Canon had become almost an obsession with composers of the late fifteenth and early sixteenth centuries. Canonic ingenuities of the most intricate and complex kind, often in the form of notational puzzles with enigmatic clues to their solution, were invented in large numbers. Canons 'cancrizans', 'per recte et retro', by augmentation, in fact all conceivable kinds of canon, 'were poured out in their hundreds by these too ingenious minds (e.g. the second Netherland school) and they were usually inserted in the one place where they were peculiarly inappropriate—the setting of the mass.'*

* Morris: 'Contrapuntal Technique', p. 52.

Palestrina's use of Canon is very different from this; he no longer seems to regard canonic device as an end in itself, but as a part of the musical texture; even when he deliberately sets out to write a series of canons, as in the mass 'Repleatur os meum,' it is clear that the canon is only a part of the musical texture; indeed, so consumate was his technical skill that even the more difficult forms of canon seem to have no cramping effect on the flow of the music.

Palestrina rarely if ever used the more abstruse forms of canonic device; mirror canons, inversions, and the like are not a part of his *materia musica*. Of the straightforward type of canon he was complete master, and considerable use is made of the device in his music, though most frequently in his earlier period.

The three most important works of Palestrina, so far as canonic writing is concerned, are the Masses 'Repleatur os meum laude', 'Ad fugam', and the six-voice 'Sine nomine'. The first two of these are relatively early works; the last was published in 1590.

In the Mass 'Repleatur' there are specimens of canon at every interval above the *vox antecedens*. They may be listed as follows:

Kyrie I—Canon at the Octave at 4 measures distance (Above).

Christe—Canon at the Seventh (minor) at $3\frac{1}{2}$ measures distance (Above).

Kyrie II—Canon at the Sixth (minor) at 3 measures distance (Above).

Gloria—Canon at the Fifth at $2\frac{1}{2}$ measures distance (Above).

Credo—Canon at the Fourth at 2 measures distance (Above).

Sanctus—Canon at the Third (minor) at $1\frac{1}{2}$ measures distance (Above).

Hosanna—Canon at the Second (major) at 1 measure's distance (Above).

Agnus Dei I—Canon at the Unison at the half measure, resolution by augmentation.

Agnus Dei II—Canon 3 in 1 at the Octave and Fifth, the resolutions appearing at 4 and 6 measures distance from the subject.

The opening of the first Agnus Dei is quoted below. It contains many features of interest. The first Tenor has the antecedent of the canon; the second Tenor, the resolution at the unison, in notes of twice the value (simple augmentation) starting at the distance of a semibreve: of the free parts, the Cantus begins with a rhythmically altered and decorated imitation of the first phrase of the canon; the Altus has a different rhythmic imitation of this, followed by an imitation of the second phrase of the canon; the Bassus starts with imitation of this second phrase (rhythmically altered) which is then repeated a fifth lower. (Ex. 187)

In the 'Ad fugam' Mass Palestrina makes much use of a form of canon which may be described as 4 in 2. One antecedent is imitated in canon at the fourth above and a semibreve distance, followed at varying distances in

Ex. 187

(B. VI. p. 169)
P. XII. p. 180

the different movements, by a second antecedent similarly treated. It also contains some ' 3 in 1 ' examples, and a ' 3 in 1 ' plus ' 2 in 1 ' in the second Agnus. The subjects of the 4 in 2 and 3 in 1 plus 2 in 1 are in most cases closely connected at the ' head ' melodically, and in the case of the 4 in 2 examples, are used antiphonally.

The three short beginnings of movements given below are worth careful study. The 3 in 1 case is an extraordinarily fine example of resolution a fifth and then a further fifth (i.e. ninth) below the antecedent.

Ex. 190 (R.IV. p. 86)
P.XI. p. 67

Trinitas in Unitate

L

The ' Sine Nomine ' Mass (P. XVIII, p. 64) seems to follow the plan of widening the distance between the antecedent and resolution in each canonic movement.   The canons are all 2 in 1, and a variety of intervals above and below is used.   The following summary gives a picture of the scheme:

Kyrie I—canon at fifth above at 1 minim distance.

Christe—canon at perfect fourth above at 1 semibreve distance.

Kyrie II—canon at octave below at 1½ semibreve distance.

Gloria—canon at major second below at 2 semibreve distance.

Credo—canon at major third above at 3 semibreves distance.

Et in Spiritum—canon at major third below at 3½ semibreves distance.

Sanctus—canon at major sixth above at 4 semibreves distance.

Hosanna—canon at major sixth below at 4½ semibreves distance.

Agnus I—canon at major seventh below at 5 semibreves distance.

Agnus II—canon at minor seventh above at 5½ semibreves distance.

The six part ' Sacerdotes Domini ' Mass has some interesting canons ' Trinitas in unitate ' with three free accompanying parts, and one without additional parts (Pleni sunt coeli).   The first reply in each case is a second above the antecedent, and the second, another second above that (i.e. a third above the subject).   These are masterly examples of Palestrina's mature technique, as the opening given below demonstrates; it should be compared with the earlier examples.

Ex.191   P. XVII. p. 116

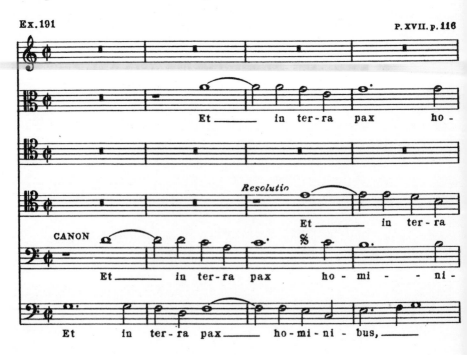

INVERSION

Two completely different technical processes are commonly referred to under the title ' Inversion '. The first is a purely melodic matter; it is often termed ' melodic inversion ' and implies the answering of every upward movement in the model by a corresponding downward step or leap in the inversion, and vice versa. The upward leap of a third, for instance, will be answered by a descending third and so forth. It is obvious that if the mode or scale in being is to be preserved the mirroring interval cannot always be strict; that is, a major third upward cannot often be answered by a downward *major* third; a minor third may be substituted; in fact major and minor intervals are, within reasonable limits, interchangeable.

The other type of inversion is contrapuntal; it is sometimes referred to as ' harmonic inversion ', or ' double, triple, etc., counterpoint.' Morris's definition is clear and concise:*

> ' Two themes or subjects are said to be in Double Counterpoint when one of them will serve either as a bass to the other's treble, or as a treble to the other's bass. (If there are three parts, all of which may similarly change places with each other, they are said to be in Triple Counterpoint, and so on.) '

The inversion is generally at the octave, tenth or twelfth (or compounds of these). In the case of double counterpoint at the octave one part keeps its position while the other moves up or down an octave; at the tenth, one part may remain while the other moves up or down a tenth; at the twelfth a similar process may be used, but, as Morris points out, ' in practice, usually either the bottom part moves up an octave and the top one down a fifth, or the top part moves down an octave and the bottom one up a fifth '.†
The technical problems and ' rules ' for solving the difficulties created by this kind of invertible counterpoint may be studied in any good text book, or more profitably, if with more complexity, in Morley's Plaine and Easie Introduction.‡ The only technical point which must be noted here is that inversions at intervals other than the octave (and fifteenth) will be free as to the quality of the interval, both melodically and harmonically.

Harmonic and melodic inversions are sometimes used in combination. Inversions in general, like most of the other ' devices ' of counterpoint, are usually a part of some more important process such as fugue or canon rather than an end in themselves.

Considerable importance was undoubtedly attached to the *practice* of double counterpoint, and to other devices of a similar nature, by theorists

* Morris: ' Contrapuntal Technique ', p. 48.
† Ibid.
‡ Morley: ' Plain and Easy Introduction to Practical Music ', ed. Harman, p. 188 ff.

and teachers in the sixteenth century. The fact that Morley devotes some eleven pages of his book to the subject, and that Zarlino is equally expansive in dealing with it, proves the point. With regard to Palestrina's use of it, it is again worth while to quote Morris:

'No one who studies Palestrina's work can doubt that he had every known device of the period at his finger-tips, and that he regarded double counterpoint in just the same light as canonic or proportional ingenuities —that is to say, as a technical discipline, to be quietly mastered and then as quietly discarded, save in so far as it could be made to serve a purely artistic purpose. At any rate he uses the device very sparingly, and most often in fugue, where he rather likes to announce a subject in two parts and then invert them in the answer.'

An examination of inversion in Palestrina's work will show that the device in both kinds is often present rather in spirit than in the letter. Instances of approximate inversion are frequent, and how telling they are! Examples of strict inversion are rare and generally of very short duration.

Turning to the first type, that is ' melodic inversion ', one example has already been quoted in the section on fugue (Ex. 182). It shows a melodic inversion starting a fifth above the ' model '; further reference will be made to this instance later (P. XXVII, p. 9) as it is an example of ' harmonic ' as well as melodic inversion.

The opening of the Motet ' Surrexit pastor bonus ' (P. V, p. 177) is an interesting instance of melodic inversion. The second tenor begins with the ' model '; the bass imitates it at two measures' distance by inversion beginning at the unison, and continuing for three measures. The Altus part (top) enters in the fourth measure (third pulse) with the model a fourth higher; the first tenor has the inversion in a rather more extended form, this time a fifth above the original and a second above the imitation of the model, and at one instead of two measures distance.

Ex.192

(R. XI. p. 79)
P. V. p. 177

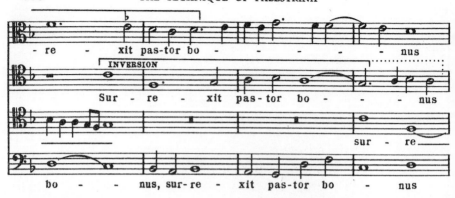

The 'harmonic' type of inversion is fairly often found in fugal leads. One example (Ex. 181, P. XIII, p. 22) has already been quoted. The inversion is at the octave as regards the model, both model and invertible counterpoint answering the first statement a fifth below.

The next case shows inversion at the twelfth (or more accurately nineteenth). It is a particularly clear-cut instance with almost four complete measures of inversion.

Ex. 193   (B. XXI. p. 21)
                                                    P. XV. p. 18

Counterpoint invertible at the tenth is rare in Palestrina's work. Such examples as may be found are usually very short in duration. The following passage from the Missa Brevis shows the process.

Ex. 194   (B. VI. p.68)
                                                              P. XII. p.50

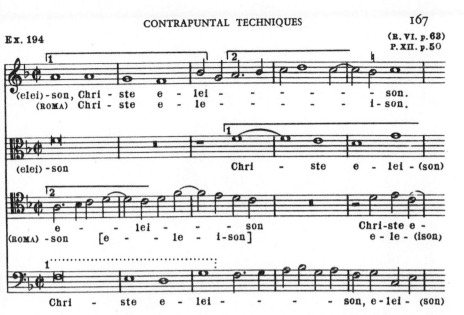

Triple counterpoint, that is, three parts each capable of inversion, is also
rare and fragmentary. The Mass 'Illumina oculos meos' contains several
passages built on three melodic phrases and variants of them. Though the
three phrases are capable of use in any position, the direct 3, 2, 1 inversion is
not used, but a very telling modification of it, in which themes 1 and 2 are
delayed, may be noted in measures five and six of the quotation.

                                                              P. XIX. p.109
Ex. 195   Missa. 'Illumina oculos meos'

Melodic and Harmonic inversions combined

One case of both ' melodic ' and ' harmonic ' inversion occurring at the same time has already been cited (P. XXVII, p. 9, see Ex. 182). Here the melodic inversion is at the fifth; the harmonic inversion is at the octave.

A further example, in which the melodic inversion is at the octave in the first statement and the harmonic inversion at the fifth below, thereby creating a melodic inversion at the fifth, is worth quoting. Though the subject is only of two and a quarter measures' duration, the process is of interest; in both cases the inversions are strict as to interval.

Ex. 196   (B. XI. p. 173)
                                                        P. IV. p. 63

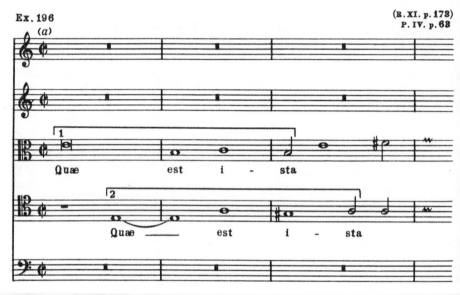

AUGMENTATION AND DIMINUTION

Augmentation and diminution in polyphony are really proportional alterations of the note values in a melodic line already heard, not necessarily bound up with the relationship of the original subject to its augmented or diminished form in contrapuntal combination. In the polyphonic age these devices were frequently and often rather mechanically applied in the treatment of a long-note Cantus Firmus. The highly developed artistic use of augmentation and diminution of thematic material of later periods (for example, in J. S. Bach's music) is only vaguely foreshadowed in polyphony.

Examples of proportional alteration of a Cantus Firmus may be found in Palestrina, especially in the earlier works, and in many cases these must be regarded as legacies from the past.

In the Hexachord Mass, for example, the Cantus Firmus first appears in breves (*Kyrie I*, Cantus II.); in the following section (*Christe*) it appears in longs (each note taking up two measures of (¢); in the second Kyrie it is given out at first in breves, followed immediately by a presentation in semibreves, and then in minims (Ex. 197a). In the first Agnus Dei the Cantus Firmus is first stated in breves, and later in dotted breves (Augmentation x 1½): (Ex. 197b).

Ex. 197

(R.VI. p. 219)
P. XII. p. 167
Kyrie II. Hexachord Mass.

(R.VI. p. 247)
P. XII. p. 189
Agnus I

The Mass ' L'homme armé ' may be regarded as Palestrina's most extensive and important excursion into the proportional procedures of the past.*

★ Compare: Obrecht, Mass 'Si dedero.'

The Benedictus is a good example of progressive diminution of the Cantus Firmus: the Cantus part has the signatures $\frac{\mathbb{C}}{\mathbb{C}}$ against $\mathbb{C}$ in the other three voices. The resulting diminutions are shown below.

Ex. 198

(R.VI.p.128 et seq)
P.XII.p.99
L'homme armé. Benedictus

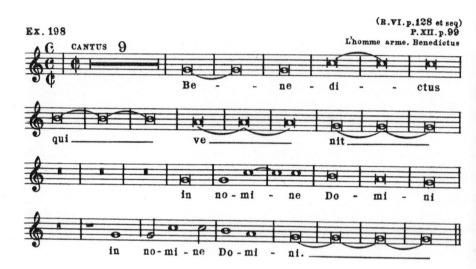

In this, as in many cases where there is a proportionally varied Cantus Firmus, the other voices pursue their way in fugal imitation on 'free' subjects, quite unaffected by the vagaries of the Cantus Firmus.

This Mass contains many other proportional variations of the Cantus Firmus. In the Gloria its delayed entry opens with a sixfold augmentation (if the $\mathbb{C}$ breve version of the theme is taken as the norm); the other voices have preceded it with fugal entries based on a diminution of the theme, but by the time the Cantus Firmus enters, a new 'point', completely independent, has superseded the one based on the C.F. diminution.

In the first Kyrie the theme appears in three-fold augmentation Θ against **O**. The second Kyrie is of unusual interest; the Cantus Firmus is here presented in three-fold diminution (*proportio sesquialtera* in combination with *diminutio simplex* $\mathbb{O}_2^3$ against **O** in the other voices). (A portion of the *L'homme armé* theme which does not appear in the example given above is used in this movement.) The other voices sing in **O**, beginning with a series of fugal imitations on a subject consisting of the opening phrase of this part of the Cantus Firmus in diminution. The force of the sesquialtera x dupla diminution is, therefore, fully felt in its delayed entry. This movement is of further importance, in that it illustrates other devices from the past, very rarely found in Palestrina; the presentation of the Cantus Firmus phrase in a manner akin to the Isorhythmic and *ostinato* techniques of an earlier period.

(B.VI. p.100)
P. XII. p.77
Missa. 'L'homme arme'. Kyrie II

Ex. 199 [Roma Text]

It is very rare that a point founded on a long-note Cantus Firmus is either extensive enough in its imitation or close enough in point of time to give the impression of diminution.   Examples such as the following are as near real diminution as is commonly found.

Ex. 200

(R. VI. p. 204)
P. XII. p. 155-156

In this instance the long-note second tenor part is imitated in melodic outline with rhythmical alterations and the interpolation of a note by the first tenor and altus, and its first four notes by the bassus. This is almost extensive enough to suggest double diminution in a very free form, but it is probably best to regard it as little more than a free imitative point founded melodically on the Cantus Firmus.

A real example of augmentation in canon has already been quoted (Ex. 187, p. 159). This device is rare, and to what extent the effect of the augmentation is realized in hearing the music is doubtful. Palestrina's attitude to all such devices·seems to be the truly musical one; he very rarely writes ingenuities for their own sake, for the most part merely hinting at device and dropping it when the process becomes or is about to become an embarrassment to the natural flow of the music.

CHAPTER IX

TEXTURES, FORM, STRUCTURE

THE problem of structure and form in the vocal polyphony of the six-teenth century is bound up to a great extent with the question of musical textures. R. O. Morris points out that three main types of procedure each achieving a characteristic texture were in common use: (1) Fugal, that is, contrapuntal imitation of a 'point', discussed in some detail in the preceding chapter; (2) Homophonic, which may most simply be described as parts moving in identical or almost identical rhythm; (3) Intermediate, that is, parts moving with rhythmic and melodic independence, but not in fugal imitation of a 'point' or 'points'. This rough classification covers the main technical processes which produced distinctive textures; in addition a whole range of contrast and variation was at the disposal of composers in the possibilities of what has been called 'vocal orchestration', the selection of different combinations of voices and number of parts singing together out of the forces in use in the various sections of the composition. This power of modifying the main types and qualities of texture placed in the composer's hands an almost unlimited range of colour and contrast.

The most important 'form' in sixteenth-century vocal music, apart from the Mass, was the Motet. It is outside the scope of this book to attempt to trace the history of the origin and development of the Motet; the imme-diate concern is to investigate Palestrina's methods of design in writing works of this *genre*.

The method which he usually adopts is the breaking up of the words which constitute the text into sections and the treatment of these sections either as self-contained entities or in groups bound together by some method (for example, by overlapping of fugal entries), the tale of the sections form-ing a coherent whole. For this purpose each or all of the 'textures' described above might be used; all the sections of the words might be treated fugally, in the free contrapuntal manner, or homophonically, or a mixture of methods could be used. The motet 'Sicut cervus' (P. V. 148) is an excellent example of an almost totally fugal treatment of the words. The text is broken up thus:

1. 'Sicut cervus desiderat ad fontes aquarum,
2. ita desiderat
3. anima mea
4. ad te, Deus.'

Each section is treated fugally.   The first section has quite an elaborate
'fugue' on a beautifully shaped subject lead by the Tenor, each voice
having two entries of at least the head of the 'point'.   The second section
has a new subject initiated by the Bassus, overlapping the first fugue; no
less than three entries of the point occur in the Bassus part.   The third subject
(anima mea) again overlaps the previous section, and is continued against
the final phrase of the words, which is treated (a) with a new fugal point
which appears in every voice before the end of the work, alternating with
the third subject, and (b) as a free contrapuntal addition to the third subject.

In the wholly (or almost wholly) homophonic type of motet, the salient
feature of the process is the use of varied voice-groupings both within the
sections and between one section and another.   This is well seen in the motet
'Cum inducerent puerum Jesum' (the second part of 'Responsum accepit
Simeon', P. VI, 50).   Here the text is treated thus:

1. Cum inducerent puerum Jesum parentes ejus
2. ut facerent secundum consuetudinem legis pro eo,
3. et ipse accepit eum in ulnas suas
4. et benedixit Deum et dixit:
5. Nunc dimittis servum tuum, Domine, in pace..

The first phrase is sung in nearly note-against-note counterpoint by first
and second Altus, first Tenor and Bassus voices: this is answered by the
Cantus, two Alti, and second Tenor, singing the same words in almost
identical rhythm.   The words 'ut facerent' are set for the four lower voices
answered by the two upper in a freely contrapuntal manner with some trace
of imitation: the rest of the line ('secundum consuetudinem') returns to
homophony (Altus I, both Tenors, and Bassus).   This is answered by a
rhythmically similar repetition of the words by Cantus, Altus II, and both
Tenors.   The third line is treated homophonically first by Cantus, Altus I
and II, and Bassus, and other four- and three-part combinations, including
some considerable inversion of the parts.   The fourth line is mainly in six-
part homophony with some non-fugal counterpoint.   The final phrase
(Nunc dimittis) is set in note-against-note style for Cantus, Altus II, Tenor II
and Bassus, answered by all six voices using very similar melodic and
rhythmic material, slightly elaborated.   Variety and contrast are obtained by
the antiphonal effect of using different combinations of voices; continuity
by melodic and rhythmic imitation within the sections, and also to a large
extent between one section and another.

As an example of the Intermediate contrapuntal type of texture the great
motet 'Tu es Petrus' (P. II, 121) with its second part 'Quodcunque
ligaveris' cannot be surpassed.   The two parts together extend for over
160 measures, and the force employed is a six-part choir.   Practically the
whole motet is written in free contrapuntal style with almost no imitation

of the fugal kind, and not very much homophonic writing. The texture is more or less uniform throughout so far as method goes, yet an almost endless variety is obtained by the disposition of the voices in three-, four-, five- and six-part groupings. The architectural building up to climaxes in which all six voices participate (ecclesiam meam . . . claves regni caelorum . . . in coelis . . . etc.) is masterly.

The process in detail bears close resemblance to that of the mainly homo- phonic motet discussed above. The opening phrase is given out by the three upper voices, and is immediately repeated by the three lower voices an octave below ; the end of the phrase is taken up again by the three upper voices and first Bassus, and so forth. The whole motet deserves the most careful study and detailed analysis. It contains much of interest from the point of view of wider formal structure.

The mixture of the different types of texture is perhaps the most important procedure in the construction of motets. For this reason a full-scale motet of this kind will now be quoted in entirety and analyzed in some detail.

Ex. 201

(R.V. p.45)
P.I.p.87

M

The first step in analyzing this splendid work is to examine the different kinds of texture and vocal groupings used. Other formal aspects of the structure will be considered later in this chapter.

The motet consists of four main sections; measures 1-48, 49-88, 89-142, and 143-166.

The first of these sections opens with a series of fugal imitations setting the words ' O beata ' (measures 1-12) making use of from one to the full five voices ; this fugal exposition leads without a break to ' et benedicta et gloriosa Trinitas ', treated in the intermediate style, more homophonic than contrapuntal, first by the four lower voices answered by the four upper, and then by the full choir (measures 13-21). The words which follow, ' Pater et Filius et Spiritus ', are set homophonically for three and four voices; ' Sanctus ' and the repetition ' et Spiritus Sanctus ' receive free contrapuntal setting in which a rising scale-passage in crotchets plays an important part; four- and five-part combinations of voices are employed (measures 22-33). Fifteen measures of ' Alleluias ' complete the section, in freely contrapuntal and partly fugal style, containing a great variety of voice groupings (measures 33-48).

The second section begins with a homophonic-plus-intermediate version of the opening subject in four and five parts (measures 49-55). The ' et gloriosa Unitas ' mirrors the ' et gloriosa Trinitas ' of the first section in homophonic-free-contrapuntal style, and the words 'Pater et Filius et Spiritus Sanctus' again follow the pattern set in the earlier part, but without the repetition of the words (measures 55-69). Another group of 'Alleluias' follows, using the material of the first setting of the word, with the parts subtly altered in layout and voice-grouping, and also in the melodic continuation of the 'points' (measures 69-88).

The third section, the beginning of the *Secunda Pars* of the motet, opens with a purely homophonic setting of the words ' O vera summa sempiterna Trinitas' for the four upper voices, followed by an answering phrase for five, three, and four voices in rather more contrapuntal style (measures 89-100); both phrases use the melodic material of the earlier openings.

' Pater, Filius, et Spiritus Sanctus' is treated in almost strict homophony, using similar material to the earlier statements of the words, but shortened and varied; the three lower voices are answered by the two Cantus parts and the Tenor, and then all five parts join together (measures 100-107).

The music and words of measures 89-107 are repeated in slightly elaborated and varied form, with different voice-groupings in measures 108-128. In place of the Alleluias of the previous sections there follows new material in the words ' Te jure laudant, te adorant, te glorificant omnes creaturae '; the setting is mainly homophonic and antiphonal, reaching a great climax in the five-part long-note treatment of the last two words (measures 129-142).

The fourth and final section starts with a homophonic statement of the words ' O beata ' for the four upper voices, using the first four-note figure of the opening fugue in the top part (measures 143-145); a repetition of the words for all five voices follows with the ' subject ' in the bass (measures 146-148). The word ' Trinitas ' is set in free contrapuntal and partly fugal style for two different three-voice combinations (measures 148-152). ' O beata Trinitas ' is again repeated, beginning with the subject in the Cantus II, five voices being used, four strictly homophonic in the first two measures, with a freely contrapuntal Tenor (measures 153-155 first pulse); on the word Trinitas a set of fugal imitations on two ' points ' begins, and this texture persists till the end of the work.

The complexities of the texture, both in regard to the type of procedure and grouping of voices, may perhaps become clearer from study of the chart given in the following pages.

MEASURE Type of Texture --- WORDS ---- CANTUS I-- CANTUS II-- ALTUS --- TENOR ---- BASSUS ----	1	2	3	4	5	6	7
	O	be - a	ta		Fugal Imitation.		

8	9	10	11	12	13	14	15	16
							Intermediate et glori - osa Tri-n	

17 mainly (Homophonic)	18	19	20	21	22	23	24	25
tas					Pa - - - ter et		Fi-li us e	Homophonic

26	27	28	29	30	31	32	33	34
Spi-ri tus Sanc - - - - tus, et Spiritus sanctus				Intermediate.				Alleluj

35	36	37	38	39	40	41	42	43
					Freely Fugal.			

44	45	46	47	48	49	50	51	52
					O	be - a ta	Homophon (Slightly Contrapunt	

53	54	55	56	57	58	59	60	61

Homophonic & Intermediate.

et glorio - sa

U - ni tas Pa-

62	63	64	65	66	67	68	69	70

-r   et Fi - li us et Spi - ri tus   Sanc - tus Alleluja

71	72	73	74	75	76	77	78	79

Freely Fugal.

80	81	82	83	84	85	86	87	88

89	90	91	92	93	94	95	96	97

Homophonic.

O   vera Summa   O   vera   Summa

98	99	100	101	102	103	104	105	106

Pa - ter Fi - lius et Spi - ritus   Sanc

107	108	109	110	111	112	113	114	115	116

Mainly Homophonic.

tus O vera summa

117	118	119	120	121	122	123	124	125	126

Intermediate.

Pa - ter Fi-li us et Spi-ri tus Sanctus

127	128	129	130	131	132	133	134	135	136

Homophonic & Intermediate.

Te jure laudant Te ado - rant Te glorifi can

137	138	139	140	141	142	143	144	145	146

Homophonic.

Om - nes cre·a tu - rae O be - a - ta

147	148	149	150	151	152	153	154	155	156

Intermediate.
(Partly Fugal)

O be-a ta Trinitas

157	158	159	160	161	162	163	164	165	166

Freely Fugal.

The grouping of the five voices can be seen clearly from the above plan. Of the 166 measures of the Motet, only two contain a single voice; three, two voices; eighteen or nineteen are in various three-voice combinations; fifty-two for four voices; the remainder mainly for the full choir and fluctuating numbers of voices.

The combinations of voices used may also be seen at a glance. They supply an extensive variety of three and four-part groupings, in kaleido-scopic permutations or clear-cut contrasts.

The main types of texture are all represented. Sometimes they are used in contrast, as for example, the homophonic ' et gloriosa ' (measure 12) after the fugal opening; sometimes they merge into one another. The balance of the types is perfectly secured, giving structural unity with unfettered variety.

The use of thematic material in this Motet will be considered later in this chapter.

THE WIDER VIEW OF STRUCTURE IN MOTETS

There is some danger in attempting to apply the formal criteria of later ages to the polyphonic period. Diatonic tonality plays such an impor-tant part in the structure of the classical period with its complete scheme of key relationships and contrasts, that most of the salient features which constitute ' form ' in that era are inapplicable to the sixteenth century. There are, however, several factors, other than textual and textural, which may reasonably claim real importance in polyphonic stucture.

In a Motet there is often present some unifying musical device; sometimes a plainsong melody is used as the basis of the work, and is treated as a Cantus Firmus around which the music is constructed; at other times the unification may be achieved by the repetitive use of thermatic material, either in the form of restatement of a whole section or the development and repetition of some prominent musical idea.

Cantus Firmus treatment

The Cantus Firmus treatment used by Palestrina in his Motets is, in most cases where this feature appears, a development of the decorated and rhythmically altered Cantus Firmus technique of the previous age, generally known as ' paraphrase ' treatment.* The Cantus Firmus, usually a plainsong melody, is taken line by line, elaborated in rhythm and melody, and often extended; in this form it is treated sectionally, often in fugal style. The process may be seen in its simplest and clearest form, perhaps, in the ' Hymni Totius Anni ' (R. XIV, P. VIII). ' Pange Lingua ', the Hymn for the first Vespers of the Corpus Christi Feast, is a good illustration, and perhaps more easily followed than some, since the Plainsong melody is well known. Many variants of the melody itself exist (some are given in the quotation below).

---

* Examples of the long-note type of Cantus Firmus in Palestrina's Motets are rare, apart from the verse by verse harmonizations of Plainsong, such as ' Lauda Sion ' and ' Veni Sancte Spiritus ' (P. VII., pp. 91, 117). An exceptional instance is ' Beatus Laurentius ' (P. I., p. 61 R. V., p. 79) where the C.F. appears in breves (second Tenor) with the last line repeated in semibreves, and around it a contrapuntal texture is woven using points free or based on the plainsong.

Ex. 202

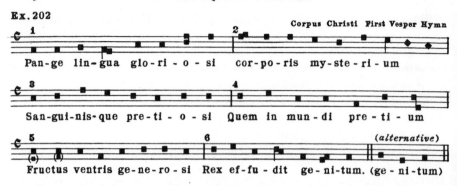

Corpus Christi First Vesper Hymn

Palestrina's elaboration of this in the top voice of the Motet (after the first line has been announced by the Tenor) is now given in full.

Ex. 203

(R. XIV. p. 74)
P. VIII. p. 57

The first line of the Hymn and Plainsong Tune is given out by the Tenor voice as Cantor. In the second line the Cantus part (in this, as in most of the Hymns, the Cantus Firmus) has a beautifully ornamented version of the corresponding line of the plainsong, which blossoms out into an extension of a further five measures. The opening of this ' subject ' is treated fugally, the Altus ' point ' (the first six notes of the subject) preceding the Cantus (C. F.) by one measure; the Tenor copies the first four measures of the Cantus in canon at the octave below at three-and-a-half measures' distance; the Bassus imitates the Altus for ten notes a fifth lower.

The third line of the Cantus, an exact melodic reproduction of the plainsong with slight rhythmic modification, is also treated fugally though rather more freely; the Bassus entry of this new ' subject ' anticipates the Cantus (C. F.) entry by three measures. In the fourth line the Cantus uses the first five notes of the plainsong rhythmically unaltered, and then breaks into a beautiful extension of the phrase for some eight measures. The first five notes of this subject (which follows the end of the third line immediately in the Cantus) are imitated at a semibreve distance by the Altus, at first accompanied by the Tenor and Bassus in free counterpoint; later both Tenor and Bassus join in the fugal imitation.

The fifth line of the Cantus, a melodic variant of the plainsong, is accompanied by (non-fugal) contrapuntal writing in the other voices. The sixth line consists of a freely varied version of the plainsong in the Cantus closely imitated by the Altus and Tenor, while the Bassus supplies a non-fugal contrapuntal part.

The two most important features which should be noted from this short examination of the hymn are: (1) in making a Cantus Firmus based on a plainsong tune, Palestrina generally reproduces the ' head ' (first few notes) of each line melodically, though with varied rhythm, in his paraphrase; the later part of each line often blossoms out into a free rhapsodic extension (for example, in three of the five four-voice lines of this hymn); (2) the variety in fugal treatment of the subjects which make up the paraphrase—leads in other voices anticipating the appearance of the subject in the Cantus Firmus, close entries in imitation, canon, delayed imitation—gives great scope for diversity and contrast, further enhanced by the use of non-fugal writing.

More elaborate treatment of a plainsong tune than that considered above is often found. A good example may be seen in the second of the Hymns (R. XIV, p. 8, P. VIII, p. 6) ' Christe Redemptor omnium '. The similarity of the first and last lines of the plainsong gives the four polyphonic verses a cohesion even greater than is normally found in these settings. This hymn is worth some detailed consideration, both on account of the great variety of procedure which Palestrina uses in the setting, and for its intrinsic beauty and interest as music.

The first verse is for Cantus, Altus, Tenor and Bassus. Following the normal practice the first line is given to a Tenor *cantor*, singing the plainsong unadorned. In the second line the Cantus Firmus, almost unvaried, is given to the Cantus voice accompanied by a free contrapuntal part in the Altus; after two and a half measures the Tenor enters with the Cantus Firmus an octave below the Cantus, accompanied by a close imitation of the 'counter-subject,' in the Bassus. In the third line the plainsong C. F. appears in undecorated semibreves in the Cantus anticipated by the Tenor at one bar; the other parts proceed in free counterpoint. The last line has two statements of the C. F. first by the Cantus, and then by the Tenor, surrounded by various kinds of imitative counterpoint.

Ex. 204   (B.XIV. p. 8)
                                                               P. VIII. p. 6

In the third verse the Cantus Firmus remains in the Cantus part; it is very close to the plainsong in all four lines, with very little rhythmic embellishment and little or no extension at the ends of lines. The voices used in this verse are Cantus, Cantus secundus, Altus, and Tenor. Below and around the Cantus Firmus the other voices weave imitative contrapuntal strands, sometimes imitating the C. F., at others developing fugal treatment of independent points. The opening of this verse is as follows:

Ex. 205   (B.XIV. p.9)
                                                               P. VIII. p.7

In the first line of the fifth verse the Cantus Firmus is transferred to the Bassus; the upper parts, Cantus, Altus, and Tenor, begin homophonically and then proceed in free contrapuntal style. In the second line the C. F., a rather more elaborate version of the plainsong, returns to the top part, the other voices singing free contrapuntal strands with some imitation. The C. F. in the third line is given to the Altus, transposed down a fourth, with a freely contrapuntal texture. For the fourth line the time changes to $\mathbb{C}^3_2$, the plainsong appearing in outline in the Cantus part with rather more homophonic writing in the other voices.

Ex. 206   (B.XIV. p.10)

(*a*)   Verse V. First line   P. VIII. p. 9

(*b*)   Fourth line   (B.XIV. p. 11)
        C.F.   P. VIII. p. 9

The seventh verse (Gloria Patri) is a much more elaborate and developed structure, using six .voices. The first line of the plainsong is given to Cantus I without elaboration; on its last note Tenor II enters with a repetition of this transposed down a fourth; in the first six measures, while the C. F. is in the Cantus, the Cantus II, Altus, and Tenor I sing free contrapuntal lines; when the C. F. is repeated in Tenor II all six voices join in, some making use of the thematic material which accompanied the first statement, at times by inversion: this process is even more striking in the second line.

The second line of the C. F. appears first in the Cantus II, and is then repeated at the twelfth below by the Bassus, the disposition of the other voices being similar to that found in the first line.

In the third line the plainsong reappears in the Cantus, against an elaborate contrapuntal texture in which a good deal of imitation of independent points as well as some close fugal work based on the C. F. is found together with completely free parts. The C. F. in this line is not repeated in another voice as in the previous lines.

The plainsong of the last line is given first to Cantus I and is later repeated by Tenor II at the octave below, again with considerable interchange of the accompanying thematic material. The whole of this final verse displays contrapuntal writing of the highest order, and a remarkable economy of material and summing up of the whole Hymn.

Ex. 207

Repetition of material

The repetition of a section later in the course of the work is a favourite structural device in Palestrina's longer motets. In the larger works cast in two distinct 'partes', the restatement of the material forming the concluding section of the first 'pars' is often found at the end of the second; this structural process is of considerable importance in binding the two 'partes' into a composite whole, producing an A-B: C-B shape. The repeated section sometimes takes the form of 'Alleluias', as in the splendid motet for double choir 'Surrexit Pastor bonus' with its 'secunda pars' 'Etenim Pascha nostra' (P. VI, p. 57); equally often an integral part of the text is repeated, as in 'Responsum accepit Simeon', where the section beginning 'et benedixit Deum' (22 measures) returns at the end of the 'secunda pars' (Cum inducerent, P. VI, p. 48 et seq.). Sometimes the repeated part comprises several independent sections; in the six-voice setting of 'O magnum mysterium' (P. I, p. 137, R. V, p. 35), a passage of forty-one measures, made up of three definite sections, 'natum

vidimus', 'collaudantes Dominum' and 'Alleluia' recurs in its entirety at the
end of the 'secunda pars' (Quem vidistis, pastores). The form in this
instance might be described as A-B C D : E-B C D.

An interesting example of the A-B-A structure within a single 'pars'
motet may be seen in 'Alleluia, tulerunt Dominum' (P. I, pp. 30 et seq.
R. V, p. 35). The first thirteen measures of the opening 'Alleluia' are repeated
with slight modification in the lower parts as the final thirteen measures of
the work. This motet is of further interest from the point of view of structure;
the material of the opening 'Alleluia' appears in curtailed and modified form
as a refrain in the middle section of the work.

THE USE OF THEMATIC MATERIAL

The danger of searching for thematic development or the recapitulation
of subjects in the sense in which these devices were used in the classical age
has already been mentioned. It is only too easy to read into certain
examples of highly wrought polyphony formal implications which are
clearly anachronistic.

There are, however, a good many instances in the motets of treatment of
material which seems to have definite formal significance. A closer examination of the motet quoted in full earlier in this chapter may show this
process.

The first 'subject' group, comprising the four-note descending figure
(A1), its continuation (A2), and the shortened leads derived from (A2) (a2),
shows a normal fugal opening. The subject-matter is not, as often with
opening fugal sections, abandoned after this treatment, but keeps recurring
through the motet, with a variety of treatment, not necessarily fugal or using
the same text; this gives it a distinct significance in the structure of the motet
as a whole. Its reappearances should be examined with care; at measure
49 (A1) appears in Cantus II, and three and a half measures later in the
Cantus I and Altus voices; (A2) appears in measure 50; at the beginning
of the second part of the motet (A1) is used in both the Cantus voices (measure 89) and again in Cantus II at measure 94 to the words ' O vera summa '.
It is also used with these words in the Altus at measure 108 and in Cantus I
and Altus at measure 113. In the final section the whole (A) group of subjects
appears: (A1) in measure 143 in the Cantus I, in measure 146 (Bassus), in
measure 153 (Cantus II); in (A2) in measure 148 (Bassus); (a2) in slightly
varied form in all the voices between measures 150 and the end. In the second
group of (A) entries (measure 49 onwards) the texture is more homophonic
than contrapuntal, and certainly not fugal; in the third case the treatment is
completely homophonic (measure 89); in the final section the opening
(measure 143) is homophonic followed by some freely contrapuntal writing
with some loosely fugal passages.

The second group of themes (B1, B2, b1) is less in extent and not so
striking. At its first appearance (B1) and (B2) are used simultaneously, set
to the words (measure 12) ' et benedicta et gloriosa ' antiphonally and
in homophonic style. A modified version (b1 plus B2) is used (measure
23) to the words ' et Filius et Spiritus '. In measures 55-59 (B1) and (B2)

reappear to the words 'et gloriosa'; the texture remains homophonic and the mode of setting antiphonal.   One further use of a modified form of (b1) may be seen at measure 128-131 in the Altus and Bassus to the words 'Te jure laudant', but this is little more than a suggestion.

The third subject, set to the word 'Alleluia' (C and its modifications c1 and c2) is closely derived from (A1) and (A2) by diminution.   It is introduced in a normal double fugal texture.   In the second set of Alleluias (measure 69 onwards) (C) appears in full in the Cantus I voice, while the other voices take up the modified or curtailed forms in imitation.   The Bassus lead (measure 72) is noteworthy, showing the close affinity which the (C) subjects have with (A1) and (A2.)

One further piece of thematic material, marked (D), akin to (A2), makes three appearances in the Tenor (measures 52-53, 138-139, 153-154) set to different words each time.   It is a striking figure moving in crotchets.

Once more it is necessary to stress the danger of wishful thinking in thematic analysis of Palestrina's music.   All that is claimed for the above commentary is that the thematic connection shown does give the motet an exceedingly close knit effect in performance.   The fact that there are many Palestrina motets* in which the same process may be observed, and that it is a process not confined to this composer in the sixteenth century makes it a matter of real importance.   The matter will be considered further in the analysis of 'parody' and 'freely composed' masses.

An interesting instance of Palestrina's use of an old formal device, a kind of *Ostinato*, may be seen in the Motet 'Tribularer, si nescirem . . .' (P. II, p. 81 R. V, p. 107).   The repetition of a short phrase at varying pitch throughout a motet was a favourite device of the earlier motet writers.†   In this work Palestrina reiterates the phrase 'Miserere mei Deus' in the Sextus (Altus) voice at intervals throughout both parts of the motet, each succeeding entry rising a step till the fifth is reached and then falling to the original pitch.   The Sextus part in the first section may be quoted:

Ex. 208

* The motets 'Ego sum panis vivus' (P. I., pp. 43 et seq. R. V. p. 54 et seq.) and   Alleluia, tulerunt Dominum' (P. I., pp. 30 et seq. R. V, p. 35 et seq.) are worthy of careful analysis in this connection.
   † Compare: Josquin, 'Miserere' in which the same ostinato Cantus Firmus is used (cited by Reese: Music in the Renaissance: p. 248).   Also, Clemens, 'Fremuit Spiritu Jesus' (bi-textual) and another setting of the words by Lassus.

Mi - se - re - re me-i De - us, Mi - se - re-re me-i De - us, Mi - se-re-re me-i De - us, Mi - se - re-re me-i De - us, Mi - se - re-re me-i De - us.

Around this *ostinato* is woven a completely independent contrapuntal texture, mainly fugal in character, in which no reference is made to the words or music of the ' Miserere mei, Deus '. The two ' parts ' of the motet have the overall A B C B form.

THE MASSES

The Masses, in their great variety and musical beauty, are, by general consent, the summit of Palestrina's achievement. From a point of view of form and structure the chief interest lies in the Mass as a *cyclic* work. The individual movements in themselves, and the subsections of the longer movements, show a formal treatment of the varying texture kind already studied in the Motet. It is with the Mass as a whole that this chapter is now concerned.

Five types of Mass may be considered in some detail. The first four of these are constructed upon pre-existent material; the last may be described as ' freely composed '.

1. The old type of Cantus Firmus Mass, in which a melody, plainsong, secular song, or some form of traditional tune, is used as a Cantus Firmus either in part or whole in the majority of movements of the Mass. Such a Cantus Firmus is presented generally unaltered melodically though with rhythmic variations; in some cases it appears in long even notes; in others, in augmentation or diminution; in others, with altered rhythms.

2. The decorated Cantus Firmus Mass, generally known as the Paraphrase Mass, in which the Cantus Firmus melody, or part of it, is broken up, ornamented melodically and rhythmically, and treated much in the manner of the freely constructed motets on a plainsong basis discussed earlier in this chapter.

3. The ' Alternation ' Mass in which plainsong and polyphony are used alternately in certain movements (e.g. Gloria and Credo).

4. The Mass founded on some already existing polyphonic composition some part of which is used, both in melody and contrapuntal texture, as the main material of most of the movements. This type of Mass is often referred to by musicologists as the ' Parody ' Mass; one even reads of a mass as ' Parodied on ' some work. Deplorable as the jargon is, it seems to have gained enough acceptance to make its use necessary.

5. The Mass which is ' freely composed ', making no definite use of pre-existent material.

Of the Masses using a Cantus Firmus which must be taken to include the first three types listed above, R. O. Morris has this to say:

'The sixteenth-century Mass on a Cantus Firmus, has, indeed, a close affinity with the modern theme and variation, and also with such cyclic symphonies as Liszt's 'Faust' Symphony and Berlioz's 'Symphonie Fantastique', in which a single thematic germ reappears in various transformations throughout all the movements of the work.'

To this apt similarity might be added the likeness to the Chorale Prelude and Chorale Variation forms of Bach and some of his fore-runners.

The five types of Mass mentioned above must now be examined more closely.

1. *The Cantus Firmus Mass.* Palestrina wrote seven masses which are generally classified under this heading. These range from the first published mass on the Antiphon 'Ecce Sacerdos Magnus' (P. XII, 1, R. I, 1), wherein the Cantus Firmus is presented in the antiquated manner with its original text throughout, to the Octavi Toni (Festum nunc celebre) (published 1600) on a plainsong Hymn, where the Cantus Firmus notes are in places broken up to accommodate the words being treated, so merging into the general texture.

In the Ecce Sacerdos Mass the Cantus Firmus, in full or in part with repetitions, appears, generally in the Tenor but also in the Cantus (Kyrie I, Agnus I), Altus I (Christe, Sanctus), and Altus II (Agnus II), as a long-note melody in all the movements except the 'Crucifixus', 'Pleni sunt coeli', 'Benedictus' and 'Osanna', where it is used in paraphrase fashion as a basis of the music. Around it the other voices weave a contrapuntal texture, sometimes, as in Agnus I, using the Cantus Firmus in diminution as a point, but more often using freely constructed points. A similarity in some of this free material may be observed, binding the various movements together even more closely than the presence of the plainsong could do.

A rather more detailed inspection of the Missa Octavi Toni (P. XX, p. 80) may suffice to give some idea of Palestrina's later Cantus Firmus methods.

The Cantus Firmus melody is as follows:

Ex. 209

Kyrie I, Christe, Kyrie II. In this section the Cantus Firmus appears in the Sextus voice (Cantus II) throughout. In the Kyrie I it is in even Breves, using the first two sections of the melody; in the Christe, sections 3 and 4 of the melody are used in simple diminution (semibreves): the remainder of the plainsong appears in Kyrie II, again in even semibreves.

Kyrie I opens with two melodically identical but rhythmically contrasted points exactly paraphrasing the first section of the plainsong and treated fugally in pairs (Tenor I and Tenor II, Bassus and Altus); the Cantus I has yet another rhythmic version of the Cantus Firmus. The second strain of the plainsong is not drawn upon directly for material, but is accompanied by new free ' points ' treated with a lot of imitation.

The ' Christe ' begins with the fugal treatment of a point reproducing the first nine notes of the third line of the Cantus Firmus in rhythmic paraphrase before the plainsong enters. The texture then becomes freely contrapuntal and imitative while the Cantus II voice sings the third and fourth lines of the melody.

In Kyrie II two ' points ' are treated fugally, one closely following line five of the Cantus Firmus, the other an independent figure which has already been heard in the Altus of the ' Christe ' seven measures earlier. The two succeeding lines of the melody are introduced and accompanied by the imitation of points paraphrasing them closely, together with free imitative counterpoint on material closely allied to the earlier free material.

This threefold movement is exceedingly close-knit, not only in the uniform type of texture, but in the secondary thematic material, which is repeated frequently throughout the three sections, as, for example, the four-note ascending crotchet figure followed by a further step to a semibreve.

The Gloria is in sharp contrast. It is mainly homophonic and intermediate in texture. The Cantus Firmus (Cantus II) appears at the rate of one note of the melody to a measure (except on one occasion), but the majority of the ' notes ' are broken up rhythmically so as to carry more than one syllable. The opening will show the process:

Ex. 210

The first section of the movement (as far as the words ' Filius Patris ') continues this method of treating the Cantus Firmus, the other parts soon becoming ' intermediate ' in texture, and making considerable use of the crotchet figure noted in the Kyrie.

The ' Qui tollis ' section uses the same breaking-up of the notes of the melody (phrases 5 and 6), preceded by a statement of phrase 5 in Cantus I in diminution. The texture remains homophonic-intermediate in style and the crotchet figures used earlier in the mass become prominent.

In the last section (' In Gloria Dei ') the time changes to 𝄵3. The Cantus Firmus appears in semibreves (diminution 3/2) (Cantus II) and is repeated (plus four notes).   The texture is again homophonic-intermediate and the four-note ascending figure (now in minims) is used in the accompanying parts.

The Credo opens in the same way as the Gloria.   The Cantus Firmus is presented in measure-length melody notes broken up, and the texture is mainly homophonic with some imitation paraphrasing the plainsong; several of the figures previously used (e.g. the ascending crotchet scale passage) are noteworthy in the accompanying parts.   At ' Et incarnatus est ' a paraphrase presentation of the Cantus Firmus is used, though the decoration is slight.   The ' Crucifixus ' is, as usual in Cantus Firmus Masses, free of the Plainsong.   It is set for Cantus I, Altus, and two Tenors, and much of the material is closely akin to the free contrapuntal figures already used; the upward crotchet scale is much in evidence towards the end of the section. The ' Et in Spiritum ' again uses the broken Cantus Firmus presentation; it is in ◖3 and very homophonic.   At ' Et unam sanctam ' the time returns to ℂ and a semi-paraphrase version of the plainsong again appears.   The final sections ' resurrectionem mortuorum ' and ' et vitam venturi ' show the Cantus, first in ◖3 |𝇋| 𝅝 rhythm, and then in ℂ with some breaking up of the long notes.

The Sanctus is built on the Cantus Firmus, unbroken, phrases 1 and 2 in breves, 3 and 4 in semibreves, 5 and 6 in ◖3 |𝇋| 𝅝.   The freely imitative contrapuntal web contains much of the material already used.

In the Benedictus (for four voices) the plainsong appears in breves using two repetitions of phrase 7 and a final repetition in semibreves against a free contrapuntal texture.   The triple-time Hosanna uses phrases 5 and 6 of the melody in breve-semibreve rhythm; the other parts are closely imitative of the Cantus Firmus.

The first Agnus has a straight presentation of the plainsong in semibreves. The accompanying voices, freely fugal, use much already familiar material. In the second Agnus the time is ◖3, and again the Cantus Firmus gives the plainsong unaltered against imitative counterpoint.

A fairly detailed analysis of this Mass has been given to show the homogeneity of these works.   Not only is the Cantus Firmus present almost all the time, giving a melodic framework to the mass as a whole, but secondary thematic material keeps recurring in the freely contrapuntal treatment. For example the figure referred to above, albeit a standard pattern in Palestrina's counterpoint, occurs too frequently (over fifty times in this Mass) to be regarded as a mere general stylistic formula.

Ex. 211

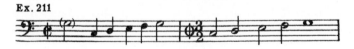

2. *The Paraphrase Mass.*   The Paraphrase type of mass follows generally the processes observed in the paraphrase motet in the treatment of a plainsong Cantus Firmus.   The lines of the melody are ornamented rhythmically and melodically, the other voices completing the texture, fugal, homophonic or intermediate.

A good example of this method will be found in the four-voice Mass
'Aeterna Christi munera' (1590. R. XV, p. 1, P. XIV, p. 1). In this Mass
there is much fugal treatment of 'points' paraphrased from the melody.
In consequence the process produces a very close thematic link from the
melodic point of view in the majority of the movements. The following
example shows the beginnings of some of the movements and gives an idea
of the varied rhythmical treatment of the melodic outline of the first phrase.

Ex. 212

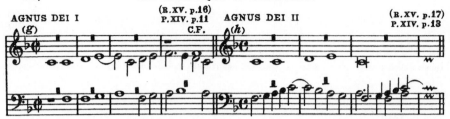

The use of secondary thematic material, often vaguely derived from the plainsong and 'developed' at various stages throughout the work as a whole, considerably strengthens the structural unity of the Mass. One such instance may be seen in the second 'Kyrie', where the two closely connected motives quoted below appear against the second line of the Cantus Firmus. Some subsequent appearances in later movements of the Mass are cited. These show considerable rhythmic and melodic variation, but their musical kinship is clear.

3. *The Alternation Mass.* The Alternation mass is a variant of the 'Paraphrase' type; in certain movements plainsong monody and polyphonic writing alternate, unbroken polyphony being used for the others. Most of Palestrina's masses of this kind were written for the Mantuan use, and in these the Mantuan versions of the plainchant were followed.

Two short extracts from the Missa in Duplicibus (Minoribus I) will illustrate the essential features of these settings. First of all the plainsong of the Kyrie (I) is shown above the Cantus part of the normal polyphonic paraphrase setting of the words. The paraphrase technique described above is used, the points reproducing the plainsong melody with remarkable clarity.

In the second quotation, the·Gloria, the alternation treatment is illustrated. The plainchant basis is given as far as ' Benedicimus te ' and the openings of the polyphonic sections, closely derived from the melody, show the ease with which the plainsong line can merge into polyphonic texture.

Ex. 214

4. *The 'Parody' Mass.* The fourth type of Mass draws upon some already existing polyphonic composition for its material. A good example of this in Palestrina's work is the six-voice 'Dum complerentur' (P. XVII, p. 85 et seq.) based on his own motet (R. V, p. 149 et seq., P. I, p. 111 et seq.).

MASS. Christe. M.11-12   P.XVII.p.87

The seven extracts from the Motet quoted above form the main thematic material of the Mass. A few other less important themes are used, but, as will be seen on closer analysis, these seven are the backbone of both the Motet and the cyclic work based on it.

The themes themselves fall into two closely related groups. A, B, and C have much in common, for example the rising fourth followed by a descending movement. D, E, F, and to some extent G are akin in the descending crotchet figures. This grouping of the subject-matter into two well contrasted patterns does much towards unification as well as contrast throughout the various movements of the Mass.

Theme A, the opening five measures of the Motet, appears with some modification and elaboration as the beginning of the first Kyrie of the Mass. The Cantus part is reproduced exactly for four measures and is continued further with some rhythmic alteration and decoration; the first Altus is unaltered for five notes, the first Tenor for ten. The subsequent appearances of A may be listed, with short comments thus:

2. *Gloria in excelsis:* ' et in terra pax '. Here the first four measures of the Cantus part are reproduced unvaried (except for the breaking of the first note to fit the new words) accompanied by three other voices (A.2, T.1, T.2) in mainly homophonic style, making use of the accompanying material of the original lower parts broken up to some extent and interchanged. The following phrase ' Laudamus te, benedicimus te ' is a clear variant of this subject with rhythmic and melodic alteration but nevertheless

closely connected with A. (A rather vague further derivation appears at ' miserere nobis '.)

3. *Credo.* ' Patrem omipotentem '. The opening of the Creed presents the Cantus part in rhythmic variation in a more elaborate contrapuntal setting. The lower three voices again draw on the material of the lower parts as heard in the motet.

4. *Credo.* ' Crucifixus '. A four-voice version very close to A, transposed down a fourth, the Cantus part now appearing in Altus II.

5. *Sanctus.* The Cantus part of A is exactly reproduced (save for alteration of note lengths to fit the new words) at the start of the Sanctus. The other voices engaged (A.I, A.II, T.II) have some elaborate contrapuntal work of a fugal character on an independent point, drawn largely from the material of the original accompanying voices.

6. *Agnus Dei I.* This movement opens with a statement of the Cantus part (exact, save for the last note) with three freely contrapuntal parts below it.

Theme B. This is closely allied to A in the important melodic rise of a fourth and subsequent stepwise descent of the top voice. In the Motet it occurs at the twelfth measure to the words ' erant omnes ' in a six-voice homophonic setting. Its first appearance in the Mass is at the opening of the ' Christe eleison ' where the Cantus melody (with slight rhythmic alteration) is treated fugally in four voices. It is used subsequently in the Mass as follows:

2. *Gloria in excelsis.* ' B ' appears at the words ' Domine Deus, Agnus Dei ', with altered rhythm and shorter note values, and is treated with imitation and variation till the end of the section.

3. *Credo.* ' Et in unum Dominum '. Here the Cantus part is exactly reproduced and the treatment is at the outset homophonic for six voices, closely resembling the Motet version, continuing in rather more elaborate freely contrapuntal style.

Another clear reference to it may be found at the words ' Passus et sepultus est '; here the theme is rhythmically altered and the note values shortened; the treatment is freely fugal for four voices.

At the opening of the section ' Et in spiritum ' considerable use is made by the lower three voices of a ' point ' made from the Cantus part and treated in imitation; this is carried on by the Cantus, Altus II and Tenor II at the words ' qui ex Patre '.

Further use is made of the theme at ' ... in remissionem ' where it appears in a six-part nearly-homophonic setting very closely related to the Motet version.

4. *Agnus Dei I.* Some resemblance may be seen at the words ' . . . mundi, miserere nobis ', though the direct connection with the subject B is less clear cut here. Again in the second Agnus at the words ' qui tollis ' a point closely related to it is used in imitation.

Theme C occurs at the opening of the Secunda Pars of the Motet. It is a double ' point ' treated fugally. The Cantus subject is closely allied to themes A and B. The ' Countersubject ' begins with an ascending figure. Its first appearance in the Mass is at the opening of Kyrie II, where both subjects are used fugally, but whereas in the Motet the Cantus and Altus I lead with the points, in the Mass it is the second Tenor and Bass which open the fugato.

2. *Gloria in excelsis.* The next important use of ' C ' is at the opening of the ' Qui tollis ' section. Here both subjects are used in a four-voice fugal exposition. A few measures later, when the words ' Qui tollis ' are repeated, both subjects appear again in rather freer imitative counterpoint for all six voices.

3. *Sanctus.* The ' Pleni sunt coeli ' section opens with a fugal treatment of both subjects, for four voices. The points, after the first entry, are used individually rather than in pairs for some twelve measures.

4. *Agnus Dei II.* The first twelve measures of this movement are taken up with an elaborate free fugal discussion of both subjects, separately or in combination.

Theme D. The first Alleluia of the Motet is set to a very striking subject with great rhythmic as well as melodic interest. It is treated in fugal fashion, the opening being given to the Cantus and Altus I in parallel thirds with a free added part. The extent of this ' theme ' in the Motet is thirteen measures. Its first appearance in the Mass is in the ' Christe eleison ' where it receives a close fugal treatment of some twenty-one measures for the four upper voices. Although the parallel-third opening is not used, much of the incidental material found in the Motet version is present.

2. *Gloria in excelsis* (measures 28-39). The words ' Domine Deus . . . unigenite ' are set to a freely fugal version of the material contained in D, with some new incidental counterpoint. This passage is preceded by a rhythmically altered working of the subject at the words ' propter magnam gloriam '.

3. *Credo.* ' Filium Dei '. The parallel-third initial entry of D reappears here and the theme is used fugally for four measures by the top four voices.

4. *Sanctus.* ' Dominus Deus Sabaoth '. Here the ' point ' with the fourth note prolonged, is used for a series of close-knit fugal imitations for some sixteen measures. (Compare with ' propter magnam gloriam ' in the Gloria; see above.)

Theme E, the third Alleluia in the motet, is closely akin to D (c.f. ' Dominus Deus Sabaoth ' mentioned above); here again the crotchet descending figure plays a large part. In the motet it is used as a fugal point, and the similarity of treatment when it appears at the words ' in Gloria Dei Patris ' in the Gloria of the mass, is very striking.

2. *Credo.* ' Et vitam venturi saeculi '. The last fifteen measures of the Credo are taken up with a closely worked fugue on subjects drawn from the points used in the motet. All six voices are employed.

3. *Benedictus.* ' In nomine Domini '. Here the subjects of the motet version are employed in extended fugal procedure for some twenty-one measures: the Tenor I version of the point in the motet extract is the more frequently used. All six voices are used, and many of the imitative entries

are at close range. This is a very interesting example of extended fugal development of a subject.

4. *Agnus Dei II.* ' Dona nobis pacem '. The Mass ends with another elaborate twenty-measure fugue on both versions of the subject as they appear in the Motet. The rising series of leads in the Cantus voice, culminating in one beginning on high G, is very impressive in its cumulative effect; it may not be unreasonable to see in this passage evidence of real melodic development.

Theme F, again, has a descending scale passage in crotchets as its most prominent feature. In the extract from the Motet two points are used together beginning in identical rhythms and mainly in thirds or sixths, the two parts becoming independent towards the close of the phrase. The additional contrapuntal part in Altus II (measures 3 and 4 of the extract) is important, as it reappears in the Mass. The first use of this subject-matter in the Mass is at the words ' Tu solus Sanctus ' in the Gloria. The closeness to the Motet version may be seen by comparing the two examples.

2. *Credo.* ' Et resurrexit tertia die secundum scripturas '. Here a freely fugal treatment of the subject appearing in the top voice of the motet extract is accompanied by variants of the other parts. Another variant of the theme is found at ' Qui cum Patre et Filio '.

3. *Sanctus.* ' Gloria tua '. A four-voice fugal setting of the point (top voice) is used here extending over thirteen measures.

Theme G consists of two subjects heard together in the Motet version; in both the descending crotchet figure is again prominent, though the first three minims of each are also thematically important. A comparison of the Motet original version of the passage and the ' Qui propter nos homines ' from the Credo of the Mass cited under it shows the closeness of the two passages, and the subtle variety which Palestrina introduces. The treatment at this point in the Mass is too long to quote in full, being some fifteen measures in length, but it repays very careful study.

2. A later appearance of G in the Credo at the words ' Sedet ad dexteram Patris . . .' is also important. Here a four-voice setting of the main subjects is carried on for some twelve measures and shows considerable diversity in treatment.

3. In the next section of the Credo at ' et unam sanctam catholicam ' a close fugal texture is woven by all six voices on the subjects for some ten measures. These three appearances of this material in the Credo are of great importance. They are not mere repetitions of a section; each has its own individual treatment and vocal orchestration. The formal significance is clear.

4. The opening of the Benedictus has a very interesting development of material obviously based on G for the double subject which is there treated fugally for some eighteen measures. The first three notes of each of the points in the motet extract are used in longer note values. The continuation of the upper subject (Altus I, Benedictus, measures 5-7) has close kinship

with the Cantus added part of F as it appears in the 'Tu solus sanctus' in
the Gloria.

This analysis of the more important material of the Mass has been undertaken in order to show something of the use of thematic development in
Palestrina's cyclic settings of the mass.   The carefully spaced and frequent
reiteration of thematic material over the work as a whole, and the variety
of treatment of the material itself suggests that sixteenth-century composers
were at least not indifferent to the potentialities of thematic repetition,
variation, and even development.

5. *The Freely Composed Masses.*   Palestrina's freely composed masses also
contain much of interest from the formal point of view.   There is often a
strong vein of thematic connection running through the works as a whole,
which, though less clearly and systematically defined than in the case of the
masses written upon already existent polyphonic compositions, and though
less obvious than the varying 'points' based on the Cantus Firmus technique
of the Paraphrase and long-note Cantus Firmus works, is, in some respects,
more important, since it shows a deliberate awareness of the formal implications of thematic repetition and development.

The famous Marcellus Mass is a good example (P. XI, p. 128, R. IV,
p. 167).

Two characteristic themes, which play a considerable part in the work as
a whole, may be cited, with some of their variants.

Ex. 216

Variants of A occur frequently throughout the Mass, most often in the
lower voices; in the second Agnus one of the modifications is used as the
opening point of a canon 3 in 1.   Some other modified appearances are
quoted below.

Ex. 217

The variants of B also play an important part. Some of these are given
below.

Ex. 218

CHAPTER X

WORD-SETTING

IT is clear that composers and theorists of the sixteenth century gave a great deal of thought to the matter of word-setting, both from the aesthetic and expressive point of view, and in connection with the actual technical processes of underlaying words. Zarlino probably reflects the views and ideals of the time accurately in the thirty-second and thirty-third chapters of his ' Istituzioni armoniche ' (1558) where he gives considerable space to both aspects of word-setting.* Morley, in the ' Plaine and Easie Introduction ', has a section devoted to ' Rules to be observed in dittying ' which is, for the most part, a précis translation of Zarlino's thirty-second chapter.

This chapter of Zarlino is concerned with ' how the harmonies are adapted to the words placed beneath them '. Zarlino begins by arguing that Plato (Republic III), though defining melody as an equal combination of speech, harmony and rhythm, nevertheless gives pride of place to speech since the sense of the words must dictate the character of the other two factors.

Morley's paraphrase of the remainder of this chapter is such pleasant reading that it seems worth while to quote most of it in full. (Spelling modernized) †:

' Now having discoursed unto you the composition of three, four, five and six parts with these few ways of canons and catches:

' It followeth to shew you how to dispose your music according to the nature of the words which you are therein to express, as whatsoever matter it be which you have in hand, such a kind of music must you frame to it. You must therefore if you have grave matter, apply a grave kind of music to it: if a merry subject you must make your music also merry. For it will be a great absurdity to use a sad harmony to a merry matter, or a merry harmony to a sad lamentable or tragical ditty. You must then when you would express any word signifying hardness, cruelty, bitterness, and other such like, make the harmony like unto it, that is somewhat harsh but yet so that it offend not. Likewise, when any of your words shall express complaint, dolour, repentance, sighs, tears, and such like, let your harmony be sad and doleful. So that if you would have your music signify hardness, cruelty or other such affects, you must cause the parts to proceed in their motions without the half notes, that is, you must cause them to proceed by whole notes, sharp thirds, sharp sixths,

---

* Translations of these chapters of Zarlino will be found in Strunk ' Source Readings ', pp. 255 et seq.
† Morley: ' Plaine and Easie Introduction ', pp. 177 et seq. (Shakespeare Facsimile)

and such like (when I speak of sharp or flat thirds and sixths, you must understand that they ought to be so to the bass). You may also use cadences bound with the fourth or seventh, which being in long notes will exasperate the harmony. But when you would express a lamentable passion, then must you use motions proceeding by half notes ; flat thirds and sixths, which of their nature are sweet, specially being taken in the true tune and natural air with discretion and judgment.

' But those chords so taken as I have said before are not the sole and only cause of expressing those passions, but also the motions which the parts make in singing do greatly help; which motions are either natural or accidental. The natural motions are those which are naturally made betwixt the keys without the mixture of any accidental sign or chord, be it either sharp or flat, and these motions be more masculine, causing in the song more virility than those accidental chords which are marked with these signs, x, ♭, which be indeed accidental and make the song, as it were, more effeminate and languishing than the other motions which make the song rude and sounding; so that those natural motions may serve to express those effects of cruelty, tyranny, bitterness, and such others, and those accidental motions may fitly express the passions of grief, weeping, sighs, sorrows, sobs, and such like.

'Also, if the subject be light, you must cause your music go in motions which carry with them a celerity or quickness of time, as minims, crotchets and quavers: if it is lamentable, the notes must go in slow and heavy motions, as semibreves, breves, and such like, and of all this you shall find examples every where in the works of good musicians. Moreover you must have a care that when your matter signifieth ascending, high heaven, and such like, you make your music ascend: and by the contrary where your ditty speaketh of descending, lowness, depth, hell, and others such, you must make your music descend, for as it will be thought a great absurdity to talk of heaven and point downwards to the earth, so will it be counted great incongruity if a musician upon the words ' he ascended into heaven ' should cause his music to descend, or by contrary upon the descension should cause his music to ascend. We must also have a care so to apply the notes to the words as in singing there be no barbarism committed: that is that we cause no syllable which by nature is short be expressed by many notes or one long note, nor no long syllables be expressed with a short note. But in this fault do the practitioners err more grossly than in any other, for you shall find few songs wherein the penult syllables of these words, *Dominus, Angelus, filius, miraculum, gloria,* and such like are not expressed with a long note, yea many times with a whole dozen of notes, and though one should speak of forty he should not say much amiss, which is a gross barbarism and yet might be easily amended. We must also take heed of separating any part of a word from another by a rest, as some dunces have not slacked to do, yea one whose name is Johannes Dunstaple (an ancient English author) hath not only divided the sentence but in the very middle of a word hath made two long rests thus in a song of four parts upon these words, " Nesciens virgo mater virum ":

Ex. 219

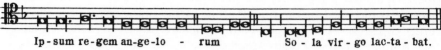

Ip - sum re - gem an - ge - lo - rum　　　So - la vir - go lac-ta - bat.

For these be his own notes and words, which is one of the greatest absurdities which I have seen committed in the dittying of music. But to show you in a word the use of the rests in the ditty, you may set a crotchet or minim rest above a comma or colon, but a longer rest than that of a minim you may not take till the sentence be perfect, and then at a full point you may set what number of rests you will. Also when you would express sighs, you may use the crotchet or minim rest at the most, but a longer than minim rest you may not use because it will rather seem a breath taking than a sigh, an example whereof you may see in a very good song of Stephano Venturi to five voices upon this ditty " *Quell' aura che spirando a Laura mia?* ", for coming to the word *sospiri* (that is, sighs) he giveth it such natural grace by breaking a minim into a crotchet rest and a crotchet that the excellency of his judgment in expressing and gracing his ditty doth therein manifestly appear.

　' Lastly you must not make a close (especially a full close) till the full sense of the words is perfect. So that keeping these rules you shall have a perfect agreement and, as it were, an harmonical consent betwixt the matter and the music, and likewise you shall be perfectly understood of the auditor what you sing, which is one of the highest degrees of praise which a musician in dittying can attain unto or wish for.'

These are necessarily theorist's precepts, and must be regarded as little more than the externals of an aesthetic problem, word-setting. It has been pointed out several times in this book that Palestrina's art is based in all its phases on restraint and moderation; it would clearly be wrong to look for complete and slavish exemplification of the theorists' 'rules' in his work, and such an attitude would tend to obliterate awareness of the much more subtle inner aesthetic spirit which shines through the music.

The precepts quoted are, none the less, good common sense for the most part, and show something of the sixteenth-century approach to the subject. It may not be unprofitable to examine them in the light of Palestrina's music, and at the same time attempt to see some of the more subtle secrets of his word-setting.

First of all, the direction concerning the setting of words implying ascension or height by rising movement, and the converse, may appear to be too obvious to warrant serious consideration. Nevertheless, this apparently naïve device is capable of producing striking and beautiful results in Palestrina's hands.

In the first of the examples quoted below, the words ' Ascendo ad Patrem meum ' are set to a melodic phrase beginning with an octave leap upwards

from a breve; the whole phrase is perfectly proportioned, and the leap is
not just an obvious piece of naïve word-painting, but an essential part of
the melodic line which expresses the words as a whole. The effect of the
passage is increased by the timing of the entries of the five voices, and their
order of entry. The opening of this splendid motet gives the impression
of triumph expressed with tremendous power and control; the rather
mechanical device of the octave leap on 'Ascendo' has been absorbed into
a far more deeply expressive process of reproducing in music the spirit of
the text.

The second example shows the word 'descendit' set to a falling crotchet
scale figure. Here again the formula appears to be quite commonplace in
its external aspect. Palestrina's treatment of the figure, and his welding of it
into the texture as a whole, is quite the reverse of commonplace. Once
more the timing and placing of the 'leads' has much to do with the beauty
of the music.

The prescription given by Zarlino (or Morley) for the expression of sorrow consists of 'sad and doleful' harmony with 'flat thirds and flat sixths', a melody using half notes (accidentals), the notes going in 'slow and heavy motions as semibreves, breves and such like'.

The setting of the words 'Timor mortis conturbat me' from the wonderful motet 'Pecantem me quotidie' quoted below, contains all the ingredients of the formula: the miracle by which Palestrina draws from them one of the most moving things in vocal music cannot be analysed, indeed, it can only be realized to the full when the music is sung. The section 'quia in inferno' shows another instance of his transformation of the simple device of taking the voices into a low register into a deeply moving musical experience.

Ex. 221   (R.VII.p.99) P.II.p.74

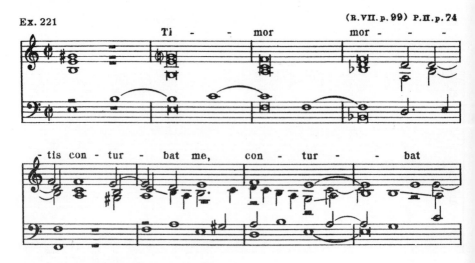

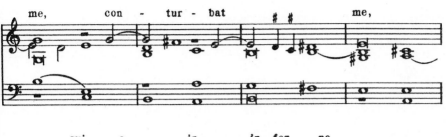

Perhaps the most beautiful expression of sadness in all Palestrina's motets is the setting of the words 'mori dignatus est' in the Easter motet 'Surrexit pastor bonus'. In this case the devices given by Zarlino are less in evidence. Several other factors contribute to the emotional intensity of the setting; the sudden change from 'major' to 'minor' 'harmonies' after the words 'et pro grege suo' is very telling; the double-choir contrast is used with extraordinary pathos; the joyful Alleluias heighten the sadness of the words 'mori dignatus est'. The most moving moment of all, in the present writer's opinion, is the entry of the second choir in the passage contained in measures five to seven of the quotation given below. The effect of this passage is something which cannot be explained by theories or words.

Ex. 222   P. VI. p. 59

The precepts for the setting of words expressing the opposite emotions of joy, exaltation, and praise are much less definite. 'Merry' harmony, the use of shorter note values, such as the minim, crotchet and quaver, and the avoidance of accidentals in the melodic line are advocated. To these may be added, from observation of the practice of Palestrina and his contemporaries, vigour of the melodic line and of the rhythm in general; this is often achieved by ascending scale passages in short note values (for example, crotchets) and disjunct movement in minims in the melodic lines, and varied or cross rhythms in the texture as a whole.

The two short passages quoted below from the Motet 'Exultate Deo' show the vigour and upsurging melodic outline as well as the excitement and tension of varied rhythm which Palestrina uses in one of his most joyous works. The word painting at 'buccinate tuba' is very graphic, and the setting illustrates most of the devices mentioned. Yet, as in the case of sorrow, it is the texture taken as a whole, the welding together of the various technical factors into expressive music, which creates the aesthetic experience of joy and praise.

The prescription for 'hardness, cruelty and other such affects' consists of a melodic line devoid of accidentals, of major thirds and sixths above the bass, and suspended fourths and sevenths to 'exasperate the harmony'. In Palestrina's church music it is useless to expect to find extreme examples of the expression of these emotions. A restrained instance may be cited, the opening of the motet 'Lapidabant Stephanum'. Here the 'natural motions . . . without the mixture of any accidental sign or chord' are used to a very great extent; major thirds as harmonic intervals abound, but few major sixths; a fair number of suspended fourths occur. A contributory device may, perhaps, be found in the disjunct nature of the melodic lines at the opening.

The use of 'flat thirds and sixths' in the 'harmony' and flats and sharps in the melodic line to express tenderness as well as sorrow is often noticeable. The quotation cited below produces the effect of calm and contemplation; the technical means used are not far removed from those of the examples of setting words dealing with grief, yet the resulting music is altogether different. A comparison between the two emotions thus expressed will demonstrate the insufficiency of externals of technique alone in word-setting.

Ex. 225

P. VI. p. 158

The concluding sections of the ' Rules to be observed in dittying ' are concerned to some extent with the actual underlaying of words. It is necessary to point out that a lot of uncertainty exists about the finer points of word underlaying in sixteenth-century polyphony. In printed part-books and manuscripts also the underlaying is often haphazard and the words and music can sometimes be fitted together only by conjecture. There is also the added difficulty that well-known texts were often omitted after the first statement, or only sketched as *incipits*.

Concerning the words, ' Dominus, angelus, filius, miraculum, and gloria ' cited by Morley, Palestrina's work seems to be remarkably free from any trace of the ' barbarism ' in which ' practitioners err more grossly than in any other fault '. A few typical examples of his setting of these words will show his care in obtaining good accentuation.

Ex. 226

(R.X. p.103)
P.XIII. p. 77

(R.X. p. 78)
P. XIII. p. 54

(a) Do - mi-nus De - us
(b) Do - mi - nus De - us

(R.X. p. 52)
P.XIII. p. 89

(R.X. p.188)
P.XIII. p.102

(c) Do - mi-nus De - us
(d) Do - mi - nus De-(us)

(R.X. p.12)
P.XIII. p.10

(R.X. p.44)
P. XIII. p. 88

(e) Glo - ri-a tu - - - a
(f) in glo - ri - a

(R.X. p.89)
P.XIII. p.66

(R.X. p.168)
P.XIII. p.120

(g) in glo - ri - a
(h) in glo-ri - a

(R.X. p.63)
P.XIII. p. 47

(R.X. p.42)
P. XIII. p.32

(i) Fi - li-us Pa - tris
(j) Fi - li - us Pa(tris)

(R.III. p.15)
P.V. p.14

(R.VIII. p.28)
P.III. p.18

(k) Tri - bus mi - ra-cu-lis
(l) An - ge-lus Do - mi-ni

With regard to the 'separating any part of a word from another by a
rest' (a survival of the 'hocket'), which Morley castigates with a pun on
Dunstable's name, Palestrina, at any rate in his sacred works, is guiltless (so
far as the writer's knowledge goes). He does not, however, carry out the
ruling 'you may set a crotchet or minim rest above a comma or a colon,
but a longer rest than that of a minim you may not take till the sentence be
perfect, and then at the full point you may set any number of rests you
will.' Even without a comma, breaks of as much as four and a half measures
may be found in a sentence. It is noteworthy that the isolated fragments
of the sentence always consist of words making sense in themselves. Three
short examples will demonstrate Palestrina's normal procedure in the
matter.

Ex. 227

(R.III. p.86)
P.V. p. 81

(a) re - ple-ti sunt o - - - mnes

spi - ri - tu san - - - - - - - cto,

The direction for the expression of ' sighs ' is clearly not concerned with the sacred music of the period.

' Lastly you must not make a close (*cadence*) especially a full close till the full sense of the words is perfect.' In this matter, as in the matter of rests in the course of a sentence, Palestrina takes a much more liberal view. Cadences, even perfect cadences complete with suspension formulae, are by no means rare at points where the sense of the words is still not complete. The passage quoted below exhibits a very definite full close after the words ' Eja ergo '. Nevertheless, Palestrina appears to take particular care not to make a break in the musical setting, either as a whole or in a single line, at a point where the portion of the words used cannot stand by themselves. An invocation, or a description of a subject, such as ' Caecilia Virgo' (see above, 227c) can stand by themselves.

Underlaying of Words

The technical process of underlaying words in the more restricted and detailed sense is, as it has been stated above, a difficult and uncertain matter upon which to give any rulings. Zarlino made an attempt, in the *Istituzioni armoniche*, Book III, 33, to clarify what was obviously a very unsatisfactory state of affairs, and although his rulings do not by any means cover the whole situation with regard to Palestrina's practice, they are worth quoting to show the sixteenth-century approach to the problems.

In his preamble to his rules he deplores the disorder to be found in setting words to music, and especially the frequent appearance of ' the musical figures so adapted to the words that the singer cannot determine or discover a suitable way of performing them.' In order to put an end to the chaos which existed in the matter he formulates the following ten rules ' which will serve both the composer and the singer '. (Translation: Strunk, ' Source Readings in Musical History ', p. 260):

Zarlino's Rules

1. A suitable figure (=note) is to be placed below each long or short syllable so that nothing barbarous will be heard. For in figured music each musical figure that stands alone and is not in ligature (apart from the semiminim and all those that are smaller than the semiminim) carries its own syllable with it. This rule is observed in plainsong also, for to each square figure is adapted a syllable of its own, excepting for the middle notes, which are sometimes treated like minims or even semiminims, as may be seen in many chants, especially in the chant for the Nicene Creed, ' Credo in Unum Deum ', which they call the *Credo Cardinale*.

2. Not more than one syllable, and that at the beginning, is to be adapted to each ligature of several notes or figures, whether in figured music or in plainsong.

3. No syllable is to be adapted to the dot placed after the figures of figured music, although this is sung.

4. It is not usual to place a syllable below a semiminim, or below those figures that are smaller than a semiminim, or below the figure immediately following.

5. It is not customary to place any syllable below the figures immediately following a dotted semibreve or dotted minim, when these following figures are valued at less than the dots, as are semiminims after a dotted semibreve or chromas (quavers) after a dotted minim; the same is true of figures that immediately follow these.

6. Should it be necessary to place a syllable below a semiminim, one may also place another syllable below the figure following.

7. At the beginning of a composition, or after any rest in the middle, the first figure, whatever it may be, must necessarily carry with it a syllable.

8. In plainsong no word or syllable is ever repeated, although one sometimes hears this done, a thing to be censured; in figured music such repetitions are sometimes tolerated—not of a syllable or of a word, but of some part of the speech whose sense is complete. This may be done when there are figures in such quantity that words may be repeated conveniently. But to repeat a thing many times over does not, in my opinion, go over well, unless it be done to give greater emphasis to words that have in them some grave sense and are worthy of consideration.

9. When all the syllables of a period, or of one part of the speech, have been adapted to the musical figures and there remain only the penultimate syllable and the last, the penultimate syllable will have the privilege of bearing a number of small figures—two, three, or some other quantity—provided, however, that it be long and not short, for if it were short a barbarism would occur. Singing in this way, there arises what many call a *neuma* which occurs when many figures are sung above a single syllable. But when figures are placed this way they offend against our first rule.

10. The final syllable of the speech will fall below the final figure of the composition if our rules are observed.

It is probably advisable to attempt to deduce a set of working rules from the first six of the provisions set out by Zarlino, and then to enquire how far they represent Palestrina's practice. These rules must, in the first instance, be understood to apply to note values in ₵.

Working Rules

I. Any white note when standing alone, that is, not as a part of a group or ligature, may carry a syllable (Zarlino Rule 1) *except* when it follows a crotchet or shorter note (Zarlino Rule 4) when it must be a part of a group.

II. A single crotchet or shorter note value does not usually carry a syllable. (Zarlino Rule 4).

III. If a weak syllable *is* placed on a crotchet another syllable may occur on the following note. (Zarlino Rule 6.)

IV. No new syllable is permitted on quaver values following a dotted minim, or on crotchet values following a dotted semibreve. (Zarlino Rule 5.)

[V. The dot of a dotted note cannot support a separate syllable. (Zarlino Rule 3.)]

[VI. Ligatures or groups of notes carry one syllable. (Zarlino Rule 2.)]

I. The first part of this rule is the common practice of the period and may be illustrated from almost any measure of Palestrina's music. The exception which implies that a white note cannot carry a new syllable after movement in crotchets or quavers seems to be observed to a remarkable degree by Palestrina himself, though his contemporaries appear to have attached less weight to the rule. Many of the cases in which Palestrina appears to change a syllable on a white note after crotchet movement are probably due to faulty transcriptions or bad printing. (The common practice outlined in Rule III will be considered in its place.)

Some instances exist where it is difficult to see how the words can be made to fit the melodic phrase without change of syllable after crotchet movement. Some examples given below will show the regular and irregular treatment.

II and III. The general ruling that a crotchet by itself cannot carry a separate syllable needs considerable qualification, so many exceptions occur. Before these are considered it must be made clear that two or more crotchets or even four quavers at the beginning of a group or ligature may carry a syllable.

Ex. 230

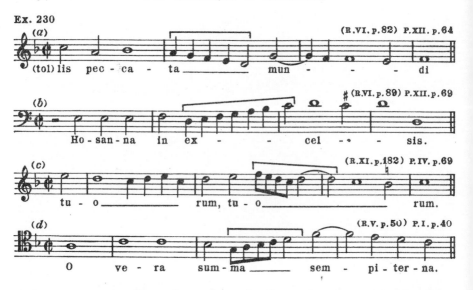

A very common figure throughout the sixteenth century consists of the rhythmic structure 'dotted minim—crotchet—minim (or longer note)'. Three separate syllables are often placed under these three notes, giving a syllable to an isolated weak crotchet, and a change of syllable on the following white note. (Zarlino Rule 6.) This underlaying of words is used so often and so freely that it must be regarded as a normal part of the technique.

Ex. 231

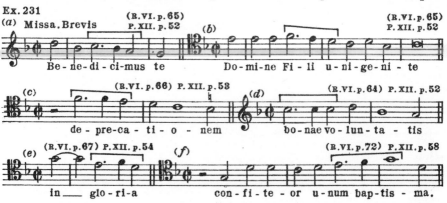

Less common are groups of two crotchets each carrying a separate syllable; nevertheless, they occur often enough to justify their inclusion in the style. Groups of four crotchets each with its own syllable also occur sporadically, and occasionally two crotchets each with a syllable are immediately followed by a group beginning with crotchet movement set to a third syllable. The examples given below illustrate these points and show a rare instance of three single crotchets each with a syllable following a dotted minim.

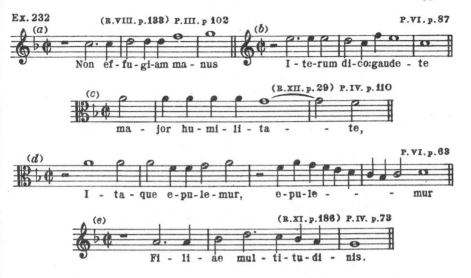

A few instances of more irregular underlaying of syllables may be quoted.

In example A above the underlaying according to the Haberl edition is
quite regular. The new Roma edition, however, gives a change of syllable
on the second crotchet of a group of four (counting the dot of the minim

as one crotchet), this syllable persisting through a group of three crotchets and a minim. This rhythmical formula is rare. B and D (if the underlaying in the Haberl edition is accepted) show a syllable on an isolated 'first' crotchet falling on a pulse beat. C is akin to A in the Roma underlaying, in that the change of syllable for the group takes place on the weak crotchet. E shows two different underlayings of the 'crotchet—minim—crotchet' rhythmic figure.

On very rare occasions a single quaver following a dotted crotchet carries a separate syllable. Two examples are given below: the second is doubtful. Examples of a change of syllable on groups beginning with a pair of quavers are to be found in the next section.★

IV. The Haberl Edition seems to take great pains to avoid breaking the rule that quavers after a dotted minim and crotchets after a dotted semi-breve must not carry a new syllable. The new Roma Edition appears to be quite prepared to allow both irregularities to occur in the early works, and it is worthy of note that Jeppesen in editing the Mantua masses (R. XVIII, XIX) seems to have few qualms about using the same means of underlaying.

The cases quoted below are worthy of careful study. In the second example the 'Roma' editor does not hesitate to place two syllables on a pair of crotchets after a dotted semibreve. The Haberl underlaying is one of the rare occasions on which the rule is broken and, in addition, a change of syllable occurs on the following minim after a pair of crotchets.

★ The passage in the Ad Fugam Mass (Et unam sanctam Catholicam Ecclesiam) which contains four instances of a syllable on a single quaver, according to the Haberl edition, is shown to be spurious (c.f. P. XI., p. 63, with R. IV. 82).

V and VI are merely notational directions.

In the sesquialtera triple times much the same processes of underlaying are found if the minim is substituted for the crotchet and so forth. The minim seems to be treated rather more freely (in word underlaying) in $\mathbf{O}_2^3$ than the crotchet in $\mathbb{C}$. This confirms the proposition that the $\mathbf{O}_2^3$ minim is 1½ times longer than the $\mathbb{C}$ crotchet. A few examples must suffice to show some of the exceptional practices already discussed in $\mathbb{C}$ as they occur in the triple times.

Repetition of words

Zarlino's eighth rule is concerned with the repetition of words of the text in their musical setting. Palestrina allows himself quite a large amount of repetition, not only of 'some part of the speech whose sense is complete' but of single words or incomplete phrases, nor does he confine this treatment to 'words that have in them some grave sense and are worthy of consideration'.

The Cantus voice in the Motet 'Misso Herodes spiculatore' (P. V, p. 60 R. III, p. 74) sings the text thus:

'Misso Herodes spiculatore,—[spiculatore,—spiculatore,—] praecepit amputari caput Joánnis Baptistae,—[caput Joannis Baptistae,]—in carcere; quo audito discipuli ejus, [—ejus,]—[quo audito discipuli ejus—] venerunt et tulerunt corpus ejus, et posuerunt illud in monumento, [—in monumento,—in monumento.]'

In the Motet 'Puer qui natus est' (P. I, p. 50 R. V, p. 64) even more repetition may be found:

'Puer qui natus est plus quam propheta est, [—plus quam propheta est,] —[puer qui natus est, plus quam propheta est;] hic est enim, de quo Salvator ait—[hic est enim de quo Salvator ait,—] [de quo Salvator ait]—: inter natos mulierum, —[mulierum,]—[inter natos mulierum,]—[mulierum,]—non surrexit major,—[non surrexit major,] —[non surrexit major,]—[non surrexit major,]—Joanne Baptista—[Joanne Baptista]— [Joanne Baptista].

Often, as may be seen especially in the second instance quoted, the repetition does emphasize an important word or complete phrase, but the choice of (for example) 'ejus' in the first quotation seems arbitrary. The real reason for much of the repetition may be Palestrina's awareness that the claims of the music and of the text must be held in just balance.

A short illustration with the music may illustrate this point.

Ex. 238   (R.V. p.15) P.I. p.14

Here the repetition of the word 'portabat' is necessary for the completion of the musical phrase.

Omission of words

Occasionally, especially in the more homophonic sections and in settings for double choir, Palestrina omits words or phrases of the text in one voice, giving it rests while other voices sing the missing words. This most often happens after a sentence has been completed, and the selection of the words sung generally makes reasonably complete sense in itself.

Sometimes, however, the omission has less satisfactory results on the sense of the words which remain. The following example shows a rather awkward situation which arise because the words 'et ceciderunt' are omitted from the Cantus part in the sentence 'Et omnes angeli stabant in circuitu throni, et seniorum, et quatuor animalium, et ceciderunt in conspectu throni, et adoraverunt Deum, dicentes: Amen.'

Nevertheless, Palestrina's treatment of the text in this wider aspect of word underlaying shows a remarkable sense of balance between the claims of the music quâ music and the words.

Penultimate Syllable

Zarlino's ninth rule is concerned with the setting of the penultimate syllable of a work or section. Palestrina often uses quite long melismata at this point when the syllable in question is long. Sometimes the lengthening-out has more than purely musical significance, and seems to be used to emphasise the meaning of the word; the setting of 'aeternum' cited below is a good instance of this.

Last Syllable

The last of Zarlino's rules deals with the final syllable of a composition or section. He implies that the final syllable and the last note should coincide. Palestrina complies with this ruling almost invariably, so far as the present writer's observation goes, *in the top voice*. The lower voices, however, are much more freely treated. Although there is some difference of opinion in the various editions on the matter (see the second example below), many clear-cut instances may be found.

Palestrina's underlaying of the text conforms to a very considerable extent to the precepts which Zarlino lays down.   There is, however, none of the stiffness in his word underlaying which Zarlino's hard and fast rules suggest. Palestrina seems to have achieved an almost perfect blend of musical and verbal claims. His underlaying of the words is almost always natural and unstrained, yet at the same time the easy flow of the music seems to be unfettered by the problems of fitting the text. The music and words run hand in hand so naturally that the technique behind the art is hidden.

Palestrina's technique in word-setting, so far as it can be judged in detail, is perhaps as perfect an example of his art as any of the other technical factors over which he showed such consummate mastery. As in these other cases, moderation and restraint are the outstanding features.

TABLE OF MUSICAL ILLUSTRATIONS

Example Number	'Roma' Reference Vol.	Page	Haberl Reference Vol.	Page	Name of Work	Measure
1	Table of Modes					
2	Dorian Melodic Shapes					
3a	R. XII	41	P. IV	119	Motet: Orietur stella	19
b	R. XII	42	P. IV	119	Motet: Orietur stella	36
4a	R. XII	44	P. IV	121	Motet: Orietur stella	75
b	R. XII	44	P. IV	121	Motet: Orietur stella	68
c	R. XII	43	P. IV	120	Motet: Orietur stella	60
5a	Phrygian melodic shapes					
b	R. XI	6	P. V	119	Motet: Commissa est	2
c	R. XI	3	P. V	117	Motet: Domine, quando	4
6	R. XI	15	P. V	126	Motet: Super flumina	29
7a	R. XI	4	P. V	117	Motet: Domine, quando	16
b	R. XI	4	P. V	118	Motet: Domine, quando	34
c	R. XI	5	P. V	118	Motet: Domine, quando	57
d	R. XI	6	P. V	119	Motet: Commissa est	18
8	Plainsong					
9	Plainsong					
10	R. VI	67	P. XII	54	Missa Brevis, Gloria	66
11a	R. III	108	P. V	86	Motet: Quam pulchri sunt	89
b	R. III	109	P. V	87	Motet: Tollite jugum meum	5
12a	R. VIII	148	P. III	114	Motet: Haec dies (a 6)	12
b	R. VII	81	P. II	61	Motet: Gaude Barbara	60
c	R. III	44	P. V	37	Motet: Lauda Zion	50
13a	R. IV	19	P. XI	15	Missa: De Beata Virgine, Hosanna	1
b	R. X	141	P. XIII	103	Missa: Secunda, a 5. Hosanna	1
14a	R. VI	118	P. XII	91	Missa: 'L'homme armé'. Credo	165
b	R. VI	127	P. XII	97	Missa: 'L'homme armé'. Hosanna	1
15a	R. VI	101	P. XII	78	Missa: 'L'homme armé'. Gloria	1
b	R. VI	115	P. XII	89	Missa: 'L'homme armé'. Credo	104
c d	R. XIV	95	P. VIII	72	Hymn 17: Vexilla Regis, v. 6	7
16	R. VI	74	P. XII	59	Missa Brevis. Sanctus	1
17a			P. XXII	72	Missa: Hodie Christus. Agnus	22
b			P. XIX	66	Missa: O Virgo simul. Gloria	1
c			P. XIX	64	Missa: O Virgo simul. Christe	16
d			P. XXII	144	Missa: Confitebor. Hosanna	39
e			P. XXII	57	Missa: Hodie Christus. Crucifixus	26
f	R. XVI	152	P. XXVII	116	Magnificat 21: Lib II. Tone 5, v. 8	15
g			P. XIX	21	Missa: In illo tempore. Agnus	43
h	R. VII	69	P. II	53	Motet: Exi cito	75
i	R. XVI	120	P. XXVII	94	Magnificat 18: Lib II. Tone, 2 v. 10	30
18a	R. III	101	P. V	80	Motet: Doctor Bonus	19
b	R. XI	78	P. V	176	Motet: Adoramus te	13
c	R. XXI	31	P. XV	26	Missa: In te, Domine. Gloria	58
d	R. IV	192	P. XI	148	Missa: Papae Marcelli. Benedictus	10
e	R. XXI	34	P. XV	29	Missa: In te Domine. Credo	13
f	R. XXI	119	P. XV	95	Missa: Delixi quoniam. Credo	12
g	R. XXI	39	P. XV	32	Missa: In te Domine. Crucifixus	40
h	R. XV	96	P. XIV	71	Missa: Nigra sum. Gloria	29
i	R. XXI	93	P. XV	74	Missa: Quam pulchra. Et iterum	50
j	R. XXI	93	P. XV	74	Missa: Quam pulchra. Et iterum	52
k	R. XXI	95	P. XV	76	Missa: Quam pulchra. Sanctus	19
l	R. XXI	93	P. XV	75	Missa: Quam pulchra. Et iterum	62
m	R. III	109	P. V	87	Motet: Tollite jugum	6
n	R. III	112	P. V	89	Motet: Tollite jugum	47
o	R. XVI	236	P. XXVII	185	Magnificat 28: Lib III. Tone 4, v. 8	7

Example Number	'Roma' Reference Vol.	Page	Haberl Reference Vol.	Page	Name of Work	Measure
18p	R. XVI	237	P. XXVII	185	Magnificat 28: Lib III. Tone 4, v. 8	22
q	R. XXI	88	P. XV	71	Missa: Quam pulchra. Credo	71
19a b c	Hypothetical					
20a			P. XXII	95	Missa: Fratres ego. Et iterum	25
b	R. VIII	145	P. III	112	Motet: Rex pacificus	32
c	R. VII	120	P. II	90	Motet: Veni, Domine	57
d			P. XXII	14	Missa: Laudate Dominum. Gloria	113
21a	R. VI	243	P. XII	186	Missa: Ut Re Mi. Benedictus	23
b			P. XXI	42	Missa: Ascendo ad Patrem. Gloria	23
c	R. V	85	P. I	65	Motet: Hodie nata est	29
d			P. XXIII	59	Missa: Beatus Laurentius. Crucifixus	20
e			P. XIX	48	Missa: Petra Sancta. Credo	57
f			P. VII	63	Motet: Ecce nunc	15
g			P. XVI	46	Missa: Emendemus. Gloria	33
h			P. XVII	72	Missa: Memor esto. Credo	40
22a	R. VII	155	P. II	116	Motet: Cantabo Domino	27
b	R. X	164	P. XIII	120	Missa: O Magnum mysterium. Gloria	137
c			P. VII 11 and 12		Motet: O pretiosum	31
23			P. VI	152	Motet: Pater noster (a 8) D	31
24a	R. VIII	63	P. III	49	Motet: O singulare praesidium	41
b	R. VIII	63	P. III	49	Motet: O singulare praesidium	42
c	R. VIII	167	P. III	128	Motet: O bone Jesu	49
25a			P. XXI	14	Missa: Regina coeli. Credo, ' Et in Spiritum '	63
b			P. XXI	85	Missa: Qual è il più. Agnus II	24
c			P. XXI	96	Missa: Tu es Petrus. Credo	27
d			P. XXII	100	Missa: Fratres ego. Sanctus	23
e			P. XXI	21	Missa: Regina Coeli. Agnus II	25
f			P. XXI	67	Missa: Qual è il più. Gloria	47
g			P. VI	87	Motet: Regina mundi	20
h			P. VI	63	Motet: Etenim Pascha	35
26	Hypothetical					
27a	R. VII	164	P. II	123	Motet: Tu es Petrus	45
b	R. XXI	72	P. XV	59	Missa: Sine nomine. (a 4). Agnus II	26
c	R. XXI	50	P. XV	42	Missa: In te, Domine. Agnus II	11
28a	R. IV	171	P. XI	131	Missa: Papae Marcelli. Gloria	9
b	R. I	8	P. X	8	Missa: Ecce sacerdos. Gloria	83
c	R. IV	175	P. XI	134	Missa: Papae Marcelli. Gloria	81
d			P. VI	120	Motet: Beata es, Virgo Maria D	33
29a	R. XVI	89	P. XXVII	70	Magnificat 15: Lib I. Tone 7, v. 8	1
b	R. XVI	161	P. XXVII	124	Magnificat 22: Lib II. Tone 6, v. 6	31
c	R. V	53	P. I	42	Motet: O vera summa	69
30a	R. VI	83	P. XII	65	Missa: Brevis. Agnus II	50
b	R. VI	81-82	P. XII	65	Missa: Brevis. Agnus II	26
c	R. XVI	236	P. XXVIII	185	Magnificat 28: Lib III. Tone 4, v. 8	88
31a	R. V	42	P. I	34	Motet: Crucem sanctam	21
b	R. V	211	P. I	157	Motet: Virgo prudentissima	82
32a	R. VI	78	P. XII	62	Missa: Brevis. Agnus I	7½
b	R. VI	78	P. XII	62	Missa: Brevis. Agnus I	15
c	R. VI	82	P. XII	65	Missa: Brevis. Agnus II	35
33	Hypothetical					
34a	R. V	150	P. I	111	Motet: Dum complerentur	21
b	R. IV	197	P. XI	152	Missa: Papae Marcelli. Agnus II	6
c			P. XX	91	Missa: Octavi Toni. Credo	75
d	R. XV	145	P. XIV	147	Missa: Sicut lilium. Credo	82
e	R. XIV	113	P. VIII	85	Hymn 21: Petrus Beatus	13
35	R. VI	81	P. XII	64	Missa: Brevis. Agnus II	20
36	R. VI	68	P. XII	55	Missa: Brevis. Credo	22
37a	R. VIII	65	P. III	51	Motet: O singulare praesidium	81
b	R. VIII	70	P. III	54	Motet: Quid habes Hester?	77
c	R. VIII	109	P. III	84	Motet: Gaude praesul	48
d	R. III	22	P. V	19	Motet: Hodie Beata Virgo	65
e	R. III	22	P. V	19	Motet: Hodie Beata Virgo	61
f	R. III	20	P. V	18	Motet: Hodie Beata Virgo	17
38a			P. VI	141	Motet: O Domine Jesu	20
b			P. VI	170	Motet: Regina Coeli D	92
39a	R. VI	67	P. XII	53	Missa: Brevis. Gloria	60

Example Number	'Roma' Reference Vol.	Page	Haberl Reference Vol.	Page	Name of Work	Measure
39b	R. V	63	P. I	50	Motet: Panis quem ego dabo	89
c	R. III	102	P. V	81	Motet: Doctor bonus	38
d	R. III	56	P. V	46	Motet: Magnus Sanctus Paulus	63
40	Hypothetical					
41a	R. XVI	111	P. XXVII	88	Magnificat 18: Lib II. Tone 2, v. 2	11
b			P. VI	122	Motet: Ave Maria (a 8)	20
42a	R. XIV	10	P. VIII	9	Hymn 2: Christe Redemptor. v. 5	5
b	R. XIV	37	P. VIII	29	Hymn 8: Ad preces nostras. v. 1	4
43a	R. XIV	143	P. VIII	107	Hymn 27: Deus tuorum militum. v. 3	16
b	R. XIV	221	P. VIII	167	Hymn 42: Prima lux surgens. v. 3	10
c			P. XXI	52	Missa: Ascendo ad Patrem. Credo, 'Et in Spiritum'	41
d			P. XXI	59	Missa: Ascendo ad Patrem. Agnus I	23
44a	R. VI	220	P. XII	168	Missa: Ut, Re, Mi. Kyrie	82
b			P. XXI	136	Missa: Viri Galilaei. Agnus II	20
c	R. XII	59	P. IV	131	Motet: Surge, Petre	20
d	R. XI	125	P. IV	29	Motet: Vulnerasti cor meum	29
45a			P. XXIII	138	Missa: Veni Creator. Credo. 'Et in Spiritum'	60
b			P. VII	12	Motet: O pretiosum	32
46a			P. VI	27	Motet: Quodcunque ligaveris	76
b	R. III	39	P. V	33	Motet: Benedicta sit	18
47a	R. VI	19	P. XII	17	Missa: Spem in alium. Credo	170
b	R. VI	70	P. XII	56	Missa: Brevis. Credo	61
c			P. XXIII	105	Missa: Assumpta est Maria: Gloria, Qui tollis	54
d	R. IV	187	P. XI	144	Missa: Papae Marcelli. Credo	193
48a			P. XXII	33	Missa: Laudate Dominum. Benedictus	40
b	R. XI	62	P. V	164	Motet: Eja, ergo	45
49	R. VI	64	P. XII	51	Missa: Brevis. Kyrie	53
50			P. XXIII	120	Missa: Assumpta est Maria. Agnus II	15
51a	R. III	112	P. V	89	Motet: Tollite jugum meum	42
b	R. III	112	P. V	89	Motet: Tollite jugum meum	45
52			P. VI	29	Motet: Assumpta est Maria	43
53			P. XXII	153	Missa: Confitebor. Agnus II	28
54			P. XXII	71	Missa: Hodie Christus. Hosanna	16
55a	R. VIII	46	P. III	36	Motet: Inclytae Sanctae Virginis	22
b			P. XXIII	97	Missa: Assumpta est Maria. Kyrie	23
56a			P. XXIII	121	Missa: Assumpta est Maria. Agnus II	48
b			P. VII	36	Motet: Ecce nunc benedicite	13
c	R. XX	125	P. XXVI	110	Litaniae Domini. (V.) D	48
57a			P. XXII	69	Missa:Hodie Christus. Benedictus	22
b	R. XIV	42	P. VIII	32	Hymn: Ad preces nostras. v. 5	43
c	R. IV	157	P. XI	120	Missa: Salvum me fac. Hosanna	19
58a	R. VIII	93	P. III	72	Motet: Jubilate Deo	71
b	R. X	33	P. XIII	25	Missa: Secunda (a 4). Hosanna	29
c	R. VI	126	P. XII	97	Missa: 'L'homme armé'. Sanctus	86
59a	R. I	3	P. X	4	Missa: Ecce Sacerdos. Kyrie	62
b	R. I	61	P. X	54	Missa: O Regem coeli. Agnus II	48
c			P. XXII	119	Missa:Confitebor. Gloria	60
60a	R. X	7	P. XIII	6	Missa: Prima (a 4) Lauda Sion. Credo	55
b	R. VI	65	P. XII	52	Missa: Brevis .Gloria	11
c	R. VI	62	P. XII	50	Missa: Brevis. Kyrie	15
d	R. X	9	P. XIII	8	Missa: Prima (a 4). Credo	96
e	R. VI	75	P. XII	60	Missa: Brevis. Sanctus	44
f			P. VII	155	Motet: Apparuit gratia	40
g			P. XVI	106	Missa: Tu es pastor. Agnus I	29
h	R. X	15	P. XIII	12	Missa: Prima (a 4). Agnus I	10
i			P. XXIII	127	Missa: Veni Creator. Gloria	31
j	R. X	131	P. XIII	97	Missa: Secunda (a 5). Credo	85
61a	R. X	105	P. XIII	78	Missa: Prima (a 5). Hosanna	10
b	R. XVI	226	P. XXVII	176	Magnificat 27: Lib III. Tone 3, v. 12	9
c	R. V	14	P. I	13	Motet: O Antoni	84
d	R. VIII	49	P. III	38	Motet: Inclytae sanctae virginis	70
62a	R. XV	39	P. XIV	29	Missa: Jam Christus. Benedictus	6
b	R. XV	45	P. XIV	34	Missa: Panis quem ego. Kyrie	15
c	R. XV	25	P. XIV	19	Missa: Jam Christus. Gloria	67

Example Number	'Roma' Reference Vol.	Page	Haberl Reference Vol.	Page	Name of Work	Measure
62d	R. XV	15	P. XIV	10	Missa: Aeterna Christi. Benedictus	30
e	R. XV	37	P. XIV	28	Missa: Jam Christus. Pleni sunt	8
f	R. XV	67	P. XIV	51	Missa: Panis quem ego. Agnus I	12
g	R. XV	48	P. XIV	36	Missa: Panis quem ego. Gloria	8
h	R. XV	45	P. XIV	34	Missa: Panis quem ego. Kyrie	13
63a			P. XVI	26	Missa: Sanctorum meritis. Gloria	66
b	R. XV	36	P. XIV	27	Missa: Jam Christus. Sanctus	32
c	R. XV	91	P. XIV	67	Missa: Nigra sum. Kyrie	35
d	R. XVII	134	P. IX	97	Offertory: 33. Sacerdotes Domini	29
e	R. XV	83	P. XIV	61	Missa: Iste confessor. Sanctus	14
f	R. XV	97	P. XIV	71	Missa: Nigra sum. Gloria	33
g	R. XV	49	P. XIV	37	Missa: Panis quem ego. Gloria	26
h	R. XV	139	P. XIV	102	Missa: Sicut liluim. Gloria	101
i	R. XV	139	P. XIV	102	Missa: Sicut liluim. Gloria	102
j	R. XV	60	P. XIV	46	Missa: Panis quem ego. Credo	160
k	R. XV	82	P. XIV	61	Missa: Iste confessor. Sanctus	6
l	R. XV	167	P. XIV	122	Missa: Nasce la gioja. Gloria	42
m			P. XXII	46	Missa: Hodie Christus. Gloria	24
n	R. XVI	145	P. XXVII	111	Magnificat: Lib II. Tone 4, v. 12	14
64a			P. XIX	48	Missa: Petra Sancta. Credo	57
b			P. XXI	74	Missa: Qual è il più. Crucifixus	22
c			P. XXIII	59	Missa: Beatus Laurentius. Credo	91
d	R. XVII	185	P. IX	138	Offertory. 45. Expectans	30
e	R. XIV	9	P. VIII	7	Hymn: Christe Redemptor. v. 3	$7\frac{1}{2}$
65a	R. X	86	P. XIII	63	Missa: Prima (a 5). Gloria	46
b			P. VI	84	Motet: Hodie gloriosa	35
66a	R. II	15	P. XXVIII	15	Madrigal. Book I. 7	9
b			P. XXVIII	162	Madrigal. Book III. 11	21
c	R. II	172	P. XXVIII	224	Madrigal. Book III. 25. (Roma. Book 1 35)	38
67a			P. XX	45	Missa: Regina coeli. Hosanna	15
b	R. X	105	P. XIII	78	Missa: Prima (a 5). Hosanna	6
c			P. XXI	55	Missa: Ascendo ad Patrem. Sanctus	45
68			P. VI	138	Motet: O bone Jesu D	61
69 a b	Worcester Mediaeval Harmony. p. 50					
70	Hypothetical					
71a	R. III	131	P. V	104	Motet: Beatus vir	61
b	R. III	133	P. V	106	Motet: Veni, Sponsa	29
c	R. VI	121	P. XII	93	Missa: 'L'homme armé'. Credo	224
72a	R. XVII	237	P. IX	175	Offertory: 57. Assumpta	58
b	R. XI	39	P. V	146	Motet: Ego sum panis	12
73a	R. I	159	P. X	133	Missa: Ad coenam agni. Agnus I	13
b	R. I	20	P. X	18	Missa: Ecce sacerdos. Credo	258
c	R. VIII	174	P. III	134	Motet: Surge, illuminare	6
74a	R. VII	187	P. II	140	Motet: Notas facite populis	36
b	R. VII	101	P. II	76	Motet: Peccantem me quotidie	61
c			P VII	129	Motet: Ave Regina coelorum	85
75a			P. XXI	108	Missa: Tu es Petrus. Agnus I	34
b	R. VII	187	P. II	140	Motet: Notas facite populis	40
c	R. XV	167	P. XIV	122	Missa: Nasce la gioja. Gloria	45
76	R. III	22	P. V	19	Motet: Hodie Beata Virgo	60
77 a b c d	Hypothetical					
78a	R. IV	66	P. XI	51	Missa: Sine Nomine. Benedictus	25
b	R. VII	105	P. II	80	Motet: Dominus Jesus	71
79	R. I	23	P. X	20	Missa: Ecce Sacerdos. Sanctus	77
80a	R. I	101	P. X	86	Missa: Gabriel Archangelus. Gloria	123
b	R. VIII	157	P. III	121	Motet: Judica me	38
81a			P. XXII	15	Missa: Laudate Dominum. Gloria	128
b			P. XXIII	125	Missa: Veni Creator. Kyrie II	$9\frac{1}{2}$
82	Gibbons: Hosanna to the Son of David					20
83			P. XVIII	141	Missa: Te Deum. Benedictus	36
84	R. XII	3	P. IV	92	Motet: Laetus hyperboreum	32
85a			P. XXII	144	Missa: Confitebor tibi. Hosanna	41
b	R. XVI	227	P. XXVII	177	Magnificat 27: Tone 3. (a 6), v. 12	30
c			P. XX	75	Missa: Quando lieta sperai. Hosanna	4
86	R. X	33	P. XIII	25	Missa: Secunda (Primi Toni). (a 4). Hosanna	16

Example Number	'Roma' Reference Vol.	Page	Haberl Reference Vol.	Page	Name of Work	Measure
87a			P. XXII	67	Missa: Hodie Christus. Hosanna	29
b	R. VIII	48	P. III	38	Motet: Inclytae sanctae virginis	55
c	R. VIII	49	P. III	38	Motet: Inclytae sanctae virginis	67
88a			P. XXII	153	Missa: Confitebor tibi. Agnus II	38
b	R. XXI	16	P. XV	13	Missa: Dies sanctificatus. Credo	174
89a	R. XXI	173	P. XV	141	Missa: Ave Maria. Hosanna	9
b			P. XXIII	44	Missa: In minoribus duplicibus. Hosanna	20
90a			P. XXIII	140	Missa: Veni Creator. Sanctus	45
b	R. XIV	95	P. VIII	72	Hymn 17: Vexilla Regis. v. 6	12
91a	R. III	11	P. V	10	Motet: Valde honorandus est	73
b	R. III	24	P. V	21	Motet: Ave Maria	43
c	R. III	60	P. V	49	Motet: Surge propera. (a 4)	65
d			P. XVIII	83	Missa: Sine nomine (a 5). Sanctus	13
e			P. XVIII	32	Missa: Veni Sponsa Christi. Sanctus	16
92	Hypothetical					
93a	R. V	182	P. I	135	Motet: Et omnes angeli	47
b	R. V	23	P. I	21	Motet: Hodie beata Virgo	68
c	R. V	86	P. I	66	Motet: Hodie nata est	50
d	R. V	120	P. I	89	Motet: Hic est discipulus	67
94e	Hypothetical					
95a			P. XX	27	Missa: Regina coeli. Gloria	46
b			P. XVIII	9	Missa: Ave Regina. Credo	37
96	R. VI	55	P. XII	44	Missa: Primi Toni (a 4). Sanctus	84
97	Hypothetical					
98a			P. XIX	14	Missa: In illo tempore. Credo	191
b	R. VI	85	P. XII	66	Missa: de feria. Christe	66
99	Hypothetical					
100	R. VI	159	P. XII	123	Missa: Repleatur os meum. Credo	185
101a	R. III	75	P. V	60	Motet: Misso Herodes	24
b	R. V	21	P. I	19	Motet: Hodie beata Virgo	29
102a	R. V	215	P. I	160	Motet: Maria Virgo	36
b	R. IV	144	P. XI	110	Missa: Salvum me fac. Credo	91
103a			P. XXIII	26	Missa: In minoribus duplicibus. Kyrie	17
b	R. V	133	P. I	99	Motet: Unus ex duobus	42
104	R. XVI	34	P. XXVII	27	Magnificat 6: Lib I. Tone 6, v. 5	22
105	Hypothetical					
106a	R. XVII	107	P. IX	78	Offertory 26: Angelus Domini	61
b	R. I	55	P. X	48	Missa: O Regem coeli. Benedictus	6
107a			P. XX	17	Missa: Descendit Angelus. Benedictus	31
b	R. IV	88	P. XI	68	Missa: Ad fugam. Agnus I	11
c	R. I	50	P. X	44	Missa: O Regem coeli. Credo	175
108	R. XI	143	P. IV	42	Motet: Surge propera. (a 5)	7
109	R. VI	66	P. XII	53	Missa: Brevis. Gloria	48
110a	R. VI	76	P. XII	59	Missa: Brevis. Sanctus	29
b	R. VI	98	P. XII	76	Missa: 'L'homme armé'. Christe	9
c	R. VI	182	P. XII	140	Missa: De Beata Virgine. Gloria	38
111	R. VI	68	P. XII	55	Missa: Brevis. Credo	21
112a	R. XVI	80	P. XXVII	63	Magnificat 14: Lib I. Tone 6, v. 2	9
b	R. IV	35	P. XI	28	Missa: Inviolata. Credo	16
113	Hypothetical					
114	Hypothetical					
115a	R. VI	81	P. XII	64	Missa: Brevis. Agnus II	20
b	R. III	41	P. V	35	Motet: Benedicta sit	63
116a	R. VI	70	P. XII	56	Missa: Brevis. Credo	59
b	R. VI	70	P. XII	56	Missa: Brevis. Credo	68
117a	R. X	164	P. XIII	120	Missa: O magnum mysterium. Gloria	137
b	R. X	125	P. XIII	92	Missa: Secunda (a 5). Gloria	97
c	R. X	101	P. XIII	75	Missa: Prima (a 5). Credo	197
118	R. XV	59	P. XIV	45	Missa: Panis quem ego. Credo	130
119a	R. VI	64	P. XII	51	Missa: Brevis. Kyrie	53
b	R. VI	67	P. XII	54	Missa: Brevis. Gloria	74
c	R. VI	73	P. XII	58	Missa: Brevis. Credo	136
120a	R. VI	5	P. XII	6	Missa: Spem in alium. Gloria	15
b	R. IV	88	P. XI	68	Missa: Ad fugam. Agnus I	8
121	R. X	2	P. XIII	1	Missa: Prima (a 4). Christe	7
122	Hypothetical					
123	R. VI	77	P. XII	61	Missa: Brevis. Hosanna	3

Example Number	'Roma' Reference Vol.	Page	Haberl Reference Vol.	Page	Name of Work	Measure
124	R. XIII	200	P. XXV	175	Lamentation 31: (a 5). Feria VI, Lect I	41
125	R. VI	79	P. XII	62	Missa: Brevis. Agnus I	30
126	R. IV	191	P. XI	147	Missa: Papae Marcelli. Sanctus	62
127a	R.XII	10	P. IV	97	Motet: Paucitas dierum	23
b	R. VII	98	P. II	73	Motet: Peccantem me quotidie	1
c	R. XIII	29	P. XXV	26	Lamentation 7: Sab. Sanct. Lect. I	64
128a	R. VII	98	P. II	74	Motet: Peccantem me quotidie	8
b	R. I	46	P. X	41	Missa: O Regem Coeli. Credo	73
129a	R. IV	55	P. XI	42	Missa: Sine nomine. Gloria	17
b			P. XXI	118	Missa: Viri Galilaei. Gloria	89
130	R. IV	25	P. XI	20	Missa: De Beata. Agnus II	41
131a	R. XV	41	P. XIV	31	Missa: Jam Christus. Agnus I	28
b			P. XXIII	89	Missa: O Sacrum convivium. Sanctus	30
132a	R. X	41	P. XIII	31	Missa: Tertia (a 4). Gloria	23
b			P. XVIII	50	Missa: Vestiva i colli. Credo	83
c			P. XXIII	11	Missa: In majoribus duplicibus. Credo	67
d			P. XVI	70	Missa: Sacerdos et Pontifex. Credo	28
133a	R. X	80	P. XIII	60	Missa: Prima (a 5). Christe	2
b	R. XV	14	P. XIV	10	Missa: Aeterna Christi munera. Benedictus	4
c	R. XV	3	P. XIV	2	Missa: Aeterna Christi munera. Gloria	4
d			P. XIX	33	Missa, Già fu chi m'hebbe. Credo	179
e	R. XX	125			Litaniae Domini (a 8)	117
134a	R. XIII	227	P. XXV	197	Lamentation 34: Sab. Sanct. Lect. I	108
b	R. XI	6	P. V	119	Motet: Commissa mea	5
135a	R. XVI	92	P. XXVII	72	Magnificat 15: Lib I. Tone 7. Gloria	23
b	R. XV	22	P. XIV	16	Missa: Jam Christus. Kyrie II	21
c	R. XV	35	P. XIV	26	Missa: Jam Christus. Sanctus	9
136			P. XIX	27	Missa: Già fu chi. Gloria	104
137a	R. XV	12	P. XIV	8	Missa: Aeterna Christi. Sanctus	2
b			P. XIX	75	Missa: O Virgo simul. Crucifixus	18
138a	R. VI	96	P. XII	74	Missa: De feria. Agnus II	38
138b			P. XXIII	88	Missa: 'O Sacrum Convivium'. Sanctus	4
139a	R. VI	81	P. XII	64	Missa: Brevis. Agnus II	20
b	R. XV	21	P. XIV	15	Missa: Jam Christus. Christe	17
c	R. VI	93	P. XII	72	Missa: De feria. Agnus I	45
140			P. XXXI	93	Hymni Feriales. IV (Feriae V) D	15
141a	R. XV	22	P. XIV	16	Missa: Jam Christus. Kyrie II	17
b	R. XV	69	P. XIV	52	Missa: Panis quem ego. Agnus II	3
c			P. XVII	17	Missa: Quem dicunt. Sanctus	56
142	R. XV	80	P. XIV	60	Missa: Iste confessor. Credo	72
143a	R. VI	129	P. XII	100	Missa: 'L'homme armé'. Benedictus	34
b	R. XVI	86	P. XXVII	67	Magnificat 15: Lib I. Tone 7, v. 2	2
c	R. XVI	11	P. XXVII	9	Magnificat 2: Lib I. Tone 2, v. 9	4
144a			P. XVI	85	Missa: Tu es pastor. Kyrie	16
b	R. III	74	P. V	59	Motet: Quae est ista	85
c	R. XI	44	P. V	150	Motet: Sicut cervus	48
d	R. XI	49	P. V	154	Motet: Ave Regina	53
145a			P. XXIII	116	Missa: Assumpta est. Benedictus	19
b			P. XXIII	121	Missa: Assumpta est. Agnus II	40
146a	R. VI	110	P. XII	85	Missa: 'L'homme armé'. Credo	12
b	R. VI	102	P. XII	79	Missa: 'L'homme armé'. Gloria	20
147a	R. VI	88	P. XII	69	Missa: De feria. Sanctus	33
b	R. VI	99	P. XII	77	Missa: L''homme armé'. Christe	27
148a	R. VI	63	P. XII	50	Missa: Brevis. Christe	4
b	R. VI	89	P. XII	69	Missa: De feria. Sanctus	41
149a			P. XX	70	Missa: Quando lieta. Credo	209
b	R. XI	96	P. IV	7	Motet: Trahe me	49
150	R. XV	48	P. XIV	36	Missa: Panis quem ego. Gloria	14
151	R. XIII	84	P. XXV	73	Lamentations 16: Sabbato Sancto. Lect.I.	107
152a	R. VI	246	P. XII	189	Missa: Ut, Re, Mi. Agnus I	29
b	R. VI	247	P. XII	189	Missa: Ut, Re, Mi. Agnus I	42
c	R. VI	247	P. XII	189	Missa: Ut, Re, Mi. Agnus I	51
153a	R. I	12	P. X	11	Missa: Ecce sacerdos. Credo	35
b	R. I	20	P. X	18	Missa: Ecce sacerdos. Credo	259
c	R. VI	98	P. XII	75	Missa: 'L'homme armé'. Kyrie	22
d	R. XIII	212	P. XXV	184	Lamentations 31: Feria VI. Lect. II	103
154a	R. XIII	140	P. XXV	122	Lamentations 23: Feria VI. Lect. II	146

Example Number	'Roma' Reference Vol.	Page	Haberl Reference Vol.	Page	Name of Work	Measure
154b	R. XIII	67	P. XXV	59	Lamentations 13: Feria VI. Lect. I	187
c	R. XIII	84	P. XXV	73	Lamentations 16: Sabbato Sancto. Lect.I.	122
155	R. XII	97–98	P. IV	158	Motet: Peccavimus	25
156a			P. XXIII	89	Missa: O Sacrum convivium. Sanctus	29
b			P. XX	120	Missa: Alma Redemptoris. Et iterum	11
c			P. VI	153	Motet: Pater noster	49
157a	R. XX	75	P. XXVI	69	Litaniae: de Beata Virgine Maria. I D	51
b	R. XX	76	P. XXVI	70	Litaniae: de Beata Virgine Maria. I D	71
158a	R. VI	26	P. XII	22	Missa: Spem in alium. Agnus I	28
b	R. VI	79	P. XII	63	Missa: Brevis. Agnus I	38
159a	R. III	27	P. V	23	Motet: Jesus junxit se	25
b	R. III	27	P. V	24	Motet: Jesus junxit se	32
c	R. VI	63	P. XII	50	Missa: Brevis. Christe	10
d			P. XXIII	99	Missa: Assumpta est Maria. Christe	19
e	R. III	31	P. V	27	Motet: O Rex gloriae	18
f	R. XV	55	P. XIV	41	Missa: Panis quem. Credo	27
g	R. I	104	P. X	88	Missa: Gabriel Archangelus. Credo	33
160a	R. VI	78	P. XII	62	Missa: Brevis. Agnus	1
b	R. XIV	153	P. VIII	115	Hymn 29: Inclyta. v. 5	5
c			P. XXIII	4	Missa: In majoribus duplicibus. Gloria	22
161	Morley: Plaine and easie introduction					
162	R. VI	174	P. XII	134	Missa: Repleatur os meum. Agnus II	41
163	R. XIV	142–3	P. VIII	107	Hymn 27: Deus tuorum militum. v. 3	6
164	R. XVI	3	P. XXVII	2	Magnificat: Lib I. Tone 1, v. 5	16
165a	R. III	110	P. V	87	Motet: Tollite jugum	18
b	R. III	109	P. V	87	Motet: Tollite jugum	10
c	R. XVI	236	P. XXVII	185	Magnificat: Lib. III. Tone 4, v. 8	6
d	R. XVI	237	P. XXVII	185	Magnificat: Lib. III. Tone 4, v. 8	19
166a	R. III	110	P. V	87	Motet: Tollite jugum meum	13
b	R. III	110	P. V	88	Motet: Tollite jugum meum	22
167	R. XVI	238	P. XXVII	186	Magnificat: Lib. III. Tone 4, v. 8	27
168a	R. III	124	P. V	98	Motet: Gaudent in coelis	87
b	R. VII	88	P. II	66	Motet: Gaude quia meruisti	99
169a	R. VII	46	P. II	36	Motet: Ascendo ad Patrem	78
b	R. XV	38	P. XIV	28	Missa: Jam Christus astra. Hosanna	7
c	R. IV	34	P. XI	27	Missa: Inviolata. Gloria	123
d	R. XIV	167	P. VIII	125	Hymn (32): Jesu corona virginum. v. 5	6
e			P. XX	104	Missa: Octavi Toni. Agnus II	11
f			P. XXIV	92	Missa: Sine titulo. Credo: Et vitam	7
170a	R. VI	55	P. XII	44	Missa: Primi Toni (a 4). Hosanna	35
b			P. XXIII	44	Missa: In minoribus duplicibus. Hosanna	27
171			P. VII	13	Motet: O pretiosum	57
172	R. XI	11	P. V	123	Motet: Anima mea turbata est	1–16
173	R. XI	8	P. V	121	Motet: Heu mihi Domine	1–10
174	R. VII	31	P. II	26	Motet: Coenantibus illis	1–10
175	R. VII	1	P. II	3	Motet: O virgo simul et Mater	1–9
176	R. XV	87	P. XIV	64	Missa: Iste confessor. Agnus II	1–6
177a	R. VIII	144	P. III	111	Motet: Rex pacificus	1–3
b			P. XX	53	Missa: Quando lieta sperai. Kyrie II	1
c	R. XV	120	P. XIV	88	Missa: Nigra sum. Hosanna	1
178	R. VII	47	P. II	37	Motet: Ego rogabo	1–9
179			P. XXIII	44	Missa: In minoribus duplicibus. Hosanna	1–9
180	R. XV	45	P. XIV	34	Missa: Panis quem ego. Kyrie	1–17
181	R. X	30	P. XIII	22	Missa: Secunda (a 4). Sanctus	1–10
182	R. XVI	11	P. XXVII	9	Magnificat 2: Tone II. (a 4), v. 9	1–7
183	R. I	1	P. X	3	Missa: Ecce sacerdos. Kyrie I	1–8
184	R. I	28	P. X	25	Missa: Ecce sacerdos. Agnus I	1–8
185			P. XXIII	88	Missa: O sacrum convivium. Sanctus	1–9
186	R. XV	17	P. XIV	13	Missa: Aeterna Christi munera. Agnus II	1–10
187	R. VI	169	P. XII	130	Missa: Repleatur os meum. Agnus I	1–11
188	R. IV	78	P. XI	60	Missa: Ad fugam. Credo	1–7
189	R. IV	89	P. XI	69	Missa: Ad fugam. Agnus II	1–10
190	R. IV	86	P. XI	67	Missa: Ad fugam. Benedictus	1–8
191			P. XVIII	116	Missa: Sacerdotes Domini. Gloria	1–12
192	R. XI	79	P. V	177	Motet: Surrexit Pastor bonus	1–8
193	R. XXI	21	P. XV	18	Missa: Dies sanctificatus. Agnus I	1–8
194	R. VI	63	P. XII	50	Missa: Brevis. Christe	7–11

Example Number	'Roma' Reference Vol.	Page	Haberl Reference Vol.	Page	Name of Work	Measure
195			P. XIX	109	Missa: Illumina oculos. Kyrie	1–8
196a	R. XI	173	P. IV	63	Motet: Quae est ista	1–3
b	R. XI	173	P. IV	63	Motet: Quae est ista	7–10
197a	R. VI	219	P. XII	167	Missa: Ut, Re, Mi. Kyrie	
b	R. VI	247	P. XII	189	Missa: Ut, Re, Mi. Agnus I	48–66
198	R. VI	128	P. XII	99	Missa: 'L'homme armé'. Benedictus	
199	R. VI	100	P. XII	77	Missa: 'L'homme armé'. Kyrie II	1–11
200	R. VI	204	P. XII	155	Missa: De Beata. Sanctus	27–35
201	R. V	45	P. I	37	Motet: O beata et gloriosa Trinitas	
202	Plainsong					
203	R. XIV	74	P. VIII	57	Hymn 13: Pange lingua. v. 1	1–43
204	R. XIV	8	P. VIII	6	Hymn 2: Christe Redemptor. v. 1	1–5
205	R. XIV	9	P. VIII	7	Hymn 2: Christe Redemptor. v. 3	1–6
206a	R. XIV	10	P. VIII	9	Hymn 2: Christe Redemptor. v. 5	1–5
b	R. XIV	11	P. VIII	9	Hymn 2: Christe Redemptor. v. 5	21
207a	R. XIV	12	P. VIII	10	Hymn 2: Christe Redemptor. v. 7	1–4
b	R. XIV	12	P. VIII	10	Hymn 2: Christe Redemptor. v. 7	7–10
208	R. VII	107	P. II	81	Motet: Tribularer si nescirem	
209			P. XX	80	Missa: Octavi Toni. Cantus Firmus taken from the Kyrie	
210			P. XX	83	Missa: Octavi Toni. Gloria	1–6
211			P. XX	80 et seq.	Missa: Octavi Toni. (Much used figures)	
212a	Plainsong					
b	R. XV	1	P. XIV	1	Missa: Aeterna Christi munera. Kyrie	1
c	R. XV	3	P. XIV	2	Missa: Aeterna Christi. Gloria	1
d	R. XV	6	P. XIV	4	Missa: Aeterna Christi. Credo	1
e	R. XV	12	P. XIV	8	Missa: Aeterna Christi. Sanctus	1
f	R. XV	15	P. XIV	11	Missa: Aeterna Christi. Hosanna	1
g	R. XV	16	P. XIV	11	Missa: Aeterna Christi. Agnus I	1
h	R. XV	17	P. XIV	13	Missa: Aeterna Christi. Agnus II	1
213a	R. XV	2	P. XIV	2	Missa: Aeterna Christi. Kyrie	30
b	R. XV	2	P. XIV	2	Missa: Aeterna Christi. Kyrie	34
c	R. XV	13	P. XIV	9	Missa: Aeterna Christi. Sanctus	27
d	R. XV	14	P. XIV	10	Missa: Aeterna Christi. Benedictus	11
e	R. XV	17	P. XIV	12	Missa: Aeterna Christi. Agnus I	24
214a	R. XVIII	1			Missa: In duplicibus (Minoribus I). (Mantua). Kyrie I	
b	R. XVIII	7			Missa: In duplicibus (Minoribus I.) (Mantua) (a) Gloria	1–5
					(b) Gloria	10–12
215a	1 R. V	149	P. I	111	Motet: Dum complerentur	1–5
	2		P. XVII	85	Missa: Dum complerentur. Kyrie	1–6
b	1 R. V	150	P. I	111	Motet: Dum complerentur	12–15
	2		P. XVII	86	Missa: Dum complerentur. Christe	1–5
c	1 R. V	154	P. I	115	Motet: Dum ergo essent	1–5
	2		P. XVII	87	Missa: Dum complerentur. Kyrie II	1–6
d	1 R. V	150	P. I	111	Motet: Dum complerentur	18–28
	2		P. XVII	87	Missa: Dum complerentur. Christe	11–22
e	1 R. V	152	P. I	114	Motet: Dum complerentur	65–69
	2		P. XVII	94	Missa: Dum complerentur. Gloria	119–124
f	1 R. V.	155	P. I	115	Motet: Dum ergo essent	18–23
	2		P. XVII	93	Missa: Dum complerentur. Gloria	96–100
g	1 R. V	151	P. I	112	Motet: Dum complerentur	42–48
	2		P. XVII	97	Missa: Dum complerentur. Credo	49–56
216a	R. IV	167	P. XI	128	Missa: Papae Marcelli. Kyrie I	1–5
b	R. IV	167	P. XI	128	Missa: Papae Marcelli. Kyrie I	1–4
c	R. IV	167	P. XI	128	Missa: Papae Marcelli. Kyrie I	2–5
d	R. IV	168	P. XI	128	Missa: Papae Marcelli. Kyrie I	18
e	R. IV	170	P. XI	130	Missa: Papae Marcelli. Kyrie II	1–4
f	R. IV	170	P. XI	130	Missa: Papae Marcelli. Kyrie II	1–5
217a	R. IV	175	P. XI	134	Missa: Papae Marcelli. Gloria	79
b	R. IV	176	P. XI	135	Missa: Papae Marcelli. Gloria	98
c	R. IV	177	P. XI	136	Missa: Papae Marcelli. Gloria	123
d	R. IV	177	P. XI	136	Missa: Papae Marcelli. Credo	1–5
e	R. IV	183	P. XI	142	Missa: Papae Marcelli. Credo	132–5
f	R. IV	186	P. XI	143	Missa: Papae Marcelli. Credo	172

Example Number	'Roma' Reference Vol.	Page	Haberl Reference Vol.	Page	Name of Work		Measure
217g	R. IV	189	P. XI	146	Missa: Papae Marcelli.	Sanctus	36
h	R. IV	189	P. XI	146	Missa: Papae Marcelli.	Sanctus	39
i	R. IV	191	P. XI	147	Missa: Papae Marcelli.	Sanctus	73
j	R. IV	194	P. XI	149	Missa: Papae Marcelli.	Agnus I	1
k	R. IV	194	P. XI	149	Missa: Papae Marcelli.	Agnus I	2
l	R. IV	194	P. XI	149	Missa: Papae Marcelli.	Agnus I	3
m	R. IV	197	P. XI	152	Missa: Papae Marcelli.	Agnus II	1
n	R. IV	201	P. XI	155	Missa: Papae Marcelli.	Agnus II	47
218a	R. IV	188	P. XI	145	Missa: Papae Marcelli.	Sanctus	16–21
b	R. IV	191	P. XI	147	Missa: Papae Marcelli.	Sanctus	69½–73
c	R. IV	179	P. XI	138	Missa: Papae Marcelli.	Credo	37
d	R. IV	181	P. XI	139	Missa: Papae Marcelli.	Credo	68½–73
e	R. IV	180	P. XI	139	Missa: Papae Marcelli.	Credo	58½
f	R. IV	186	P. XI	144	Missa: Papae Marcelli.	Credo	183
g	R. IV	195	P. XI	150	Missa: Papae Marcelli.	Agnus I	22
h	R. IV	196	P. XI	151	Missa: Papae Marcelli.	Agnus I	42
i	R. IV	201	P. XI	155	Missa: Papae Marcelli.	Agnus II	47
j	R. IV	193	P. XI	149	Missa: Papae Marcelli.	Benedictus	26
k	R. IV	180	P. XI	139	Missa: Papae Marcelli.	Credo	65
219	Morley: Plaine and Easie Introduction. p. 178						
220a	R. VII	42	P. II	33	Motet: Ascendo ad Patrem		1–8
b			P. XVI	71	Missa: Sacerdos et pontifes. Credo		45–51
221	R. VII	99	P. II	74	Motet: Peccantem me quotidie		29–44
222			P. VI	59	Motet: Surrexit Pastor (a 8)		37–50
223a	R. XII	88	P. IV	151	Motet: Exsutate Deo		1–8
b	R. XII	90	P. IV	153	Motet: Exultate Deo		42–53
224	R. V	110	P. I	83	Motet: Lapidabant Stephanum		1–17
225			P. VI	158	Motet: Salve Regina		78–end
226a	R. X	103	P. XIII	77	Missa: Prima (a 5). Sanctus		36
b	R. X	73	P. XIII	54	Missa: Quarta (a 4). Sanctus		13
c	R. X	52	P. XIII	39	Missa: Tertia (a 4). Sanctus		19
d	R. X	139	P. XIII	102	Missa: Secunda (a 5). Sanctus		11
e	R. X	12	P. XIII	10	Missa: Prima (a 4). Sanctus		29
f	R. X	44	P. XIII	33	Missa: Tertia (a 4). Gloria		91
g	R. X	89	P. XIII	66	Missa: Prima (a 5). Gloria		113
h	R. X	163	P. XIII	120	Missa: Tertia (a 5). Gloria		131
i	R. X	63	P. XIII	47	Missa: Quarta (a 4). Gloria		38
j	R. X	42	P. XIII	32	Missa: Tertia (a 4). Gloria		41
k	R. III	15	P. V	14	Motet: Tribus miraculis		3
l	R. VIII	23	P. III	18	Motet: Angelus Domini		1
227a	R. III	36	P. V	31	Motet: Loquebantur		54–61
b	R. XI	17	P. V	128	Motet: Quam pulchri sunt		27
c	R. VIII	11	P. III	10	Motet: Cantantibus organis		20–30
228	R. XI	60	P. V	162	Motet: Eja ergo		1–5
229a	R. V	122	P. I	91	Motet: Sicut lilium		20
b	R. V	127	P. I	95	Motet: Quam pulchri sunt		27
c	R. V	170	P. I	127	Motet: Quodcumque ligaveris		25
d	R. V	140	P. I	104	Motet: Cum pervenisset		85
e	R. V	144	P. I	107	Motet: Viri Galilaei		68
f	R. V	144	P. I	107	Motet: Viri Galilaei		68
g	R. V	57	P. I	45	Motet: Ego sum panis		60
h	R. V	157	P. I	117	Motet: Dum ergo essent		60
230a	R. VI	82	P. XII	64	Missa: Brevis. Agnus II		28
b	R. VI	89	P. XII	69	Missa: De feria. Sanctus		35
c	R. XI	182	P. IV	69	Motet: Quam pulchri sunt		27
d	R. V	50	P. I	40	Motet: O vera summa		6
231a	R. VI	65	P. XII	52	Missa: Brevis. Gloria		7
b	R. VI	65	P. XII	52	Missa: Brevis. Gloria		24
c	R. VI	66	P. XII	53	Missa: Brevis. Gloria		46
d	R. VI	64	P. XII	52	Missa: Brevis. Gloria		4
e	R. VI	67	P. XII	54	Missa: Brevis. Gloria		71
f	R. VI	72	P. XII	58	Missa: Brevis. Credo		118
232a	R. VIII	133	P. III	102	Motet: Susanna ab improbis		51
b			P. VI	87	Motet: Regina mundi		19
c	R. XII	29	P. IV	110	Motet: Ave, Trinitatis		35
d			P. VI	63	Motet: Etenim Pascha		26
e	R. XI	186	P. IV	73	Motet: Duo ubera tua		32

Example Number	'Roma' Reference Vol.	Page	Haberl Reference Vol.	Page	Name of Work	Measure
233a	R. I	41	P. X	37	Missa: O Regem Coeli. Gloria	62
b			P. XVI	70	Missa: Sacerdos et Pontifex. Credo	27
c	R. XI	152	P. IV	48	Motet: Dilectus meus mihi	33
d			P. XXIII	11	Missa: In majoribus duplicibus. Credo	66
e	R. IV	171	P. XI	131	Missa: Papae Marcelli. Gloria	9
234a	R. VII	155	P. II	116	Motet: Cantabo Domino	27
b	R. XX	148	P. XXVI	128	Litaniae Sacrosanctae Eucharistiae D	50
235	R. IV	82	P. XI	63	Missa: Ad fugam. Credo	98
236a	R. I	16	P. X	15	Missa: Ecce sacerdos magnus. Credo	161
b	R. VI	85	P. XII	66	Missa: De Feria. Christe	1
c	R. I	128	P. X	107	Missa: Ad coenam agni. Kyrie II	9
d	R. I	29	P. X	26	Missa: Ecce sacerdos. Agnus I	33
e	R. XVIII	69			Missa: In duplicibus minoribus II. Credo	161
f	R. XVIII	97			Missa: Beata Mariae Virginis I. Gloria	110
237a	R. X	14	P. XIII	11	Missa: Prima (a 4). Hosanna	57
b	R. X	54	P. XIII	41	Missa: Tertia (a 4). Hosanna	45
c			P. XXI	43	Missa: Ascendo ad Patrem. Gloria	47
d	R. III	45	P. V	38	Motet: Lauda Sion	66
e	R. V	14	P. I	13	Motet: O Antoni emerita	83
238	R. V	15	P. I	14	Motet: Senex puerum	11
239	R. X	48	P. XIII	36	Missa: Tertia (a 4). Credo	78
240	R. V	180	P. I	134	Motet: Et omnes Angeli	14
241a	R. III	135	P. V	107	Motet: Veni, Sponsa Christi	64
b	R. VII	130	P. II	97	Motet: Hierusalem, cito veniet	80
242a	R. VI	77	P. XII	61	Missa: Brevis. Benedictus	35
b	R. I	156	P. X	130	Missa: Ad coenam Agni. Benedictus	43
c	R. VII	69	P. II	53	Motet: Exi cito	78
d	R. VII	64	P. II	50	Motet: Rorate coeli	86

SHORT BIBLIOGRAPHY

Agricola, Martin. *Musica Figuralis Deudsch*

Apel, Willi. *The Notation of Polyphonic Music* (Fourth Edition, 1953).   The Medieval Academy of America, Cambridge, Mass.

Aron, Pietro. (O. Strunk : *Source Readings*)

Artusi. *L'arte del Contraponto*

Bukofzer, Manfred F. *Studies in Mediaeval and Renaissance Music.* J. M. Dent & Sons, London, 1951

Coates, Henry. *Article on Palestrina* (Grove's Dictionary ; Fifth Edition)
Palestrina (Master Musicians series). J. M. Dent & Sons, London, 1938

Coussemaker, C. E. H. de. *Scriptorum de Musica Medii Aevi* (4 vols.)

Dart, R. Thurston. *The Interpretation of Music.* Hutchinson's University Library, London, 1954

Fulda, Adam de. (Gerbert : *Scriptores*)

Gerbert, M. *Scriptores Ecclesiastici de Musica Sacra Potissima* (3 vols.)

Glarean, H. *Dodecachordon*

Jeppesen, Knud. *Counterpoint.* Williams & Norgate Ltd., London, 1950
The Style of Palestrina and the Dissonance (Second Edition).   Oxford University Press, London, 1946

Marchetto of Padua. (Gerbert : *Scriptores III*)

Morley, Thomas. *A Plaine and Easie Introduction to Practicall Musicke*, 1597. (Shakespeare Association Facsimiles. Introduction by E. H. Fellowes.) Oxford University Press, London, 1937
A Plain and Easy Introduction to Practical Music. Edited by R. A. Harman, with a Foreword by R. Thurston Dart. J. M. Dent & Sons, London, 1952

Morris, R. O.   *Contrapuntal Technique in the Sixteenth Century.*
                Clarendon Press, 1922, 1934
                Article on Polyphony (Grove's Dictionary ; Fourth
                Edition)

Reese, Gustave.   *Music in the Middle Ages.* J. M. Dent & Sons, 1941
                Music in the Renaissance. W. W. Norton & Co.,
                New York, 1954

Sachs, Curt.   *Rhythm and Tempo.* J. M. Dent & Sons, London,
                1953

Samson, J.   *Palestrina.* Geneva, 1940

Strunk, Oliver.   *Source Readings in Musical History.* W. W. Norton
                & Co., New York, 1950 ; Faber & Faber,
                London

Terry, R. R.   *G. da Palestrina* (Heritage of Music series). Oxford
                University Press, London, 1927, 1948

Tinctoris.   *Diffinitorium Musicae* (Coussemaker : *Scriptorum*)
                Liber de Natura et Proprietate Tonorum

Zarlino.   *Istitutioni armoniche*

COLLECTED EDITIONS OF THE MUSIC OF PALESTRINA

Breitkopf and Härtel (1862-1907). Edited by Haberl and others. (33 vols.)

" Roma " Edition (1947 : in progress). Edited by Casimiri and others.
(21 vols.)

INDEX